WAY OF THE SIGN |IV >> VOL. 1

CARTPOWER

WAY OF THE SIGN IV

ARTPOWER™

Designer: Wang Anlei
Chief Editor: Mo Tingli

Address: Room C, 9/F., Sun House, 181 Des Voeux Road Central, Hong
Kong, China
Tel: 852-31840676
Fax: 852-25432396

Editorial Department
Address: G009, Floor 7th, Yimao Centre, Meiyuan Road, Luohu District,
Shenzhen, China
Tel: 86-755-82913355
Fax: 86-755-82020029

Web: www.artpower.com.cn
E-mail: artpower@artpower.com.cn

ISBN 978-988-12616-5-6

Printed in China

Signage and Wayfinding Graphics

We are surrounded by banal, uninteresting and ineffective signs. Every day we are assaulted by signs that try to shout above the cacophony of the world around us. Each sign is an opportunity.

There are many considerations when you approach a signage project. The fundamental criteria are clarity and simplicity. But signage can do more than just point people in the right direction. It can enhance their experience. As well as being clear and informative, it can be engaging, inspiring and intelligent. Beautifully designed and beautifully made.

One of the reasons we love doing this type of work is its physical nature. It gets a designer away from the computer screen and into the real world.

The size and positioning of signs is key, but equally important is the use of materials and how they sit in a space. The choice of typeface, colour and words needs careful thought. Signage is an extension of an organisation's identity into a physical space. It is as important as any other part of the identity. We love taking an identity from paper into the real world.

We have been fortunate to work on a great range of signage schemes, from Twickenham Stadium to an installation at Kew Gardens. It's wonderful that we get to work with amazing architects, engineers, writers, manufacturers and craftsmen from around the world to help realise these three-dimensional forms that people interact with every day.

We are still finding our way. Each project comes with its own complexities – no two are ever the same. There are always unexpected challenges to overcome, but that's what makes this type of work so interesting and rewarding. We learn from every project we do.

Jim Sutherland is the co-founder of hat-trick design in London. The company has completed branding and wayfinding projects for Twickenham Stadium, Natural History Museum, Horniman Museum, Prostate Cancer UK, Land Securities, Rambert Dance, Stockwell Park, Centre Point and Almacantar.

Jim Sutherland – hat-trick design

CONTENTS »

Institute of Electrical Engineering, Stuttgart University, Signage System Redesign

Design Agency:
Büro Uebele

Client:
Universitätsbauamt Stuttgart
Und Hohenheim

Photography:
Daniel Fels

Project Team:
Katharina Moritzen, Felix Rabe,
Katrin Theile, Andreas Uebele

Principal Typeface:
Neue Helvetica

A chance to remedy our earlier mistakes is something we all often wish for later in life, and in our professional lives, too. The signage system designed by our office 15 years ago – and since unchanged – looked good, but in corridors where lighting levels can be subdued it was hard to read. The understated lettering in purple and black echoed the architecture, but didn't contrast strongly enough with the silver-coloured background strips. Now the whole thing's been spruced up, freshly painted in fluorescent colours, and finished off with lettering in black – a sharp and effective contrast. The result is clear to see – the messages stand out in vibrant neon shades against the grey concrete walls, proclaiming: read this! Here! Now!

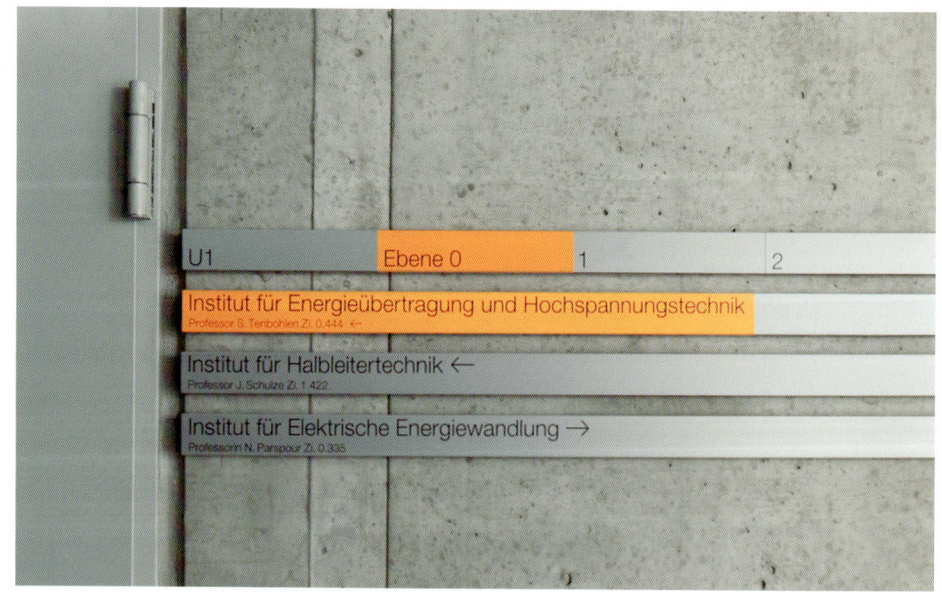

Ebene U1 | 0 | 1 | 2

Institut für Energieübertragung und Hochspannungstechnik
Professor S. Tenbohlen Zi. 0.444

Institut für Halbleitertechnik ←
Professor J. Schulze Zi. 1.422

Institut für Elektrische Energiewandlung →
Professorin N. Parspour Zi. 0.335

Institut für Nachrichtenübertragung

Fachbereich Elektrotechnik und Informationstechnik (IVEL INFOTECH)

Design Agency:
Foreign Policy Design Group

Client:
Sifang Art Museum, Nanjing, China

Sifang Art Museum, Nanjing, China

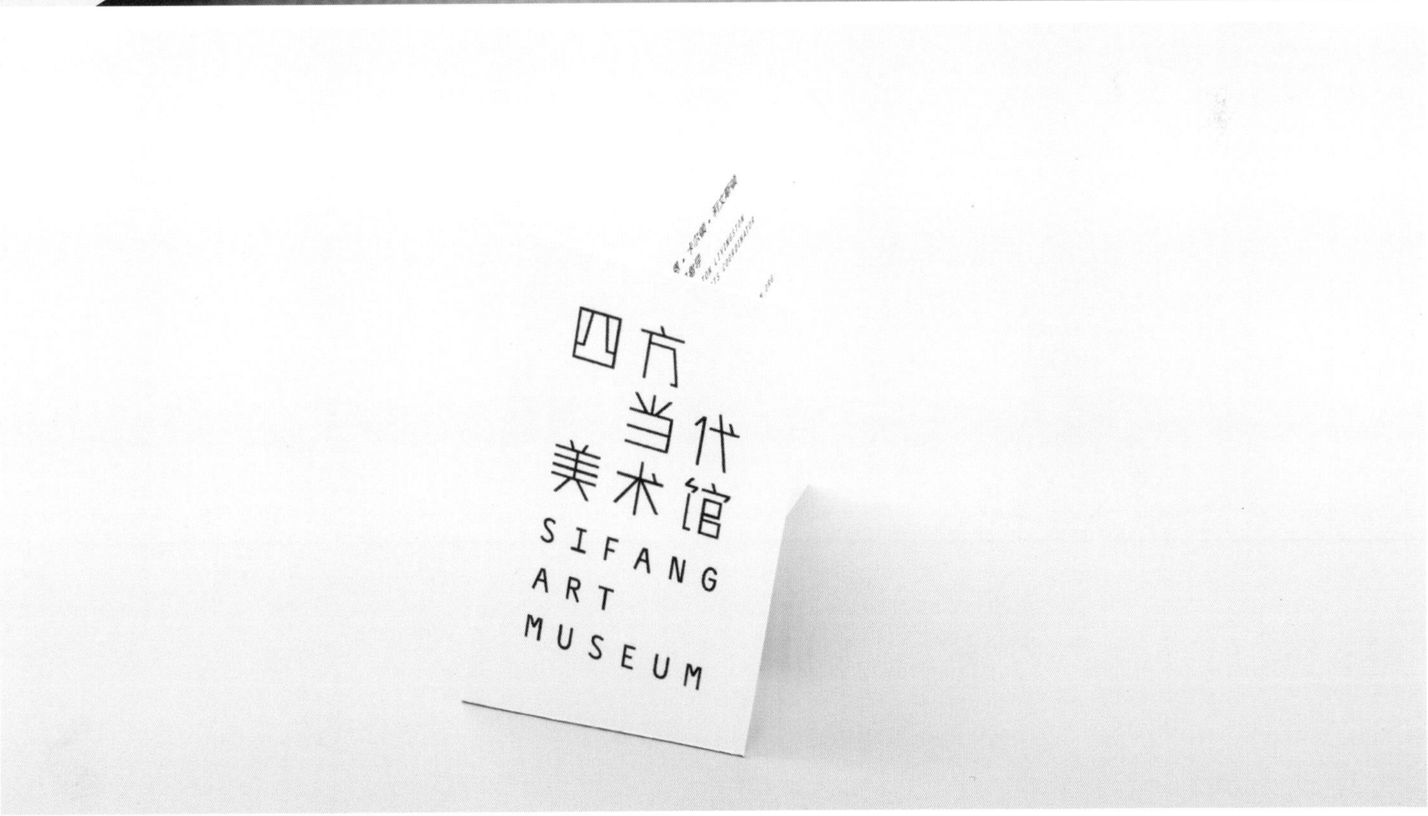

LOWER GALLERY
负一层展厅 ∨

Set within the gentle terrain of Laoshan in Nanjing, the architecture of Sifang Art Museum is a well-constructed mix of harsh angularity with an elegant appeal whereby the asymmetrical structure hovers in space. Every view angle yielding a different trapezoidal perspective; the collateral system adopts the trapezoidal form. The Chinese saying - Strength within Gentleness - is inspired by bamboo - the material and form used for landscaping and parts of the structure. This underpins the brand identity, describing the gentle landscape where in old China, scholars and artists took recluse to master their craft or refine their thinking. The demure also balances the masculinity of the architecture. White, is also a canvas a museum would function as.

WASHROOMS
卫生间

01
∧ ∨
B1

RECEPTION
< 接待处

MUSEUM SHOP
> 美术馆商店

CAFE
> 咖啡厅

WASHROOMS
> 卫生间

Spa Iconography and Signage Concept

Design Agency:
Esadore Creative

Designer:
Mohammad Hamed Zeinali

Client:
Nine Degrees Spa

Nine Degrees is a Middle Eastern spa concept created by ESADORE International, and the inspiration for it was to develop a unique spa brand that keeps Middle Eastern traditions alive, whilst increasing public knowledge and understanding of the value and vital importance of Health and Relaxation within daily living and leisure time.

ESADORE Creative designed a signage concept for Nine Degrees Spa. The task was creating a bilingual (English-Arabic) spa and wellness-oriented way finding system that easily and instantly communicates with the guests and visitors, relying on the idea of being simple and universally understandable.

The signage has to speak Nine Degrees brand identity, so it needs to carry out the specific color palette, typography and the tone. We created a flexible signage concept and tailored a communication strategy, which makes us able to develop it based on the buildings' architectural and interior characteristics. The pictograms and iconography elements were created to reflect the relaxing environment of a spa.

Unicamp Convention Center Signage

Design Agency:
Estúdio 196 Branding & Design / DuoDesign Comunicação Visual

Architect:
Zanettini Arquitetura Planejamento e Consultoria

Client:
Universidade Estadual de Campinas – Unicamp

Rendering:
Cling

The University of Campinas – Unicamp, in Brazil, decided to build a convention center in which to promote academic and cultural activities. These activities looked to benefit the Unicamp and the region of Campinas. Its signage needed to be clear and intuitive to guide users through a large and diverse space. The linear concept we adopted permeates the entire environment, providing fluid and continuous guidance for the users. The use of dark and light tones to differentiate between the external and internal totem stands respectively, and the use of red and orange colors to identify each of the wings make the spatial organization more understandable. With a clean and contemporary design, the project comprises totem stands, panels, direct applications on walls, floor signs and even pictograms, which all integrate seamlessly with the architecture. The signage system transmits values such as modernity and avant-gardism; synonymous with the identity of the university.

Filas A-G

A1

A1

Filas A-G

Auditório
Unicamp

A

Alimentação

Sanitários
Elevadores

Salas de Reuniões

Acesso
Filas P-V
Acesso
Filas G-O
Acesso
Filas A-F

UNICAMP

CENTRO DE
CONVENÇÕES

Acesso
Passarela
Estacionamento

Bridgepark Muengsten

Design Agency:
F1rstdesign.Com

Designer:
Christopher Ledwig, Olivia Ferguson Losier, Judith Cleve

Photography:
Christopher Ledwig

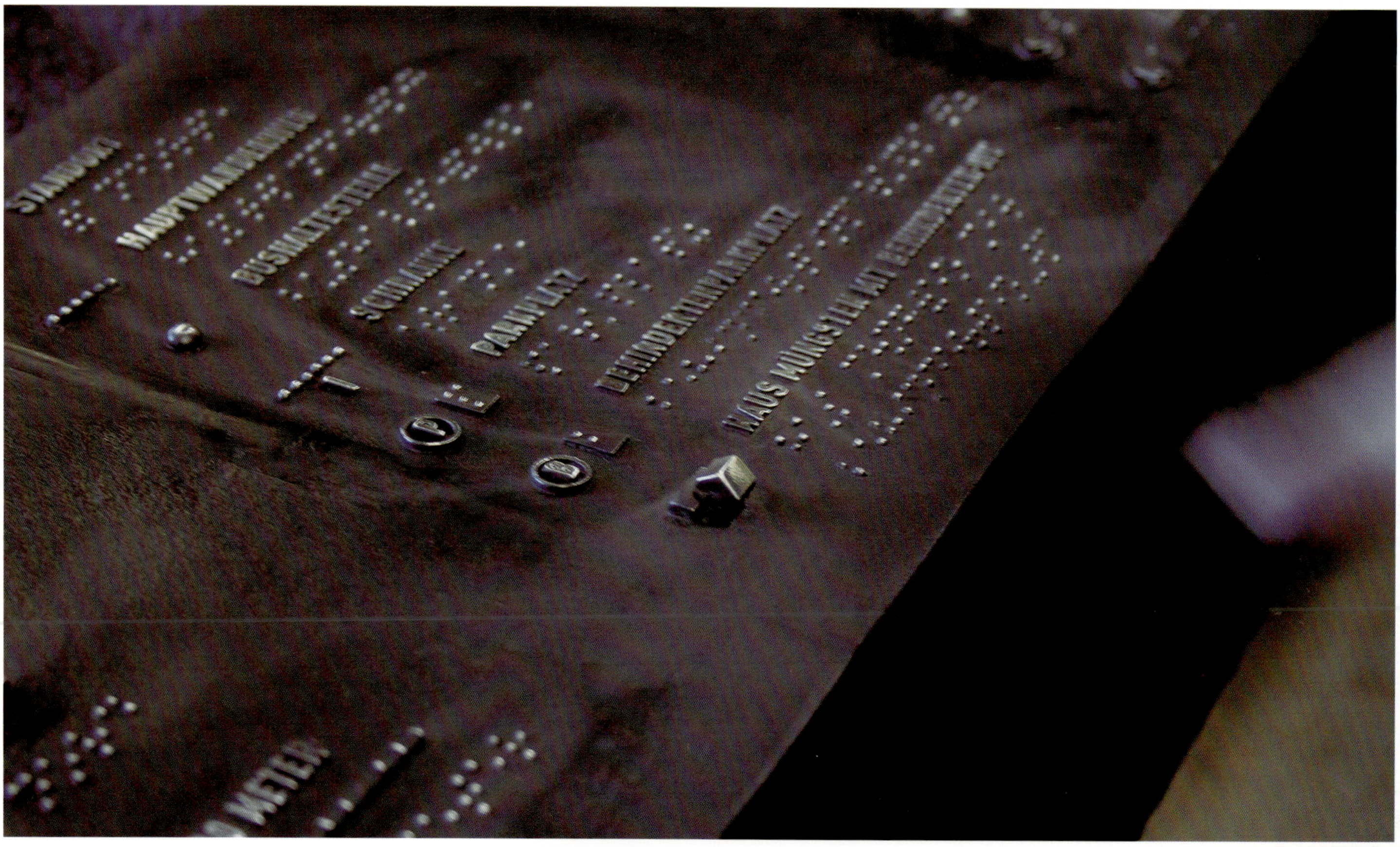

Problem
The Muengstener Brücke – Germany's highest railway bridge – runs across the river Wupper inbetween the cities of Solingen and Wuppertal. A landscape park has been developed during the regional aid program Regionale 2006. There is a hiking trail leading from the bridge to the castle Schloss Burg.

Objective
The aim is to make the landscape park and main hiking trail accessible for the blind, visually handicapped and challenged persons as well as visitors in general.

Method
Concept, design and implementation of a barrier-free wayfinding system. The core element is a cast iron model with tactile symbols and braille texts that has been developed in close cooperation with blind persons. Many different production methods from lowtech to hightech have been used in the fabrication process.

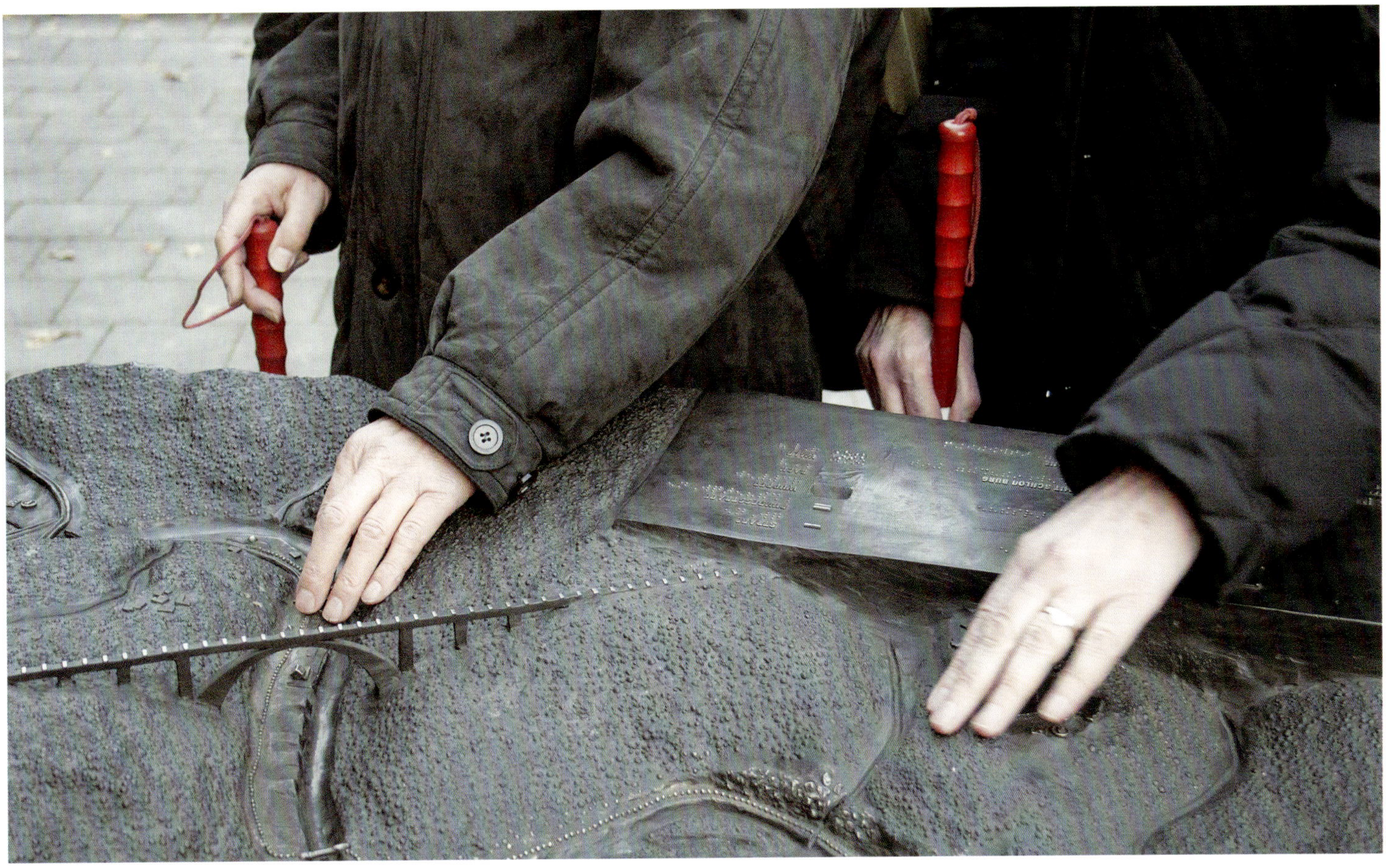

O | R | P
Group Practice

Architecture:
Rischko Architects, Oliver Rischko

Corporate Design & Wayfinding:
F1rstdesign.Com

Designer:
Christopher Ledwig, Sebastian Schneider

Photography:
Christopher Ledwig, Oliver Rischko

Problem
Four doctors from three disciplines come together to create an innovative practice and need an interior design, corporate design and a wayfinding system.

Objective
Conception and design of an interior and corporate design that communicates both the practice community and the individual disciplines.

Method
By color coding both the equipment and the practice interiors are ordered. The discreet use of color along with generous white space sets a medical appearance.

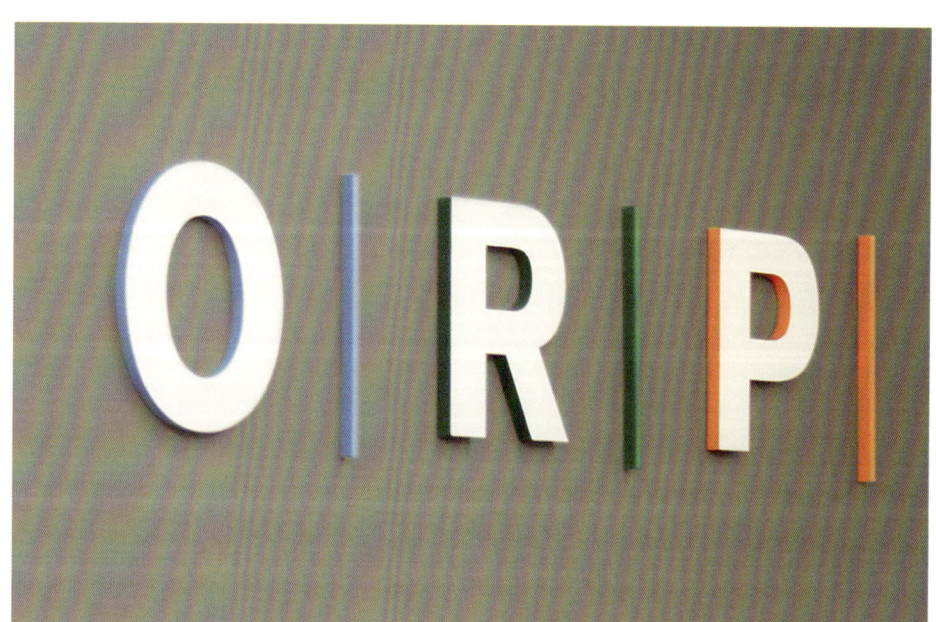

Talk to Torino
Speaks Out

Designer:
Gabriele Marchi, Diego Federico,
Marco Condello, Antonio di Summa

RETROBOTTEGA
bold

Aa
ABCDEFGHIJKLM
NOPQRSTUVWXYZ
abcdefghijklmn
opqrstuvwxyz
0123456789

Talk To was carried out in 2011 as a final project at the European Institute of Design in Turin (class of Graphic Design) by Marco Condello, Diego Federico, Gabriele Marchi and Antonio di Summa.

It's a micro signage system for pedestrian that uses the urban context as framework, and it aims to guide pedestrians by accompanying them through the city's points of interests.

Composed of a customized set of pictograms and typeface, language and voice of Turin, Talk To uses three colors to distinguish main thematic areas: orange for art and culture, blue for services and green for leisure and spare time.

The entire 'Talk To' system has been designed with the characteristics of the stencil in order to be applied in the most immediate, versatile and less invasive way on frameworks offered by the urban space.

The experimental stage has been developed in Turin's 'Barriera di Milano' district in collaboration with the Municipality of Turin and the cultural centre 'Urban Barriera'.

A special thanks to Professor Piero De Macchi for his valuable advice concerning the Retrobottega Bold typeface designing process.

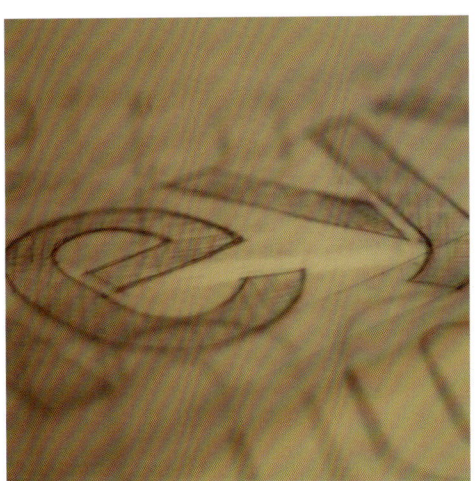

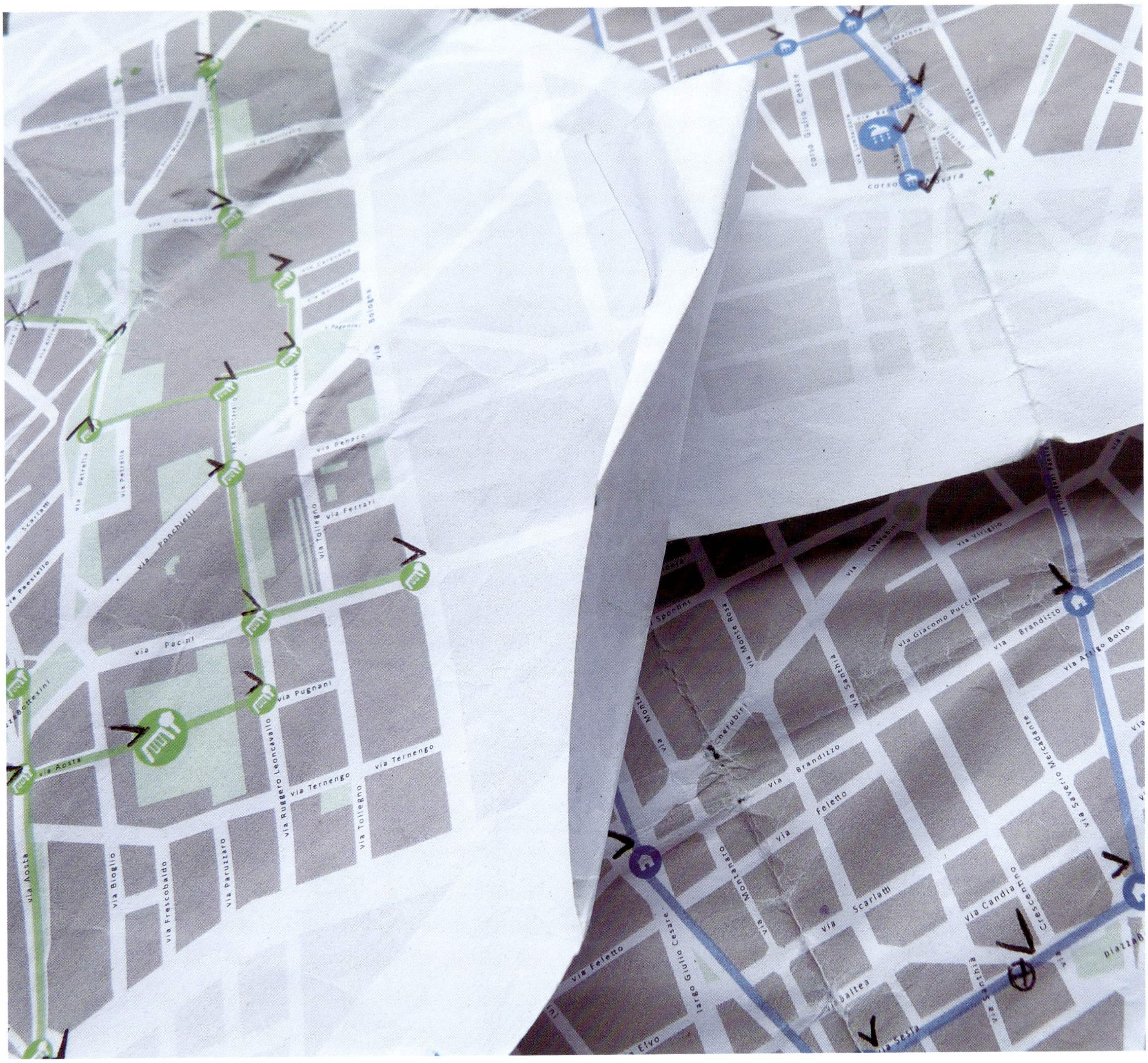

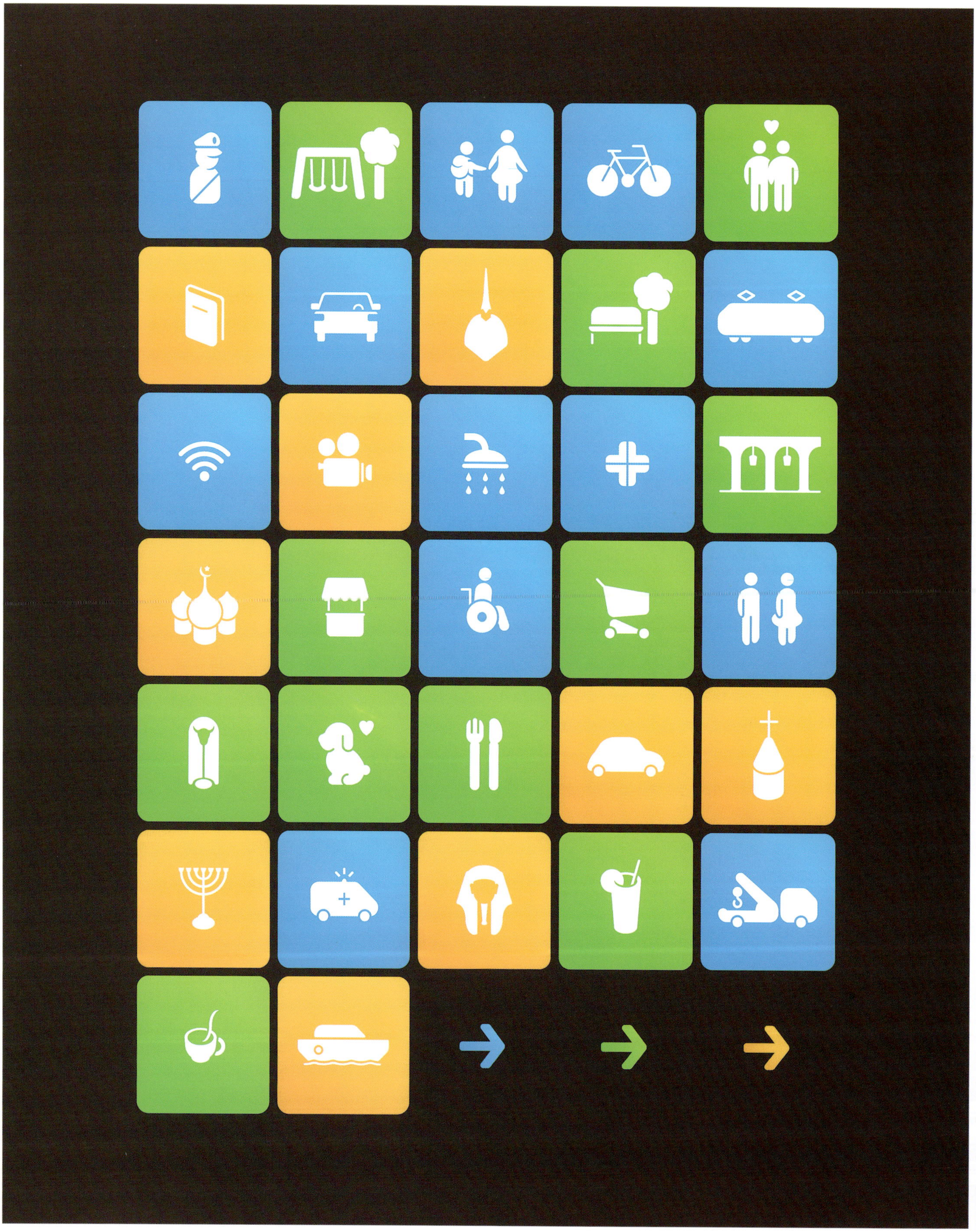

Wayfinding Design for Limkokwing University of Creative Technology

Designer:
Syaza Za'ba

The concept of the wayfinding design is transformation. The isometric or triangle design technique is used in the wayfinding design. This is to represent the transformation of the triangle shapes forming into another shape. Phoenix bird is a symbol of inspiration at Limkokwing University. An idea of transforming four special birds into a phoenix is executed. The four birds are owl, peacock, eagle and hornbill. They are chosen based on each characteristic that could represent the symbol of phoenix. Each bird will represent a building. Moreover, the characteristics of the chosen birds also represent the students and workers in the university. Black signboard is used in the design to maintain its theme colour in Limkokwing University. Plus, black also represents the elegant look of Limkokwing Building. The signage is also displayed on the black empty wall to brighten up the environment. The font used in the design is Helvetica. The font was chosen based on its sleek lines and modern sensibility structure. It is also a simple font and it supports a readable and reading process to have a clear communication.

THE EAGLE

1	STUDENT SERVICES MARKETING RECEPTION MOSQUE
2	HUMAN RESOURCE ACADEMIC ADMIN. UNIT FACULTY MANAGER CORPORATE BOARDROOM INTERNATIONAL STUDENT SERVICES
3	HALL OF FAME

THE PEACOCK

G	SECURITY CONTROL ROOM RESOURCE WINGS RADIO DIGITAL IMAGING LIMKOKWING ENGLISH CENTRE SEMINAR HALL 1
1	KNOWLEDGE RESEARCH CENTRE INTERNATIONAL STUDENT ACTIVITY CENTRE LIBRARY
2	THE GALLERY CENTRE FOR MALAY STUDIES FACULTY CENTRE FOR INDUSTRY RESEARCH AMD ARCHI
3	FASHION GALLERY FASHION WORKSHOP 1-3 BATIK WORKSHOP CLASS 68-81

THE OWL

G	WORKSHOP PHOTO STUDIO 1-4 CLASS 1-10 LECTURE THEATRE 1-3
1	LAB 1 - 30 IT
2	CLASS 43-67 LECTURE HALL 1-7 MATERIAL RESOURCE ROOM
3	CLASS 82-96 ILLUSTRATION 1-3 DRAWING B-C

THE HORNBILL

G	CLASS 11-12 REGISTRY FINANCE BURSARY
1	CLASS 13-23 FACULTY
2	CLASS 24-42 DRAWING A
3	CLASS 97-115 DRAWING D

THE EAGLE   THE PEACOCK   THE OWL   THE HORNBILL

CLASS
64

Voskresenskoe Entertainment Center Identity and Wayfinding

Design Agency:
Tomatdesign

Designer:
Maxim Arbuzov, Marina Vlasova, Andrey Tarakanov

Photographer:
Denis Vasilyev

Боулинг
Bowling

Фитнес
Fitness & Gym

Информация
Info

Уважаемые посетители, для удобства перемещения в нашем комплексе, основные функциональные зоны - бассейн, боулинг и тренажерный зал - имеют свой цвет. Кроме этого, следуйте линиям на стенах, которые укажут вам направление, и содержат полезные пиктограммы. Желаем приятного время-препровождения!

Бассейн
Swimming pool

We developed a wayfinding which is also an identity for new health and entertainment center opened within Voskresenskoe club-hotel near Moscow.

One of the tasks was not only to create comfortable navigation system, but also to position the center as an independent place that offers services also for people who live near the hotel territory in Voskresenskoe district. Thus we didn't use the identity of the hotel.

First of all we considered the existing architect project: not so big space, but long and dark corridors, which resembled labyrinth. The navigation based on bright colors that also help to orient better and creates special emotional background. Pictograms and wayfinding elements were placed right on the walls as super graphics. The line system became an additional element of comfort. They code the functional zones of the center and lead you all the way to the target.

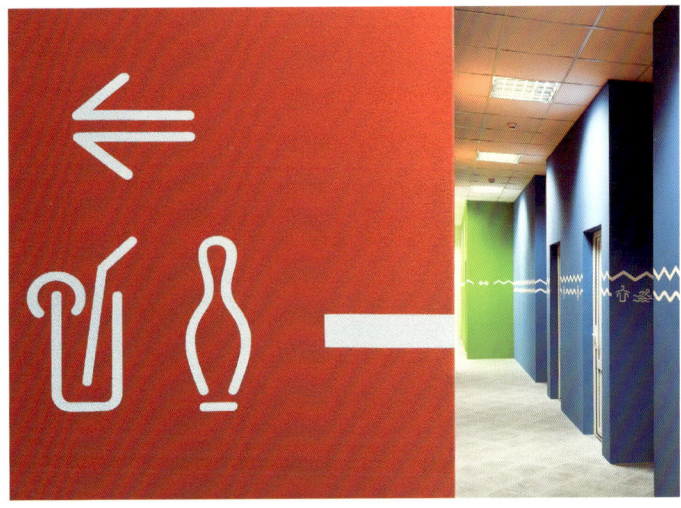

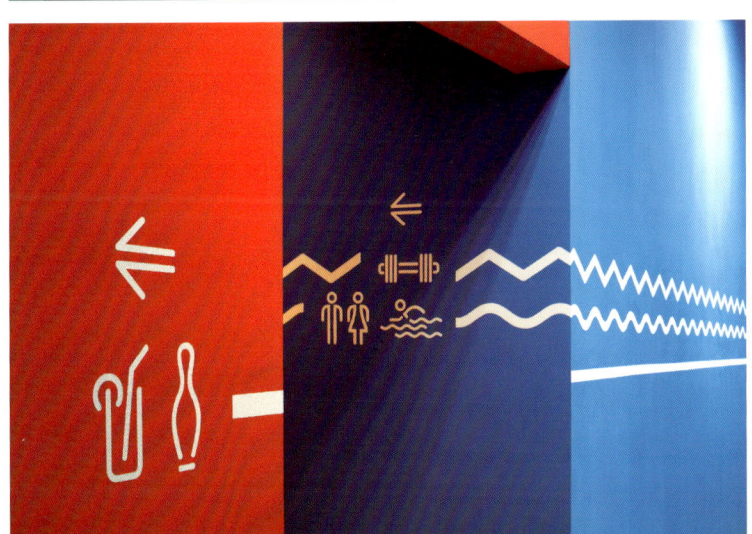

Wayfinding System of Faculty U16

Designer:
Veronika Bártlová

Design Studio:
Faculty of Visual Arts - Visual
Communications Studio

Client:
Tomas Bata University in Zlin

Ateliér 3D design
Studio of 3D Design ❮

Ateliér vizuální komunikace
Studio of Visual Communications ❮

2

❮ Pracovna učitelů **216**
❯ Počítačová učebna **204**
❮ Ředitel ÚVT **220**
❮ Asistenka ÚVT **217**
❮ Technologické pracoviště **203**

❯ WC
❯ VÝTAH

It is the concept of the new wayfinding system for the Faculty of Visual Arts in Zlin.

Whole idea is based on the combination of using simple typography and two additional lines, which goes along with the whole building.

The wayfinding system applies the corporate faculty colour. It is made from the plastic wall stickers.

Dílny
Workrooms

Ateliér 3D design
Studio of 3D Design

Ateliér vizuální komunikace
Studio of Visual Communications

Ateliér design skla
Studio of Glass Design

Ateliér design obuvi
Studio of Shoe Design

Ateliér prumyslový design
Studio of Product Design

Kreslírna
Drawing room

Ateliér design oděvu
Studio of Fashion Design

Ateliér prostorová tvorba
Studio of Spatial Design

1   2   3   4

Ateliér design skla
Studio of Glass Design

Ateliér design obuvi
Studio of Shoe Design

Ateliér prumyslový design
Studio of Product Design

3

> Dílna 310
> Pracovna učitelů 304
> Sklářská dílna 318
> Pracovny
> Seminární místnost 317
> Tisková místnost 317

> WC
> VÝTAH

Prostate Cancer UK

Design Agency:
hat-trick

Design Director:
Gareth Howat, Jim Sutherland

Designer:
Rory Brady, Gareth Howat, Jim Sutherland

Client:
Prostate Cancer UK

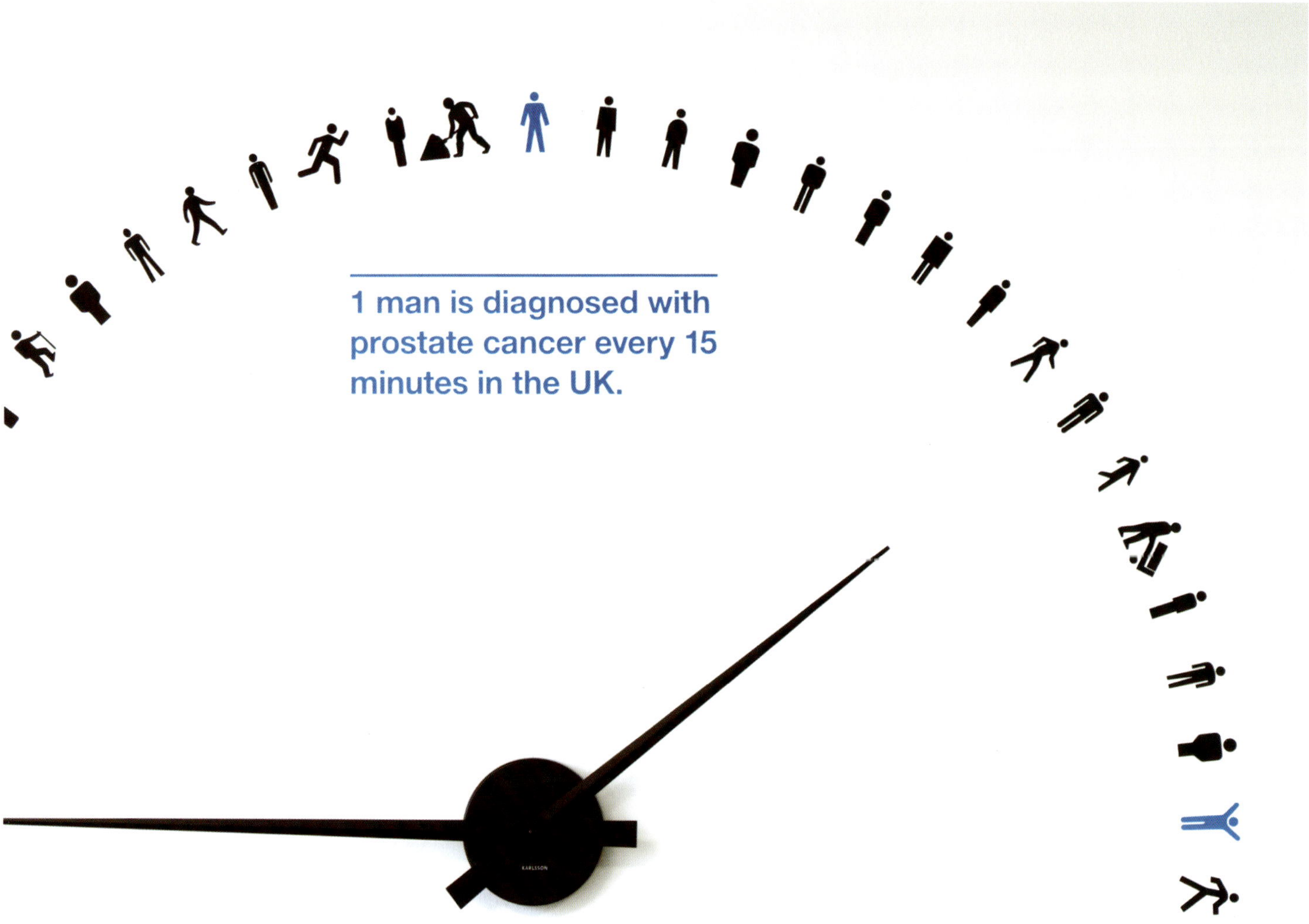

1 man is diagnosed with prostate cancer every 15 minutes in the UK.

Prostate Cancer UK wanted to rebrand with a bold new identity to help them reach more men as this cancer is predicted to become the most common form by 2030. As part of the rebrand we created a 'man of men' icon from many symbols of men in different settings & positions. Their offices were then furnished with this new identity.

1 in 9 men in the UK will get prostate cancer at some point in their lives. We needed to raise the profile of the charity for every man. Prostate Cancer UK's offices were the perfect opportunity to extend the new identity, immersing their staff in the new, bold visual style & key messages of the organization.

We created a 'man of men' icon from many images of men in different settings & positions. This reflects the number of men affected by the disease & is symbolic of men working together to find solutions. This also communicated that the disease affects all kinds of men. The offices were furnished with these life-size icons, a photo wall of iconic men & we also designed a clock to bring one of their key messages to life – the fact that every 15 minutes a man is diagnosed with prostate cancer.

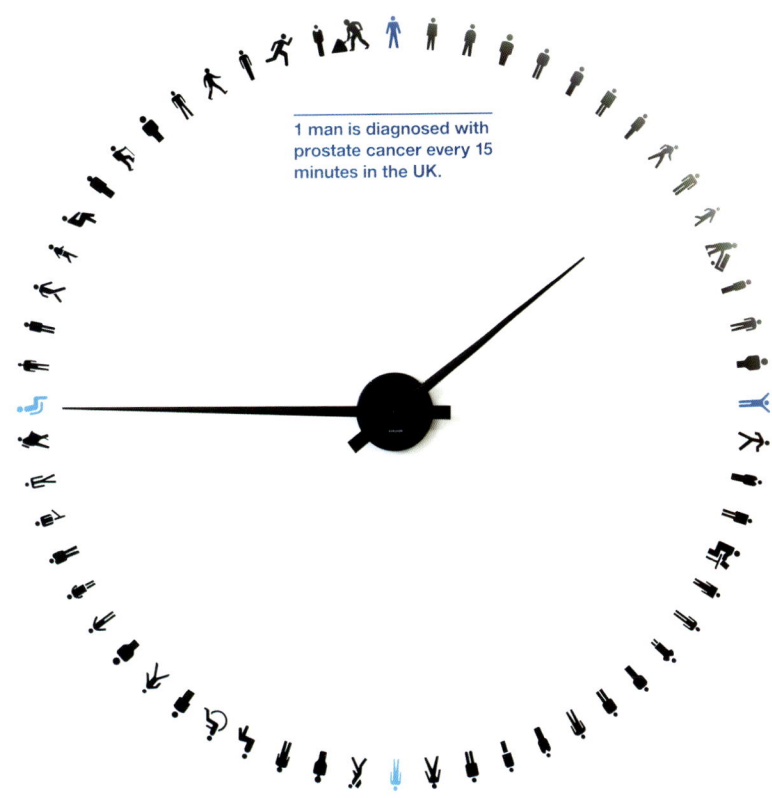

1 man is diagnosed with prostate cancer every 15 minutes in the UK.

PROSTATE CANCER UK

The enthusiasm and dedication of the charity is inspiring and I am very pleased to be a volunteer.

It has been a real support to talk to Dad and it is interesting how many people open up about their own cancer experiences once I've told them about mine.

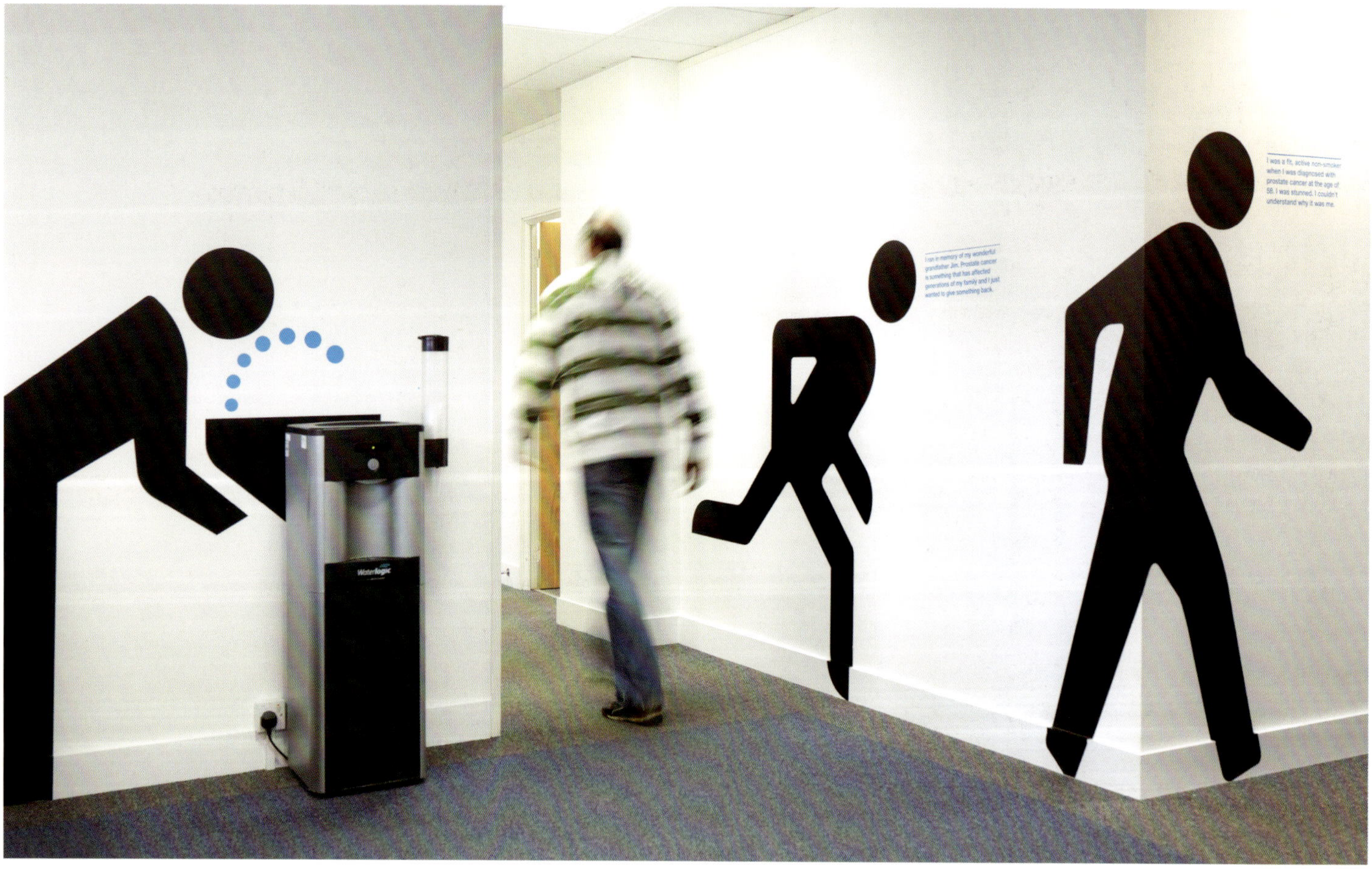

I was a fit, active non-smoker when I was diagnosed with prostate cancer at the age of 58. I was stunned. I couldn't understand why it was me.

I ran in memory of my wonderful grandfather Jim. Prostate cancer is something that has affected generations of my family and I just wanted to give something back.

Rambert Dance Company – Hoarding

Design Agency:
hat-trick

Design Director:
Gareth Howat, Jim Sutherland

Designer:
Rory Brady, Gareth Howat, Jim Sutherland

Client:
Rambert Dance Company

Rambert is Britain's national company for contemporary dance.

Photo
Hugo Glendinning
—
Dancer
Miguel Altunaga

ur new home will be a centre where the world's greatest choreographers, composers and designers will work together to create amazing dance.

Photo
Hugo Glendinning
–
Dancer
Eryck Brahmania

Rambert Dance Company is Britain's flagship contemporary dance company. Established in 1926 by Polish dance teacher Marie Rambert, the company has built a reputation of consistently delivering an exciting and innovative programme.

In March 2009 Rambert was given the green light to build a new purpose-built home in the heart of London's Southbank. Along with our appointment to rebrand the company, we were also commissioned to design a series of hoardings for use around this new site.

Our approach was to use iconic images of Rambert dancers, but angled so they reflected the idea of movement and broke out of the edge of the hoarding to attract attention.

Zetland House

Design Agency:
Bunch

Client:
Zetland House

Creative Director:
Denis Kovac

Singwriter:
Nicolai Sclater

Zetland House is a unique and striking warehouse-style office property, situated in the heart of Shoreditch, London. The building was originally a Print Works for The Bank of England. Today, it has been refurbished with modern businesses in mind, whilst maintaining its existing structure and original period features.

Bunch was invited to devise a new signage system and update the original branding. Inspired by almost extinct ghost signs from the surrounding area, the new signage looks both contemporary and familiar. In close collaboration with Nicolai Sclater, a traditional East London signwriter, original designs were drawn by hand and applied directly to the walls and onto everything from large scale signage to external and internal wayfinding and courier signs.

Bunch would like to acknowledge the invaluable help given to us by Adam J. Evans/Ordinary.

ZETLAND
HOUSE

LOFT STYLE
OFFICES

MEETING
ROOMS

BIKE PARK

GYM

BASEMENT
GALLERY

LIFT THREE

LIFT

3

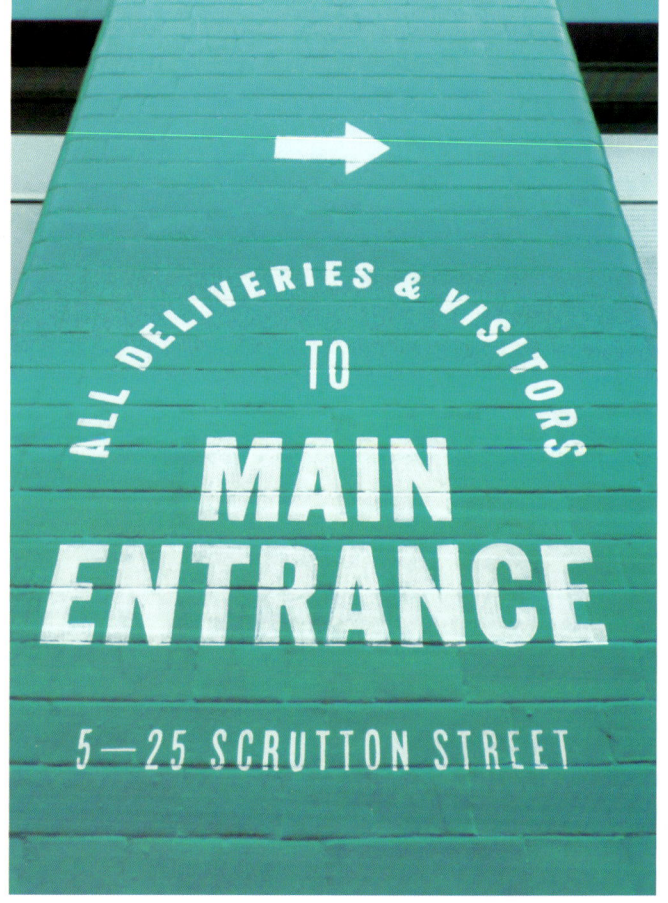

ZETLAND HOUSE

5—25 SCRUTTON STREET
ZETLANDHOUSE.COM

LOWER GROUND

A THE VAULT GYM
B SIGNAL GALLERY
C THE VAULT GYM
D CAFÉ Z
E PORTLAND APARTMENTS
F 7DIGITAL
G PAPER MACHE TIGER

GROUND

A SHUTL
B MYLAKO
C MINNOW FILMS
D BLACKBRIDGE COMMUNICATIONS
E VYRE
F VYRE
G VYRE

FIRST

A IMAGE LINE COMMUNICATIONS
B EMPOWERING LEARNING
B2 JACOB BAILEY
C SPINACH BANKSTHOMAS
D ALMEIDA CAPITAL
E MAXXIMA LABMED IML SWIM
F THE LATE NIGHT SALON
G STYLESIGHT

SECOND

A EMPEROR
B EMPEROR
C EMPEROR
D WAY TO BLUE
E BOSSA STUDIOS
F IOGEN
G IOGEN

THIRD

A TOWNSHEND LANDSCAPE
ARCHITECTS
C PLUCK UK / DEMAND MEDIA
D OPTIMITY
D1 POWSTER
D2 SPOTLESS INTERACTIVE
D3 AVANTI CONSULTING

THIRD

E1 DRAGONFLY FILM & TV
E2 ASITE
F1 TYRRELL KATZ
F2 BEAUTIFUL WORLD
F3 EGELNICK AND WEBB
G EGELNICK AND WEBB

FOURTH

A AUGUST
B AUGUST
C AUGUST
D AUGUST
E SOMESUCH & CO
F CAFÉDIRECT
F2 CAFÉDIRECT

BLOCK H
109 —123 CLIFTON

LG RHAPSODY
G SKILLED CAREERS
1 CHALAYAN
2 TONY FRETTON ARCHITECTS
3 SQUIZ

SCRUTTON STREET
5—25
MAIN
ENTRANCE

Barbal Signage

Design Agency:
Gen Design Studio

Designer:
Carla Ribeiro

Photography:
Leandro Veloso

Creative Director:
Leandro Veloso

Client:
Barbal

This signage was developed for Barbal which develops weighing technology such as bascules, scales and measuring systems.

With FF NETTO as a starting point, we further developed and added some pictograms properly contextualized with BARBAL's new plant.

The pictograms' system had to be related to the company's values and look and feel, translating a technological appearance. With these details, we believe the brand communicates an organized and competitive image, distinguishing itself from competitors.
When designing the platforms to implement the signage, we took advantage of the company's tools and materials and got the client directly involved with the production process. Barbal manufactured all the plates.

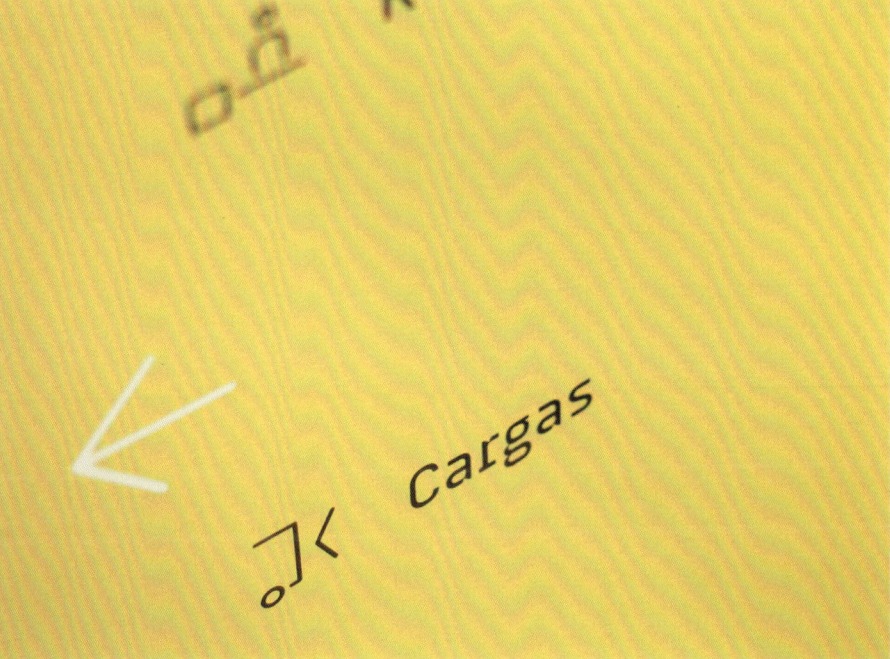

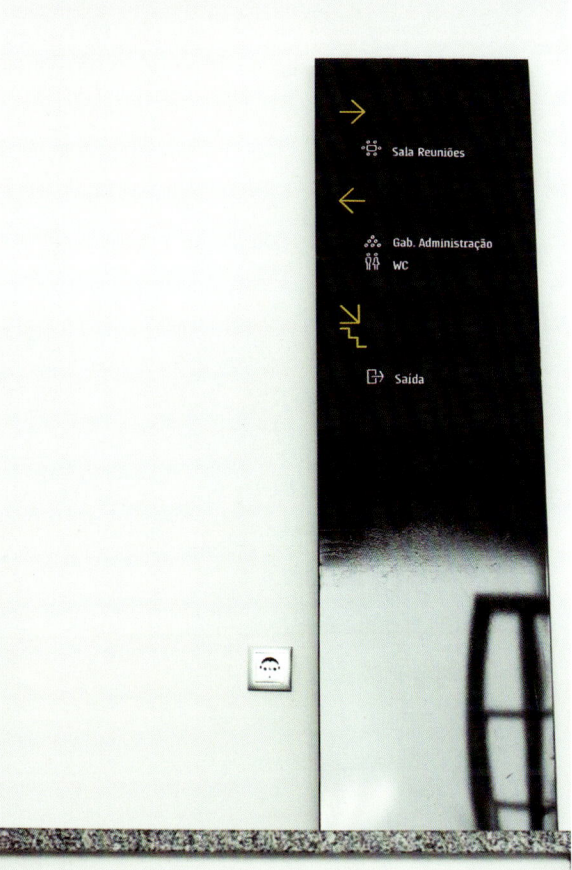

Mendes Júnior
Signage System

Design Agency:
Greco Design

Designer:
Gustavo Greco, Tidé, Ricardo Donato,
Fred Fita, Flávia Siqueira, Dani Pires

Client:
Mendes Júnior

Photography:
Rafael Motta

Mendes Júnior company has been active in the civil construction industry in Brazil and around the world, undertaking construction projects for highways, railways, subways, ports, hydroelectric dams, thermoelectric plants, oil and gas projects, among others. The family of pictograms and numbers created for the signage system was based on a diamond's (symbol of the instituition) shape and proportions.

Recepção

Extintor de
Incêndio

Mangueira de
Incêndio

Client:
SEBRAE-MG

Design Agency:
Greco Design

Photography:
Rafael Motta

Deisgner:
Gustavo Greco, Zumberto, Tidé, Victor
Fernandes, Alexandre Fonseca

Pentomino
Signage System

SEBRAE-MG (Small Business and Entrepreneur Support Agency) offers a set of tools that can be combined in order to generate a broad range of different solutions for the development of small and micro businesses. The signage system created for the institution was based on the pentomino puzzle. Just as is done at SEBRAE, different pieces are combined to generate multiple results. The family of pictograms and numbers created is the result of these combinations. In a light and playful manner, the Pentamino pictograms translated the entity's mission into a visual plan, expanding the brand personality into new and unprecedented contact points.

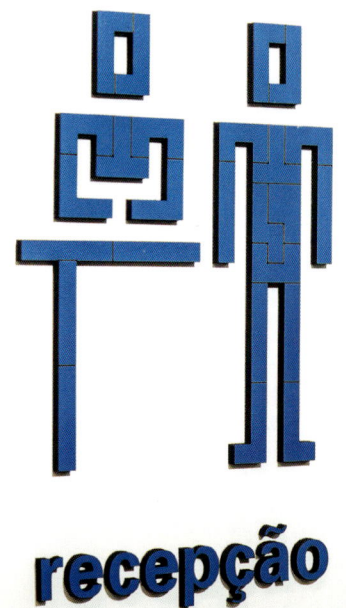

recepção

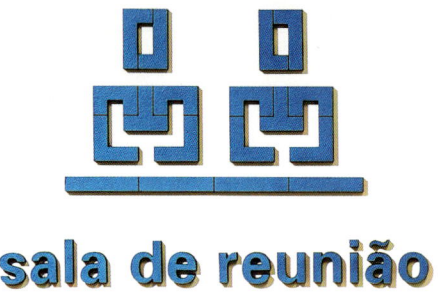

sala de reunião

copa

Designer:
Alex Swatridge, Laura Bowman, Tim Donaldson,
Gareth Howat, Jim Sutherland

Client:
Network Housing Group

Design Agency:
hat-trick

Design Director:
Gareth Howat Jim Sutherland

Network Housing (Stockwell Park)

Network Housing asked us to design a wayfinding system for the Stockwell Park Housing estate. The estate had a wide variety of buildings and surfaces within it, so the signage needed to be adaptable. The signs were required to be clear and simple, with the aim of helping both the first-time visitor and also residents of the estate. The signage was intended to help the estate feel more accessible and welcoming.

Our concept was based on a modular system of tiles, combined with a bespoke palette of patterns. This palette was created by a selection of local artists and designers, all based on the local history, architecture and culture of the area. This delivered a balance of both functionality and personality. The tile system allowed the signage to adapt to a range of surfaces and configurations to suit the variety of surroundings.

Federal Hospital Klagenfurt

Design Agency:
bauer – konzept & gestaltung

Client:
KABEG

Photography:
bauer – konzept & gestaltung

A wayfinding and colour guidance system developed for one of the biggest new built hospitals in Central Europe. The systematic wayfinding system is based on hubs which lead patients and visitors through the whole hospital complex. Specific colours define different areas and support a quick orientation: Applied on floors, and used as font and background colours, they lead from parking garage to the patient's room. The typeface used has a strong contrast and a narrow spacing: by increasing the font size, its legibility for elderly and handicapped people is assured. Patients have different ways to ambulances as visitors have their own routes to the patient's rooms.

Station D

N4

N4
Ebene 0

Besucherweg
Ebene 0

Besucherweg

Klassestation 4 N4

Station K S4

Stationäre Aufnahme

N1 Klassestation 1

N2 Klassestation 2

S1 Station G

S2 Station H

Stationäre Aufnahme

↑ Ambulanzen

← Notfall
ⓘ Information

S3/F3
Ebene -1

OK Open
Cultural House

Design Agency:
bauer – konzept & gestaltung

Photography:
bauer – konzept & gestaltung

Client:
OK Center

An internal and external information sign system was developed for the newly converted cultural hub in the old city center of Linz, consisting of two exhibition spaces, offices, restaurants and a large square. The concept was to consider the historic and the contemporary architecture, as well as the whole urban surrounding. The information sign system was made from embossed and coated metal plates which react to the backgrounds and the surfaces. White and grey plates were used indoors, whereas black and rusting steel was used for the outside areas. A strong identity by using a specifically developed typeface and corporate pictographs.

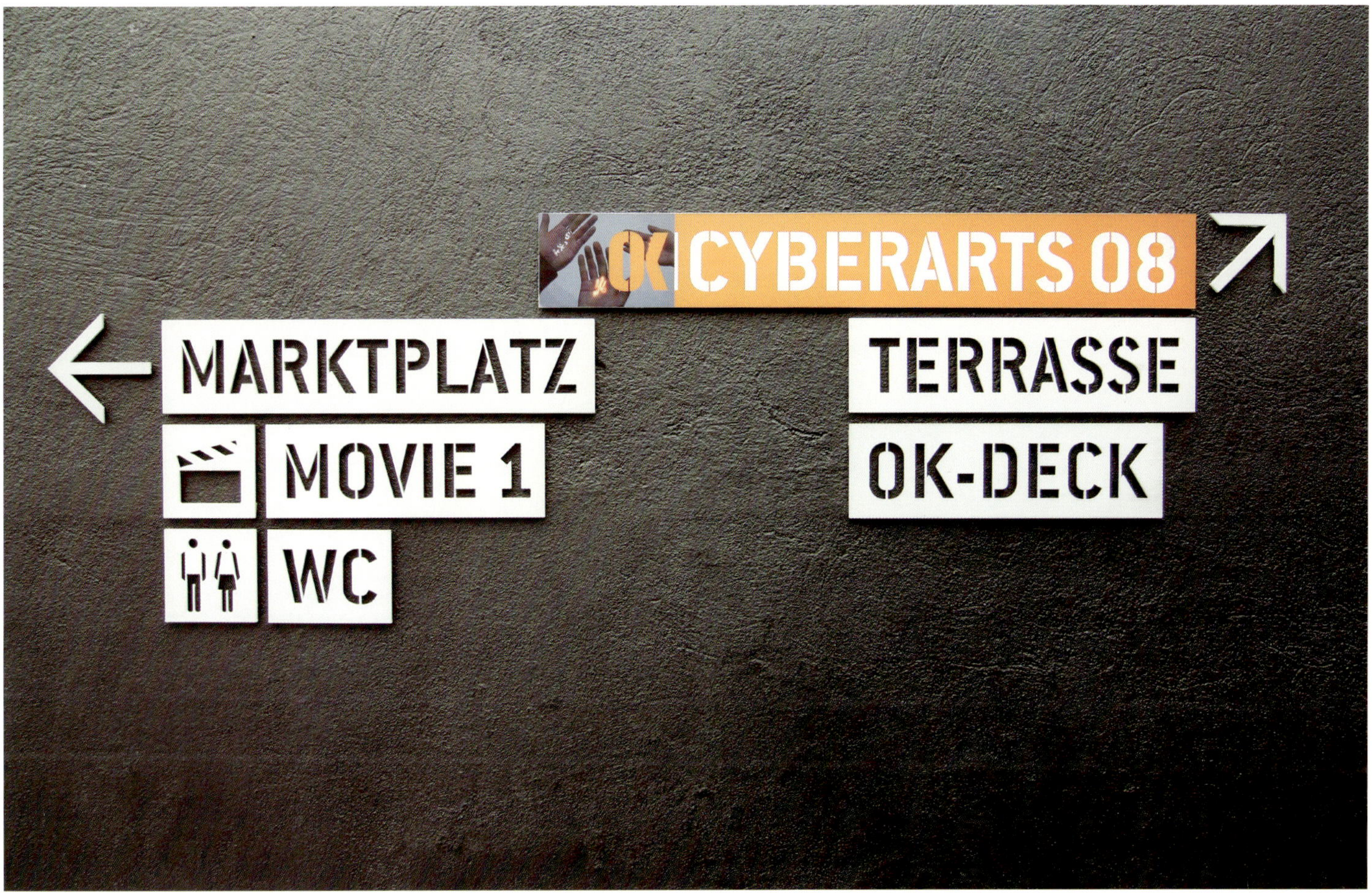

abcdefghijklmnopqrstuvwxyz

ABCDEFGHIJKLM NOPQRSTUVWXYZ

1234567890

Chasopys Signage System

Designer:
Igor Skliarevsky

"Chasopys" (Ukrainian for "Magazine") is one of the most popular and comfortable places in Kyiv (Ukraine) to socialize, have meetings, work, hold events and give presentations. The visitors don't pay for food or drinks, but for the time they spend. The space is divided into thematic zones, each of which is intended for different activities — from watching a movie with a small group of friends or having a conference to working alone over a cup of coffee in a quiet setting. There are 7 halls in total, spread over two stories. It's not easy to find your way around all of this, so new visitors are greeted at the entrance by hosts who provide them with a map of the building and take them on a small tour. Besides the map, a clear and simple signage system was developed that speaks to the user in simple language rather than in code or symbols. For example, the sign on the Office reads, "Here you can scan and copy documents and use a projector, flip-chart and fast Internet for video-conferences." Some of the signs are made of material on which users can write with chalk, so hosts and visitors of "Chasopys" can supplement the navigation with up-to-date information on what will take place in the building and when.

Кінозал

Тут можна переглянути
фільм з медіатеки
або подивитись світ

Дванадцять

Тут можна розрахувати,
відсканувати, скористатися
проектором, фліпчартом
та видрукним швидкісним
інтернет-з'єднанням

Резерв
17.00

Вбиральня

Сходи

Настільний футбол,
турнік, куточок
речей ручної роботи

Камінна

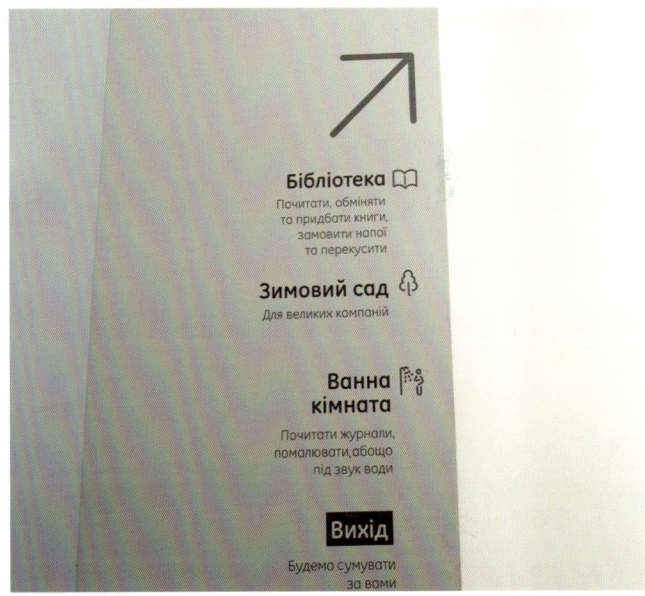

Бібліотека

Почитати, обміняти
та придбати книги,
замовити напої
та перекусити

Зимовий сад

Для великих компаній

Ванна
кімната

Почитати журнали,
помалювати, абощо
під звук води

Вихід

Будемо сумувати
за вами

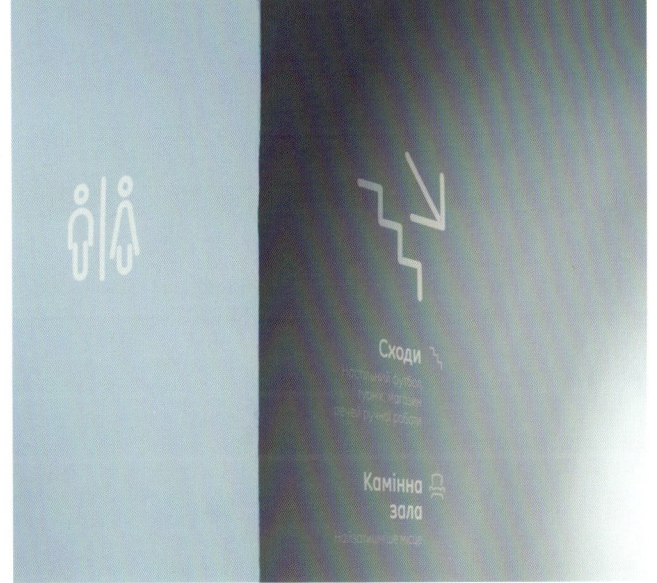

Сходи

Настільний футбол,
турнік, куточок
речей ручної роботи

Камінна
зала

Elisava School
of Design Signage

Designer:
Albert Trulls, Javi Sastre

Client:
Elisava. Barcelona School of Design and Egineering

Elisava is one of the leading design schools in Spain and it is located in Barcelona's city center.

The school moved to a new building next to one of the most iconic landmarks in the city, Les Rambles, to which a signage had to be designed. The school decided that this signage had to be carried out by the students, and Albert and Javi designed this proposal that became the basis for the final signage.

The interior distribution of the new headquarters had a huge 'plaza' in the middle and, from there, many dead end corridors emerged forming a quite confusing hallway network. Moreover, almost all all the walls were grey, which generated an unpleasant feeling of disorientation on the visitor's mind.

Albert and Javi's proposal aspired to solve this confusing sensation just after the visitors had entered the building by placing a powerful graphic signage in the middle hall. These metallic surfaces placed in each floor had a big letter on one side and some more precise directions on the other. This first boards helped the students locate their destination and, on the go, other signs would give them more accurate information, including maps, classes, toilets, offices, etc.

The external signage had also to be taken into account so Javi and Albert's proposal was to place a huge vinyl logotype of the school in the Les Rambles facade. This was an effective way to show to all pedestrians that Elisava was now there.

Wayfinding Deakin Library

Designer:
Kine Halland

Client:
Deakin University Library

Photography:
Kine Halland

The development of a strategic Wayfinding and Navigation proposal for Deakin University Library, was an assignment in the last semester of Bachelor of Creative Arts at Deakin University.

This Wayfinding design proposal complements the library interior through shape, curve and colour. The concept is built on the rotated D-shape in the Deakin University emblem and all elements of the design are based on this shape to create a cohesive look for the wayfinding system.

The colour palette is strong and fresh and is used to colour code the library sections and levels. The three levels are divided by three main colour groups, while each section of the library has been given its own colour.

Three forms of library maps are implemented in the wayfinding system; main signboard, wall print, and pocket maps. The colour coding of levels and sections as well as the well distributed maps make the navigation of the library intuitive and effortless.

The wayfinding proposal is based on a systematic and sophisticated iconographic design strategy. The basic shape applied throughout the design, from each pictogram to signage and supporting elements, is designed with recognisability and consistency in mind. The colour coding of levels and sections together with the well distributed maps make the navigation of the library intuitive and effortless.

 Arts and recreation

 Literature

 Social Science

 Religion

 Science

 Technology and applied Science

 Journals

 Computer science, information and general works

 Language

 Philosophy and Psychology

 K-Law

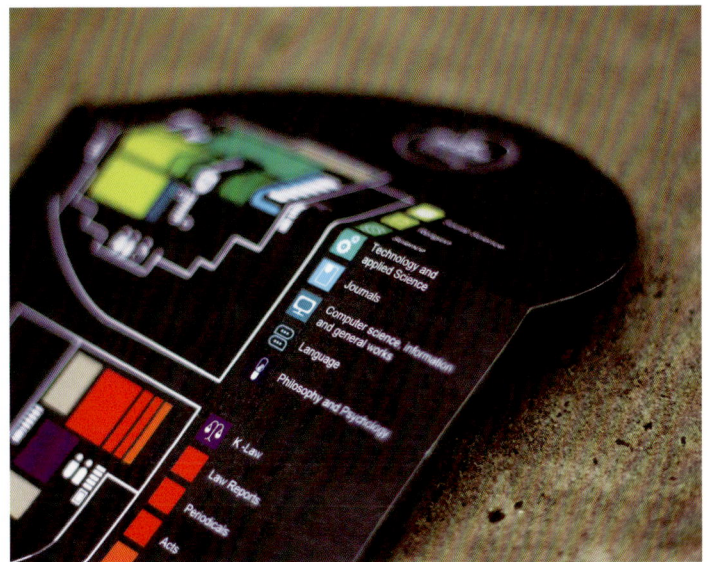

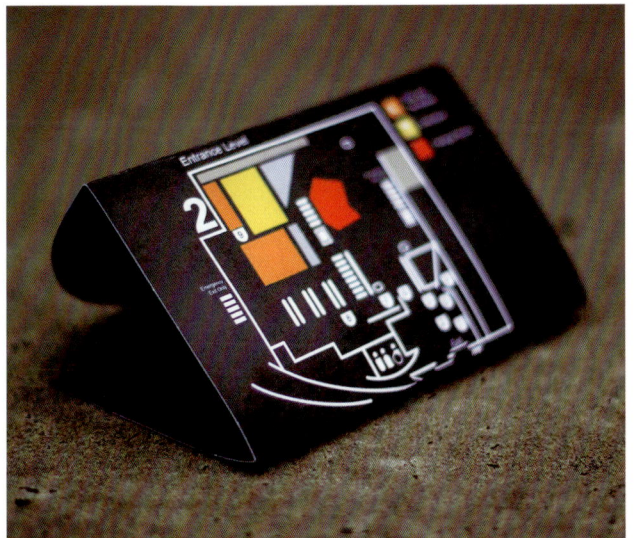

The Space Program

Design Agency:
Foreign Policy Design Group

Photographer:
Jovian Lim

The Space Program is a location-specific project that endeavours to revitalize ordinary spaces by providing a unique experience that is part museum, store and installation.

Re-interpreting and re-capturing the charm of ordinary spaces within a city, The Space Program seeks to redefine and re-engage visitors where they can learn about local culture in an unconventional context. Intended as part museum, part retail store and part installation; it features a curated mix of objects where design, intellect and contemporary culture meet. Globally expandable as a concept, the goal is to embed The Space Program within different cities around the world, such that each new insertion introduces a renewed appreciation of the space.

THE
SPACE
PROGRAM

is a location-specific global project that
aims to revitalise ordinary spaces by
providing a unique experience that is part
museum, store and installation.

A PROJECT BY
FOREIGN POLICY
DESIGN GROUP
WITH UNLISTED
COLLECTION

THE
SPACE
PROGRAM

THE
SPACE
PROGRAM

is a location-specific global project that
aims to revitalise ordinary spaces by
providing a unique experience that is part
museum, store and installation.

Signage and Wayfinding for UPTEC Innovation Center

Design Agency:
Claan

Designer:
Clara Vieira, Andreas Eberharter

Client:
Science and Technology Park of University of Porto

Photographer:
Clara Vieira, Andreas Eberharter

With the opening of the Innovation Center in Porto the building itself had to become the communication catalyst of UPTEC's values. Claan created a signage system and tailored a communication strategy which expands beyond the walls to turn the Innovation Center into a landmark and communicate through the signage the aspects of research, experimentation and science. The initial hospital like corridors has become full of color and life through the invasive graphics across the space and the creation of illusion. After all science and research are also about creativity and discoveries and the lab signage has taken playfulness and joy into the space.

Claan identified a different approach to innovation as the signage system should be bold, young and dynamic at the same time. By using an anamorphic typography process the studio established a connection between simple numbers and scientific measurements and challenged the conventional idea that innovation can only be realized in high-technology.

The eye height of an average visitor was defined as approximately 1,65m and the numbers are 2,8m. This reference served as the "sweet spot" from which the corridor of the laboratories was perceived in the moment a visitor stepped into the intersection of the entrance hall and that corridor. As the five entrances to the laboratories are aligned on the same wall, the numbers could be visualized in perfect shape and size from that point of view. As soon as an observer leaves the position to approach each laboratory entrance the numbers become bigger and bigger until the point of total distortion. The real measurements of number 5 which is the most away from the entrance to the corridor, is 7m long.
Beside identifying the laboratories in the building and leading the visitors, the bright luminous red color represents forbiddance and creates a natural blocker before knocking or stepping into the sterile research facilities.

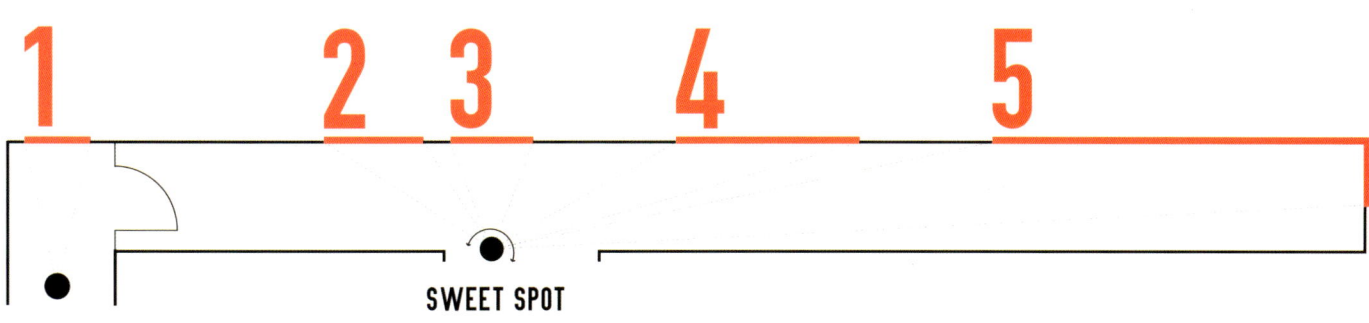

SWEET SPOT

[Observer Vantage Point, 1.65 m height]

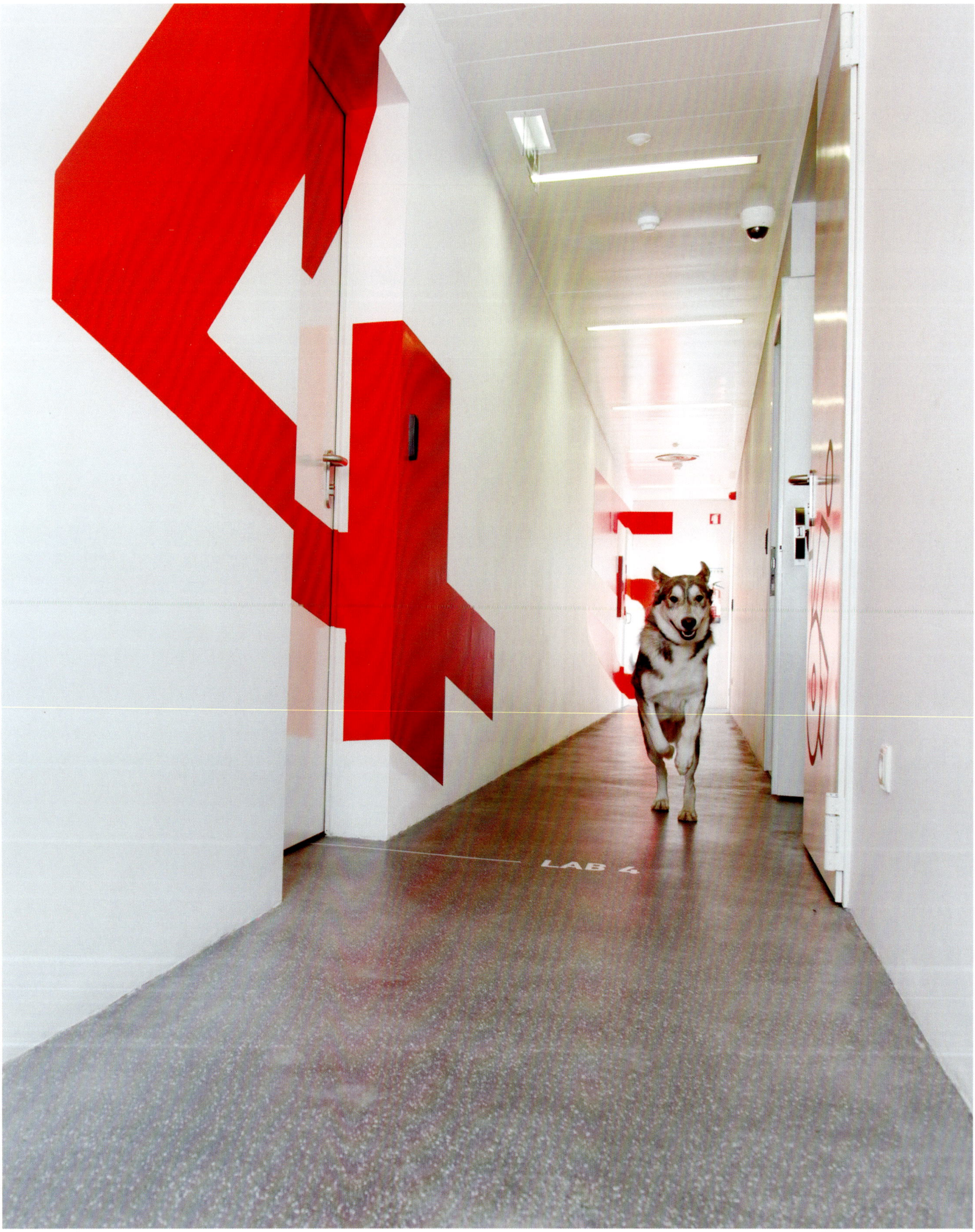

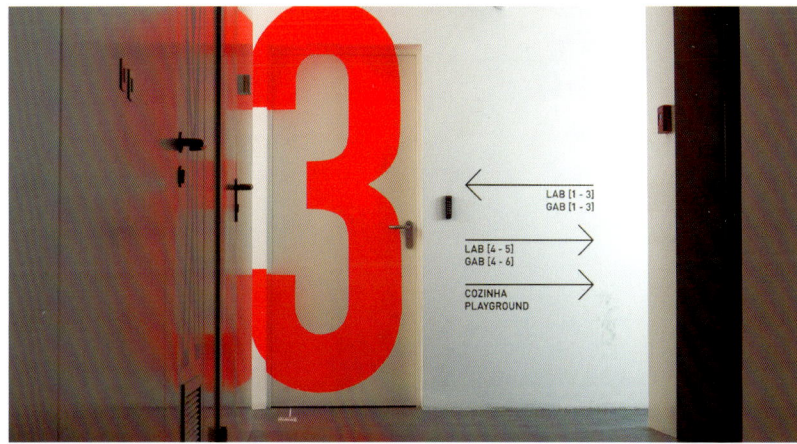

LAB [1 - 3]
GAB [1 - 3]

LAB [4 - 5]
GAB [4 - 6]

COZINHA
PLAYGROUND

[PISO 1]

University's Art and Design Center Signage

Designer:
Kittaya Treseangrat

This project was initiated as a redesign of my University's Art and Design Center - I focused on making navigation of space and environment more accessible, while also improving the visual aesthetic of the area. I attempted to impart a sense of movement and life, while adding the visual effect of three dimensional objects to what was once a fairly drab and uninteresting locale. The bands of color guide the eyes along the length of the building, providing an energetic beacon for first-time and frequent visitors alike. My hope was to create a more inspirational place for art students to congregate and learn in.

Photography:
Kevin Killey Photographics

Designer:
Jason Spencer

Client:
Hardy Milazzo, the Australian Taxation Office

Design Agency:
KS Design Studio

Art Director:
Karin Seja

ATO Adelaide (Australian Taxation Office)

The ATO Adelaide fitout brings together several ATO sites into one building located over 14 floors. The Signage and Wayfinding package designed by KSD captures the ATO strategic direction to engage and motivate ATO staff by contributing to the process of creating a professional and inspiring work place.

Emphasis was placed on creating a strong connection and sense of ownership between the Interiors, the site, the users and the local community. Staff were invited to submit photographs of their most memorable experiences within South Australia. This ignited the concept for naming each level after an iconic South Australian region and to integrate the images as translucent super graphics to become part of the building's fabric.

At least one image from all those who contributed was included in the foyer display. This installation makes for a dynamic communication tool amongst staff.

Times Museum

Design Agency:
250 Gramm / WX-Design

Client:
Times Museum / Guangdong Museum of Arts

Designer:
Nivard Thoes

Photography:
250 Gramm

Wayfinding & Environmental graphics for the new branch of the Guang Dong Museum of Art designed by distinguished architect Rem Koolhaas (O.M.A).

Dutch typographic designer Nivard Thoes created a tailor-made bilingual typeface for English and Chinese lettering, designed with stencil features for sign-panels and interior graphics applied directly on concrete walls and flooring for a total space of 28,000 square meters.

The conceptual approach was inspired by the architects original intention of creating a 'printed museum' merging graphics into it's interior. To achieve the fusion of 2 dimensional elements into space the signage was developed as a second skin, directly applying lettering on the interior surface. The industrial style way-finding approach was combined with secondary wall mounted sign-panels made of stainless steel with laser-cut lettering.

109

Kwa Mai Mai

Designer:
Osmond Tshuma

Studio:
Department of Graphic Design (University of Johannesburg)

Lecturer:
Sidhika Sooklal

Photography:
Osmond Tshuma

The wayfinding system for Kwa Mai Mai was an assignment undertaken by Osmond Tshuma at the Department of Graphic Design (University of Johannesburg) in 2012.

The project required the creation of a brand identity, pictograms and a set of environmental graphics that were impactful, useful and potentially unique and could communicate information to a specific target group in a persuasive and professional manner.Kwa Mai Mai is a place where one can find any Zulu traditional regalia in Johannesburg; one is able to meet Sangomas (Traditional healers) who use real animal parts to cure sicknesses. The logo concept of the Kwa Mai Mai is derived from the African wooden masks; the shape also echoes a fingerprint, creating a suggesting that each Sangoma is different from another because of different ancestral spirits (Zulu: Amadlozi). The shapes, dots and the colour are all linked to native South African tribes.

The visual language is inspired by Southern African patterns. The visual language is designed in a way, which gives honour to the African tribes. The visual language has a "sense of place", and it enhances the place's visual appeal and identity, and ultimately making Kwa Mai Mai more memorable to residents and visitors. The visual language also reassures and encourages exploration/ wandering and discovery hence making people can engage with the place.

KWA MAI MAI

Pottery

Umqombothi
(Traditional Beer)

Imikhonto nezivika
(Spear & Shields for sells)

Telephone

Herbs

Dried fruits

Ampitheatre

Taxis

No photographs

Thcela & Empande
(Mixed roots)

Dcaba
Herb Incisions

Parking

Traditional Regalia

Tuck Shop

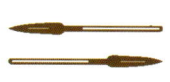

Direction arrows

Rest Rooms

Divination

Khuthala
Pre School

Casa del Lector. Identity / Signage System

Designer:
Alberto Corazón, Oyer Corazón

Client:
Fundación Germán Sánchez Ruipérez

Photography:
Ricardo Santonjal+D+Art

Casa del Lector (Reader´s House) is one Technical Center of Fundación Germán Sánchez Ruipérez. It opened its doors on Oct 2012, but Alberto Corazón and Oyer Corazón had been working on its signage system and identity since June 2009, on a work-in-process that involved the architect, the interior designers and the Client.

Reader's House is the "short name" of the International Center for Research, Analysis, Development and Promotion of Reading, pioneer in the "cultural understanding" of the act of reading. The focus is on the reader, not on reading, nor in books. The Center is located in the former Madrid´s Slaughter house.

For the Identity Signage of Casa del Lector, we created the typeface Futura Lectora, a thickened version of Renner's Futura. Inside we have used many different fonts, letters, words... steel, neon, vinyl, and Dibond, among other materials.

Refracted Light

Design Agency:
P-06 Atelier

Designer:
Giuseppe Greco, Miguel Matos

Photography:
João Morgado | FG+SG

Design Director:
Nuno Gusmão

Client:
Ciência Viva

This intervention is part of an overall environmental graphic design project that we designed for the Pavilion of Knowledge (a science museum in Lisbon, Portugal). The focus of this specific intervention was the museum entrance, where we wanted to create a strong identity that could somehow suggest a little bit of its "curious" scientific contents. The concept was to make an analogy with the effect of light refraction, like a "rainbow". Big window openings were covered with colored transparent film, along with suspended plexiglass colored panels, (that were at the same time the support for communication and signage information). The sunlight variations during the day and the inner artificial light during the night, provide the intervention with a constant ambiance mutation.

Photography:
INTO

Designer:
Richard Wise

Fabrication:
Signbox

INTO University Partnerships Head Office Signage

The signage created for INTO University Partnerships' head office in Brighton, UK, reflects the main elements of INTO's brand. Glazing manifestation is achieved with sweeping curves in translucent red combined with lettering in frosted glass effect vinyl – used for the word 'welcome' in 24 languages at the main entrance, and the company's mission statement across the glazed wall of the board room. The corporate typeface Neo Sans is used as fret-cut and vinyl lettering to indicate spaces such as meeting rooms and hot desks while red vinyl symbols wrapped onto the pillars or applied to the glazing indicate dining areas, printers and tea points.

Inspirational student profiles from INTO's centres across the world are placed throughout the office and a set of university partner plaques adorn the walls of the meeting rooms on all three floors. These are a reminder to staff of the company's achievements and values.

INTO University of East Anglia Wayfinding Signage

Designer:
Richard Wise

Art Direction:
Andy Uren

Fabrication:
Signbox

Photography:
Signbox, INTO

The INTO University of East Anglia Centre for international students in Norwich, UK, is a joint venture between INTO University Partnerships and the University of East Anglia. The way-finding signage for the centre guides people throughout the building and enhances the student experience. Brightly coloured Stealth monolith signs initially lead you to the academic and residential entrances where you are presented with location maps indicating the sections and rooms on each floor. A combination of colour and isolated elements of INTO's brand are used to visually distinguish each floor level in a way that works in harmony with the contemporary nature of the building, providing students and staff with a stimulating environment in which to live, work and learn.

Wayfinding for the Institute of Genomic Research

Designer:
Stephanie Demeter

The Institute of Genomic Research was a wayfinding project I did for a class at Ball State University. Each student was required to redesign a building using wayfinding. The real-life building I was assigned was The Institute of Genomic Research, a company that deals with a lot of science. With a lot of the company's focus being on genetics, I based the logo off of genetic sequencing images and what some charts showed. At the entrance, the viewer is welcomed by the company logo. It introduces them to The Institute of Genomic Research. Each decision point is marked with repetitive colored bars with symbols for each department. These color-bar-paths function as the unique wayfinding device. Walls are repeatedly marked with signage to aid in helping the viewer find their way at each decision point. The stairs act as an aiming device where viewers can reestablish their position. It contains a legend of which departments are on each floor further guiding you to your desired location. Its bright colors make it easy to locate. Each department has its own identity and color, making easy differentiation between departments. The font used is Futura Condensed Medium, giving off a clean and innovative appeal. Wayfinding for the Institute of Genomic research was designed and photographed by myself at Ball State University Arts and Journalism Building.

Elevator

Food

Restrooms

Stairs

Restrooms

Restrooms

Food

Stairs

Elevator

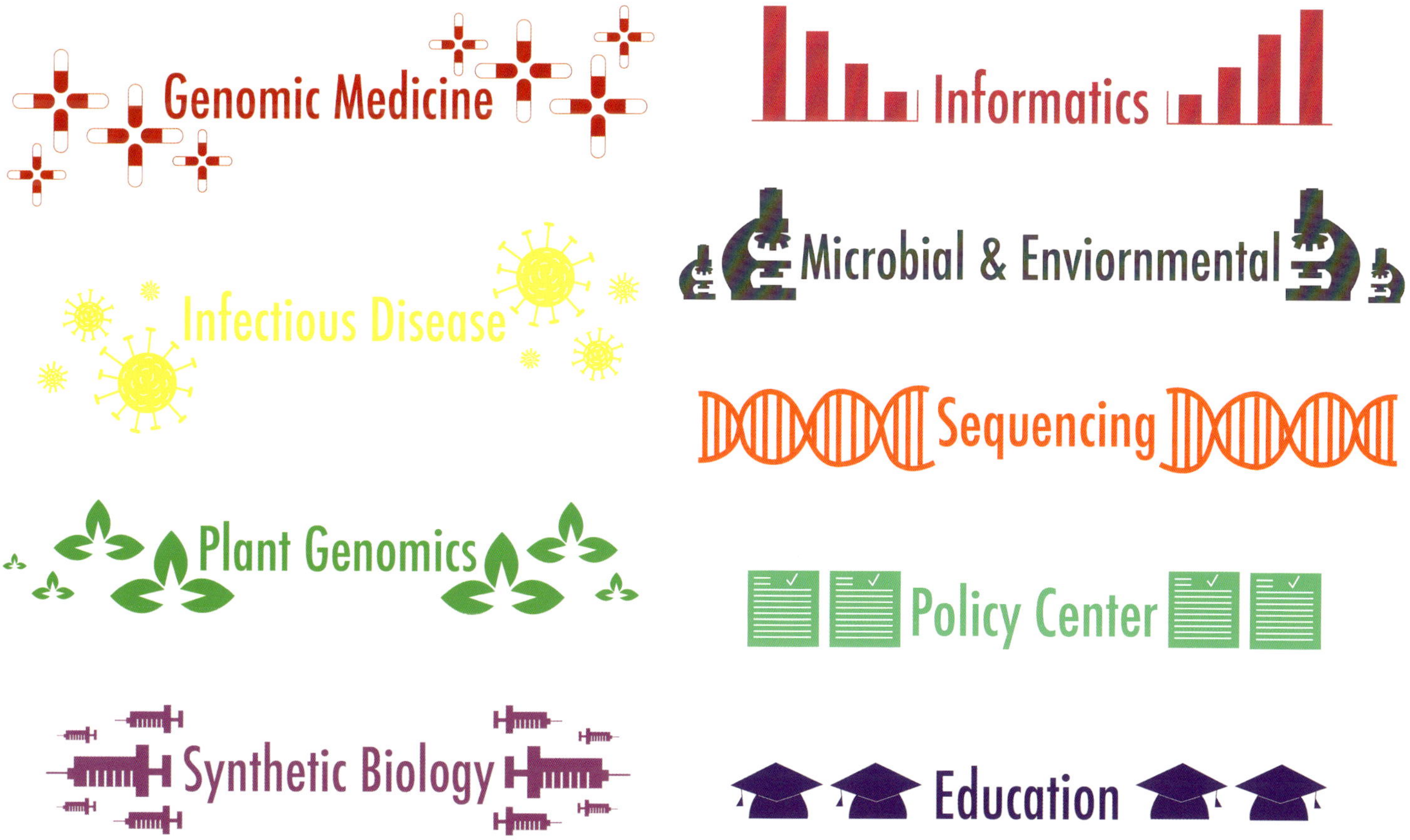

Genomic Medicine

Informatics

Infectious Disease

Microbial & Enviornmental

Sequencing

Plant Genomics

Policy Center

Synthetic Biology

Education

139

Signage and Wayfinding System for the Chamber of Labor (Arbeiterkammer/AK) of Vienna

Design Agency:
Bohatsch und Partner

Photography:
Pez Hejduk, Andreas Soller

The AK is the legal representation of Austria's workers, employees, and consumers. It provides free legal advice to all its members and acts as a think tank for employees' interests.

This design project involved conceiving and realizing a signage and wayfinding system for the main AK building. By converting, renovating, and expanding the AK building, built in the 1950s, the responsible office of architects gave the building a completely new feel without losing its original character. The hall porter's lodge at the entrance, the consultation area, and the info desk became central "distributing points." The various requirements of diverse user groups were a pivotal factor in designing the visual guidance system.

There are three different groups of visitors: visitors who have an appointment need to get their swipe card at the porter's lodge in order to get access to the different floors in the building where main and subsidiary distributors help them find their way; visitors seeking legal advice need to get as directly as possible to their consultants in one of the three consultation pavilions characterized by hanging glass beams with the three-dimensional letters A, B, and C; users of the library (AK Bibliothek) can see the entrance to the library – marked by a three-dimensional, stylized book in bright red – from far off.

I. STOCK

Signage and Wayfinding System for the School Center Krems

Design Agency:
Bohatsch und Partner

Client:
The School Center Krems

Photography:
Andreas Soller

Developing a wayfinding and orientation system, the studio aimed at communicating the positive synergy between the different school types. The campus contains many rooms that can be used by any of the three schools. Only the kindergarten has its own separate building attached to a public car park. The architects (NMPB Architekten) developed their concept for the school from a cuboid form from which elements were cut out. Bohatsch und Partner started to use the resulting elevation views as the basis for their design approach. Using and showing a clear construction process also fit in well with the idea of the campus, allowing students to comprehend the design principles behind the building.

This approach can be seen best by having a close look at the wallpaper design for the school and the kindergarten. The wallpaper shows the various elevation views combined in many variations. Each school has its own color code. As there is space that is used by all schools together, the approach emphasized the synergy by combining the colors on elements used in shared space. Good examples are the wallpapers which are used in all shared spaces and on the signs for rooms.

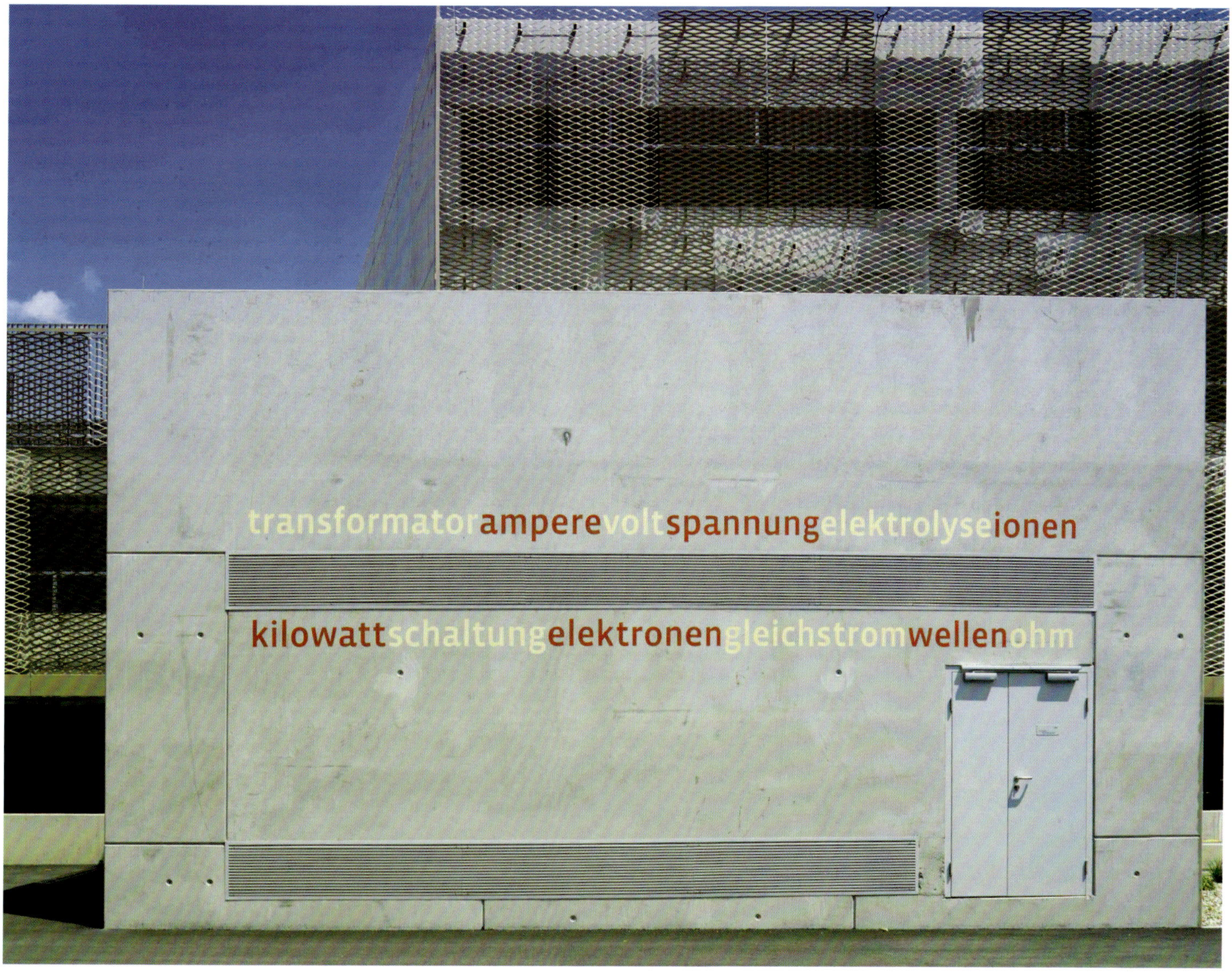

transformatoramperevoltspannungelektrolyseionen

kilowattschaltungelektronengleichstromwellenohm

Parkhaus

120 von Krems

Stadtrichter und Kammergraf. Ebenso reich wie angesehen der irdische Reichtum jedoch nicht erfüllen konnte, vertarbe ermönch.

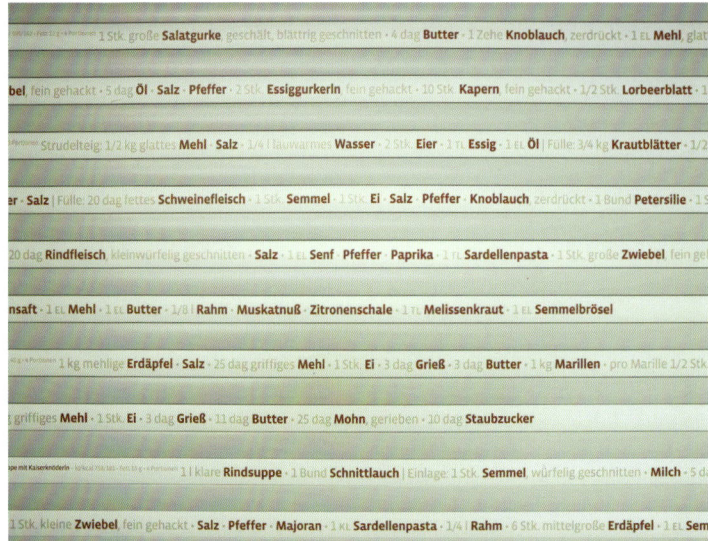

1 Stk. große **Salatgurke**, geschält, blättrig geschnitten · 4 dag **Butter** · 1 Zehe **Knoblauch**, zerdrückt · 1 EL **Mehl**, glatt

bel, fein gehackt · 5 dag **Öl** · **Salz** · **Pfeffer** · 2 Stk. **Essiggurkerln**, fein gehackt · 10 Stk. **Kapern**, fein gehackt · 1/2 Stk. **Lorbeerblatt** · 1

Strudelteig: 1/2 kg glattes **Mehl** · **Salz** · 1/4 l lauwarmes **Wasser** · 2 Stk. **Eier** · 1 EL **Essig** · 1 EL **Öl** | Fülle: 3/4 kg **Krautblätter** · 1/2

er · **Salz** | Fülle: 20 dag fettes **Schweinefleisch** · 1 Stk. **Semmel** · 1 Stk. **Ei** · **Salz** · **Pfeffer** · **Knoblauch**, zerdrückt · 1 Bund **Petersilie** · 1 S

20 dag **Rindfleisch**, kleinwürfelig geschnitten · **Salz** · 1 EL **Senf** · **Pfeffer** · **Paprika** · 1 TL **Sardellenpasta** · 1 Stk. große **Zwiebel**, fein gel

nsaft · 1 EL **Mehl** · 1 EL **Butter** · 1/8 l **Rahm** · **Muskatnuß** · **Zitronenschale** · 1 TL **Melissenkraut** · 1 EL **Semmelbrösel**

1 kg mehlige **Erdäpfel** · **Salz** · 25 dag griffiges **Mehl** · 1 Stk. **Ei** · 3 dag **Grieß** · 3 dag **Butter** · 1 kg **Marillen** · pro Marille 1/2 Stk.

griffiges **Mehl** · 1 Stk. **Ei** · 3 dag **Grieß** · 11 dag **Butter** · 25 dag **Mohn**, gerieben · 10 dag **Staubzucker**

1 l klare **Rindsuppe** · 1 Bund **Schnittlauch** | Einlage: 1 Stk. **Semmel**, würfelig geschnitten · **Milch** · 5 da

1 Stk. kleine **Zwiebel**, fein gehackt · **Salz** · **Pfeffer** · **Majoran** · 1 KL **Sardellenpasta** · 1/4 l **Rahm** · 6 Stk. mittelgroße **Erdäpfel** · 1 EL **Sem**

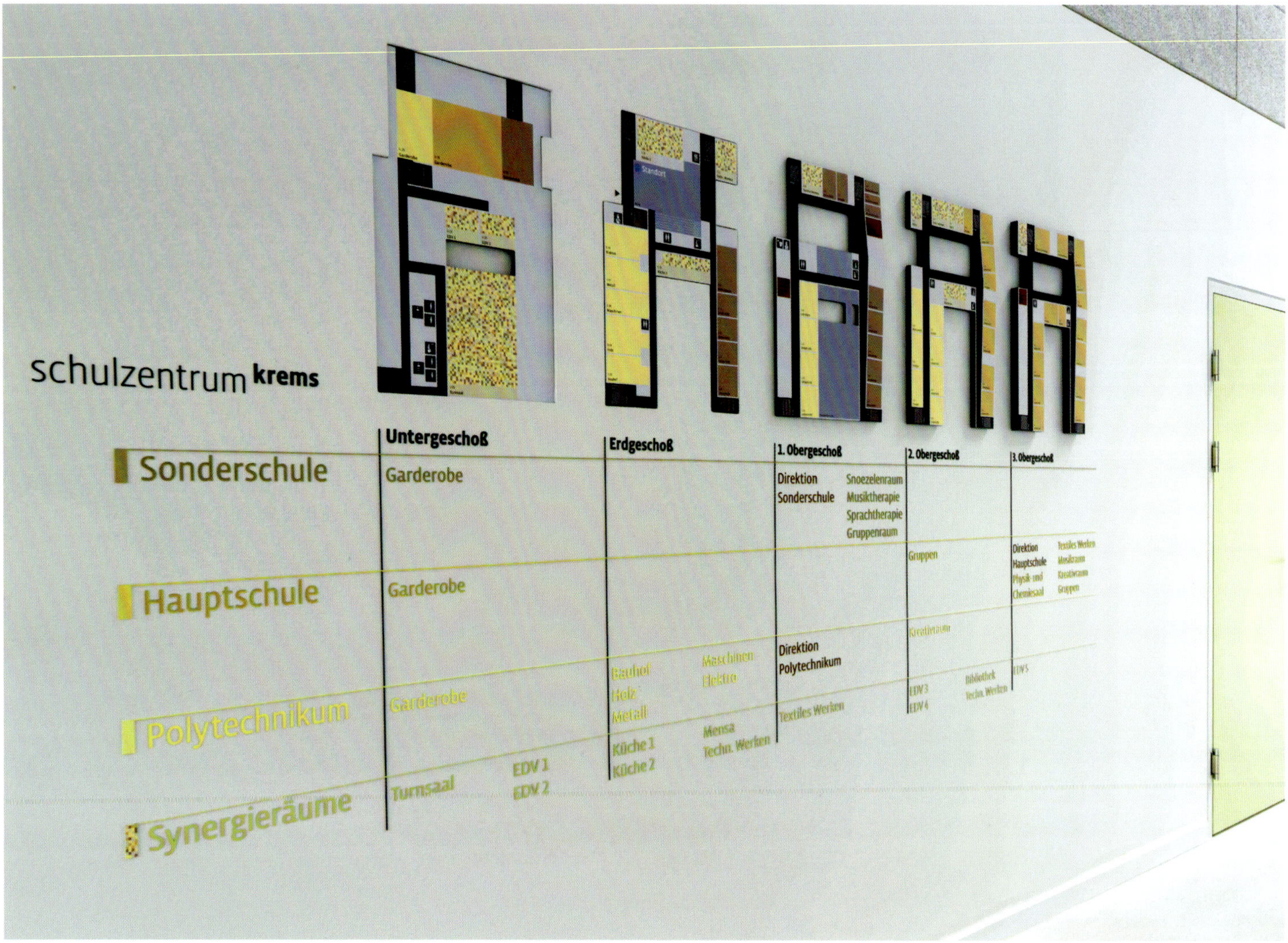

schulzentrum **krems**

	Untergeschoß	Erdgeschoß	1. Obergeschoß	2. Obergeschoß	3. Obergeschoß
Sonderschule	Garderobe		Direktion Sonderschule / Snoezelenraum / Musiktherapie / Sprachtherapie / Gruppenraum		
Hauptschule	Garderobe			Gruppen	Direktion Hauptschule / Physik und Chemiesaal / Textiles Werken / Medizraum / Kreativraum / Gruppen
Polytechnikum	Garderobe	Bauhof / Holz / Metall / Maschinen / Elektro / Küche 1 / Küche 2 / Mensa / Techn. Werken	Direktion Polytechnikum / Textiles Werken	Kreativraum / EDV 3 / EDV 4 / Bibliothek / Techn. Werken / EDVS	
Synergieräume	Turnsaal / EDV 1 / EDV 2				

1. Stock

Erdgeschoß

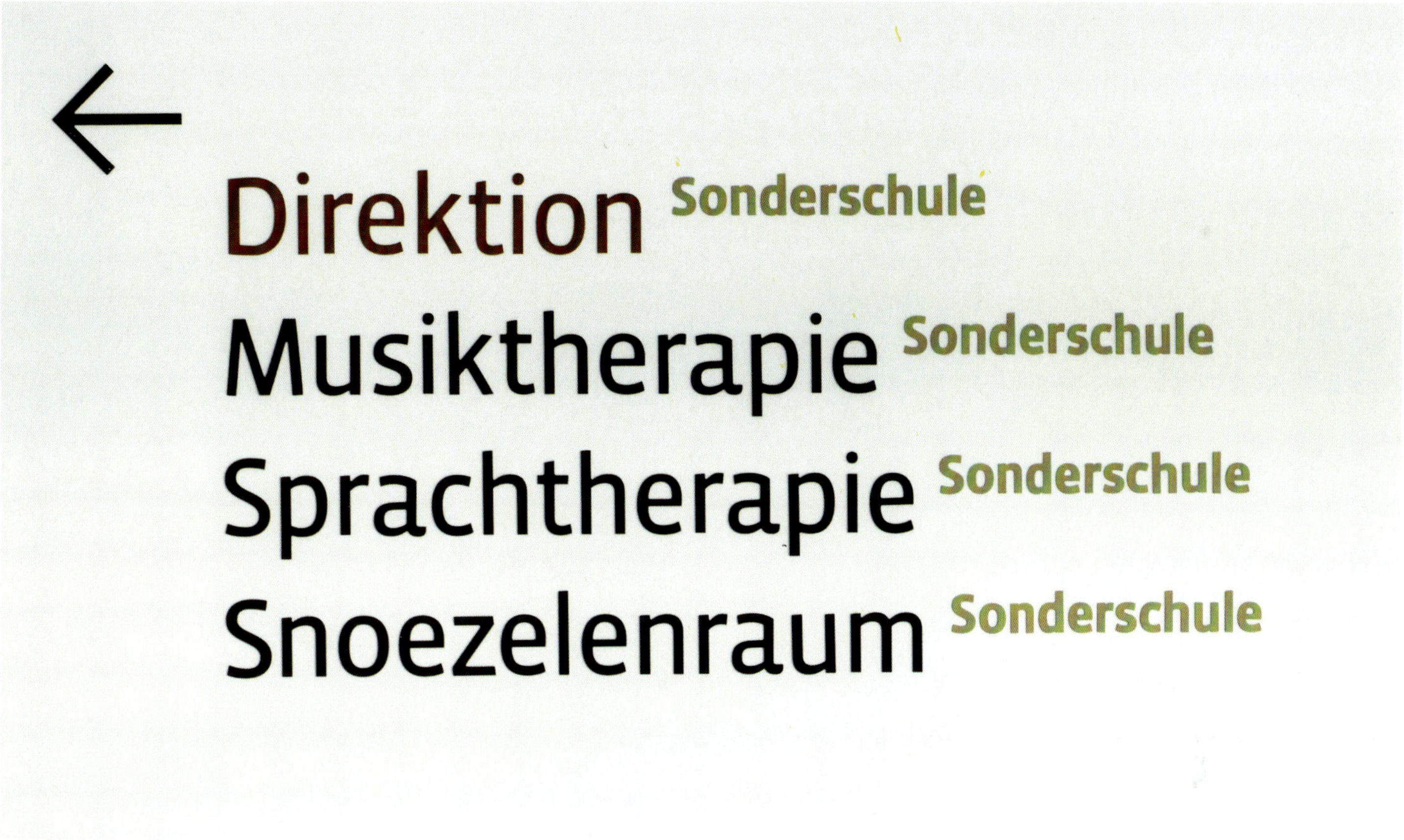

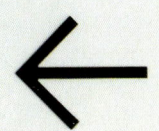

Direktion Sonderschule

Musiktherapie Sonderschule

Sprachtherapie Sonderschule

Snoezelenraum Sonderschule

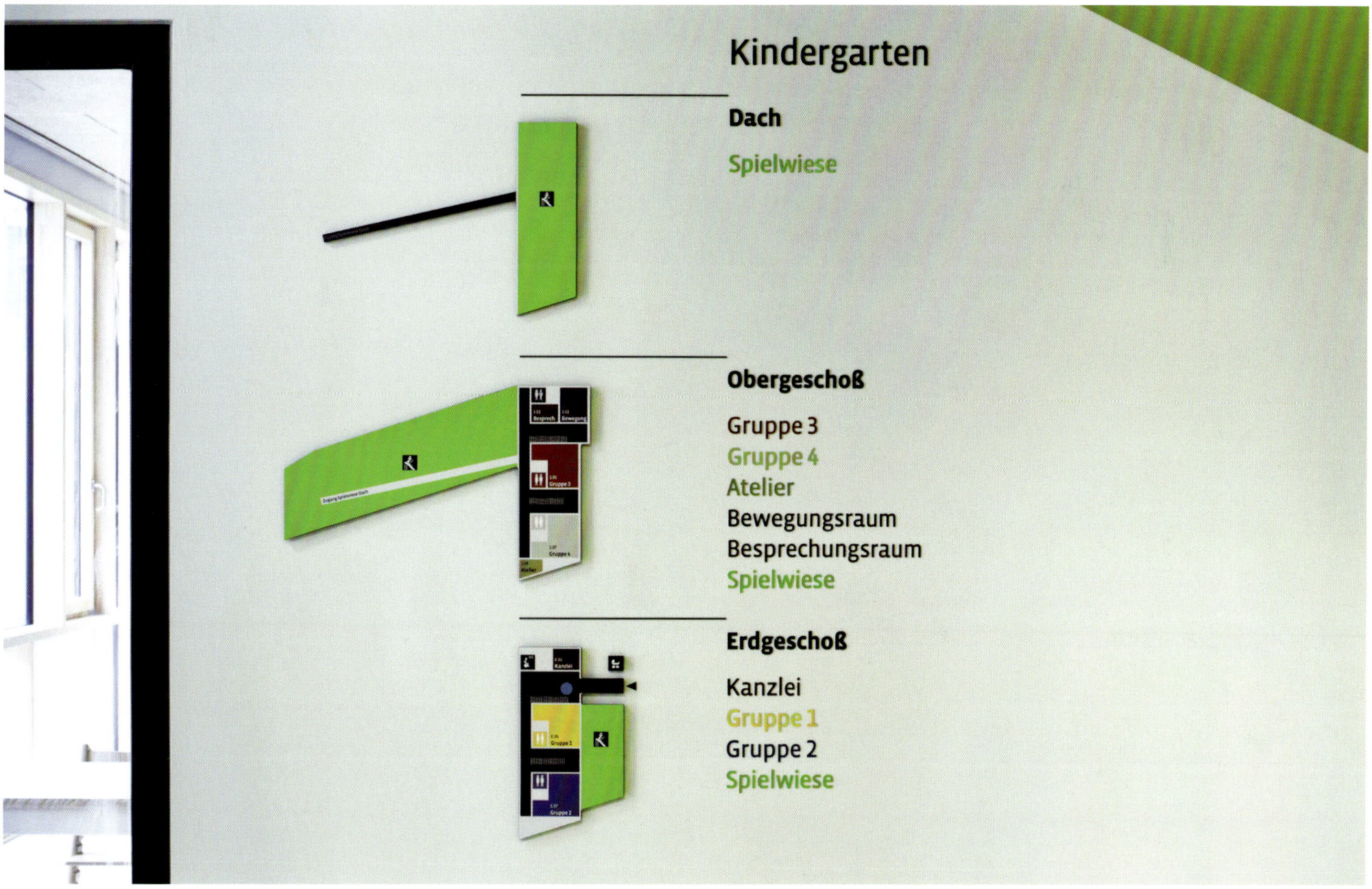

Kindergarten

Dach

Spielwiese

Obergeschoß

Gruppe 3
Gruppe 4
Atelier
Bewegungsraum
Besprechungsraum
Spielwiese

Erdgeschoß

Kanzlei
Gruppe 1
Gruppe 2
Spielwiese

Aargau School of Design

Design Agency:
feinform, Zurich

Graphic Designer:
Andrea Gmünder

Client:
Schule für Gestaltung Aargau, Aarau

Photography:
Jean-Claude Jossen, St.Gallen

Large colorful type decorates the white corrugated sheet metal façade. Set into the depressions of the trapeze corrugated sheets, the characters form a delicate composition, visible only to passers-by and not to be understood as information, but rather as subtle artistic intervention.

In the color-neutral new building, painted white throughout, the lettering provides splashes of color and takes up the idea of overlapping colors as used in the school's current corporate design.

Particular attention has been paid to typography. There is a multitude of fonts, each subordinately labeled with its name, designer and year of creation – a didactic flight of fancy, which extends beyond type to include colors and their technical terms as used in print (Pantone) and architecture (NCS), respectively.

The part of the eye-catcher is played by the isometric drawing decorating the lobby, an abstract representation of the entire complex. Orientation is ensured through generous directions, painted directly onto the white walls using stencils, a technique taught at this school.

The result is a lively, artistic, and playfully didactic, generous guidance and signage system fully taking into account this school of design's purpose and character.

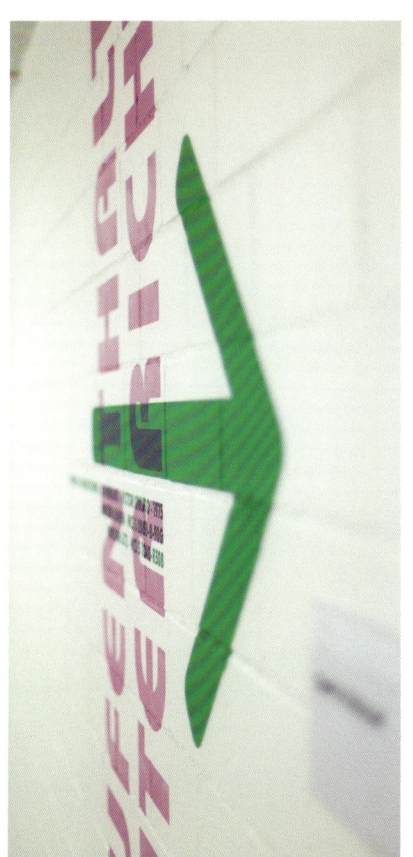

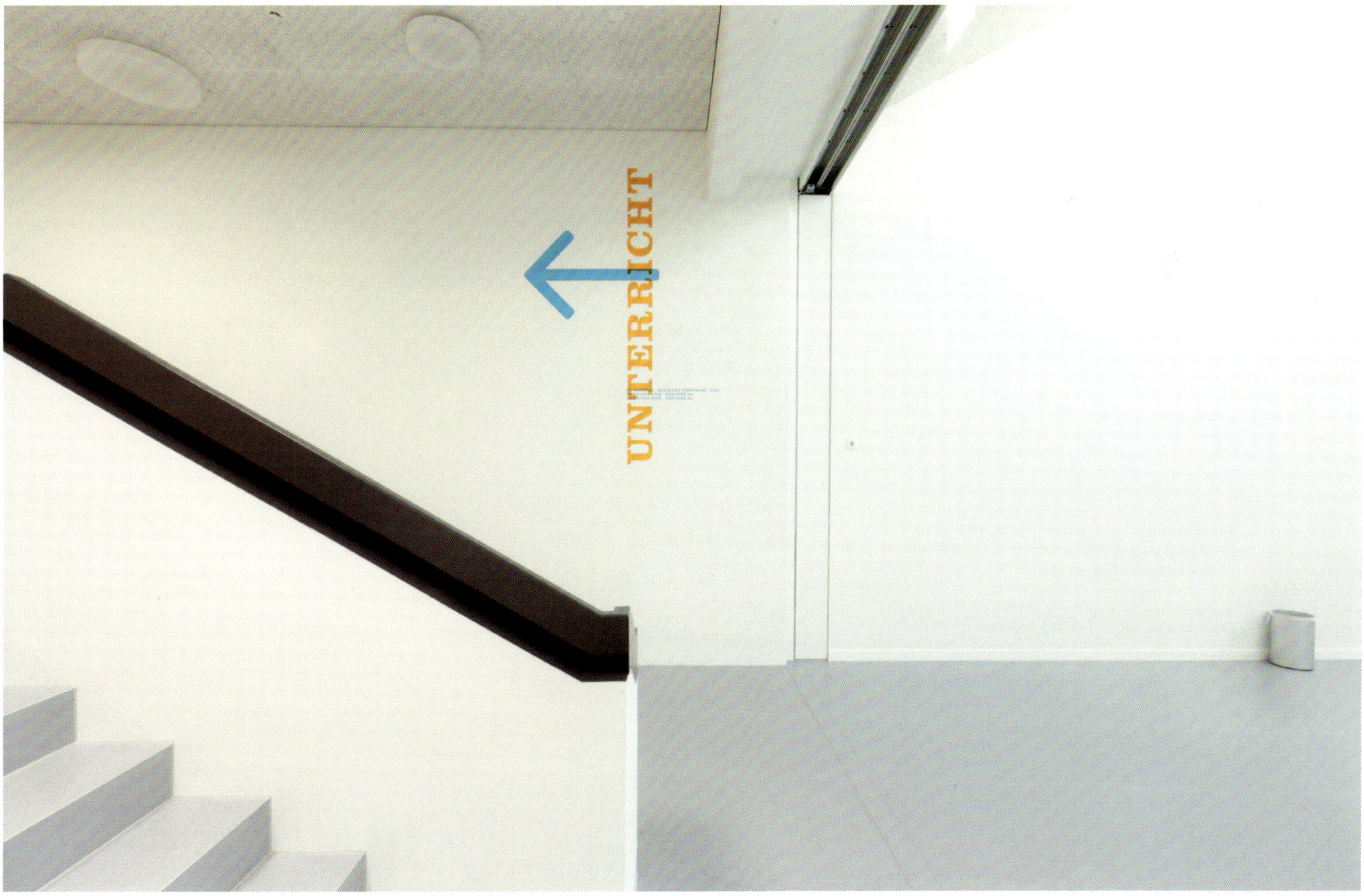

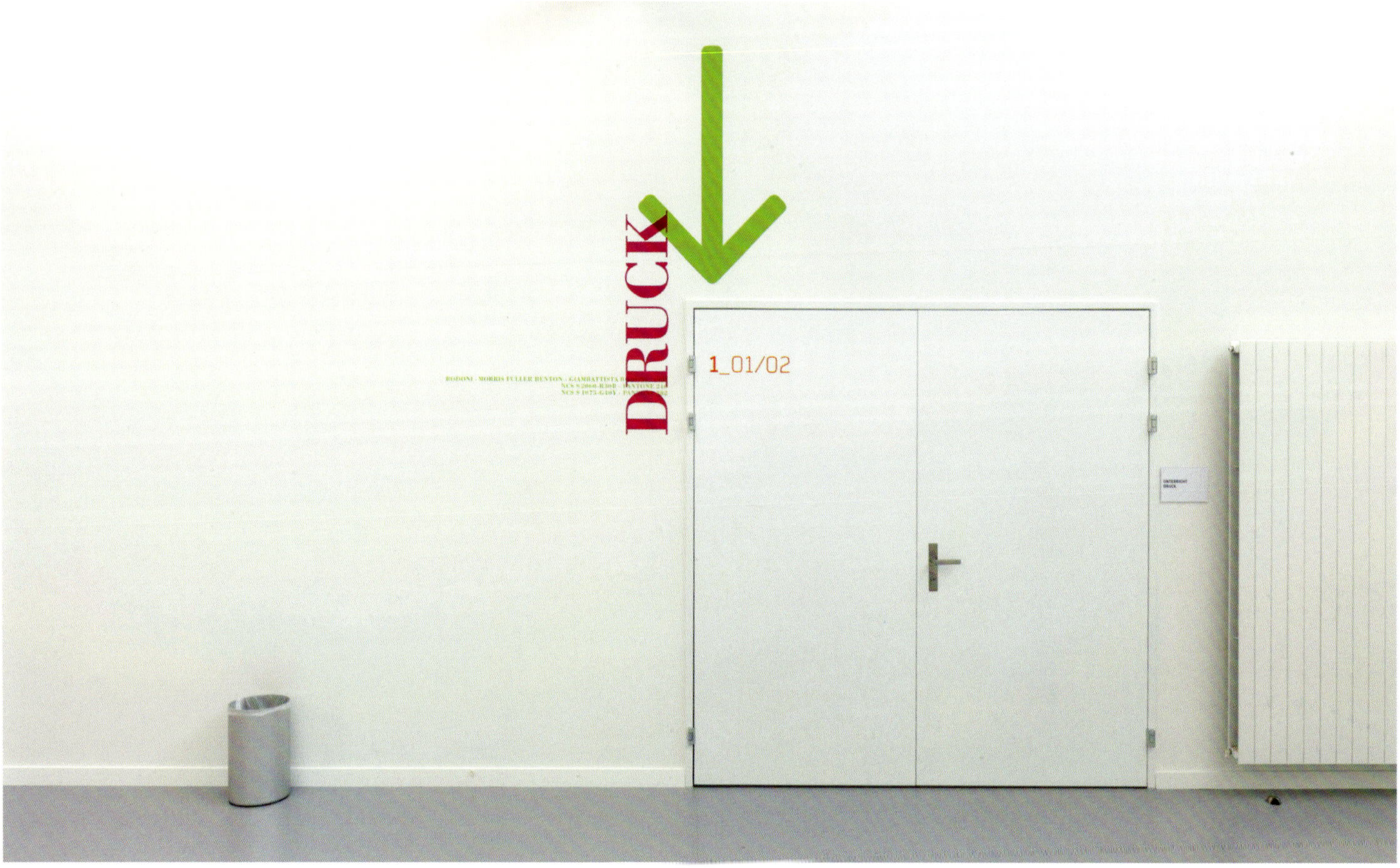

1_01/02

DRUCK

ATELIER

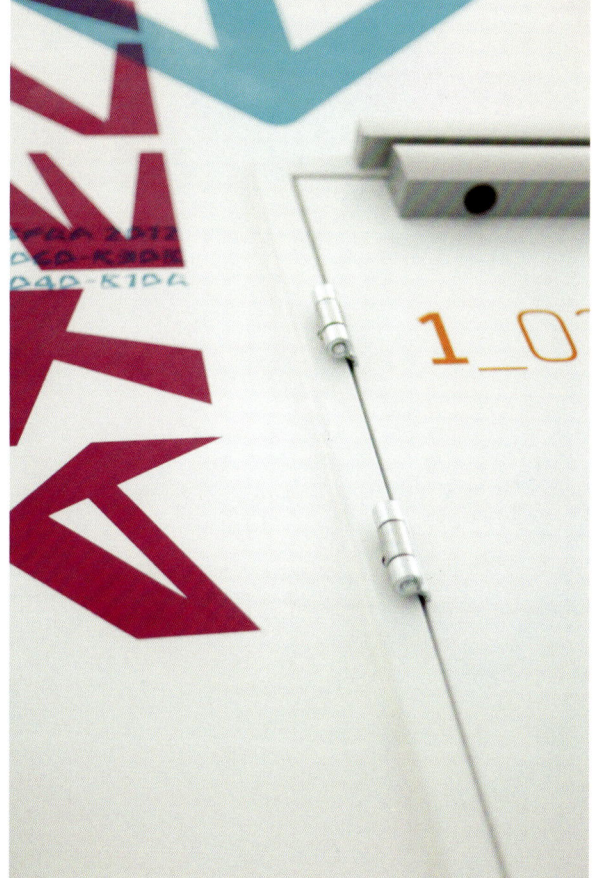

SITZUNG
UNTERRICHT

E_08

SITZUNG

BIOME · CARL CROSSGROVE · 2012
NCS S 1040-B10G · PANTONE 630
NCS S 0580-Y90R · PANTONE RED 032

1_0

DATA SEVENTY · 808
PANTONE 311 ·
PANTONE 382 · NCS S

Forum St.Katharinen

Design Agency:
feinform, Zurich

Client:
Notenstein Privatbank AG, St.Gallen

Graphic Designer:
Andrea Gmünder

Photography:
Jean-Claude Jossen, St.Gallen

The aim of the Forum St.Katharinen signage concept was to bridge the gap, through appearance, lettering and information, between the historic background of the location and the here and now. Using previously existing elements (colors, shapes and materels) for guidance, this connection was established – in harmony with the contemporary architecture and its current purpose.

KIRCHE ST.KATHARINEN >

KIRCHE
ST.KATHARINEN

KIRCHE
ST. KATHARINEN

FORUM ST. KATHARINEN

DIE MAUERN DES FORUMS REICHEN AUF EINE BEWEGTE GESCHICHTE BIS INS JAHR 1228 ZURÜCK.
IM BEWUSSTSEIN DIESES ERBES WURDE DIE ANLAGE 2012 ERNEUERT UND RÜCKSICHTSVOLL ERHALTEN.

GAMMA
SAAL

DELTA
SCHLATTERSTUBE

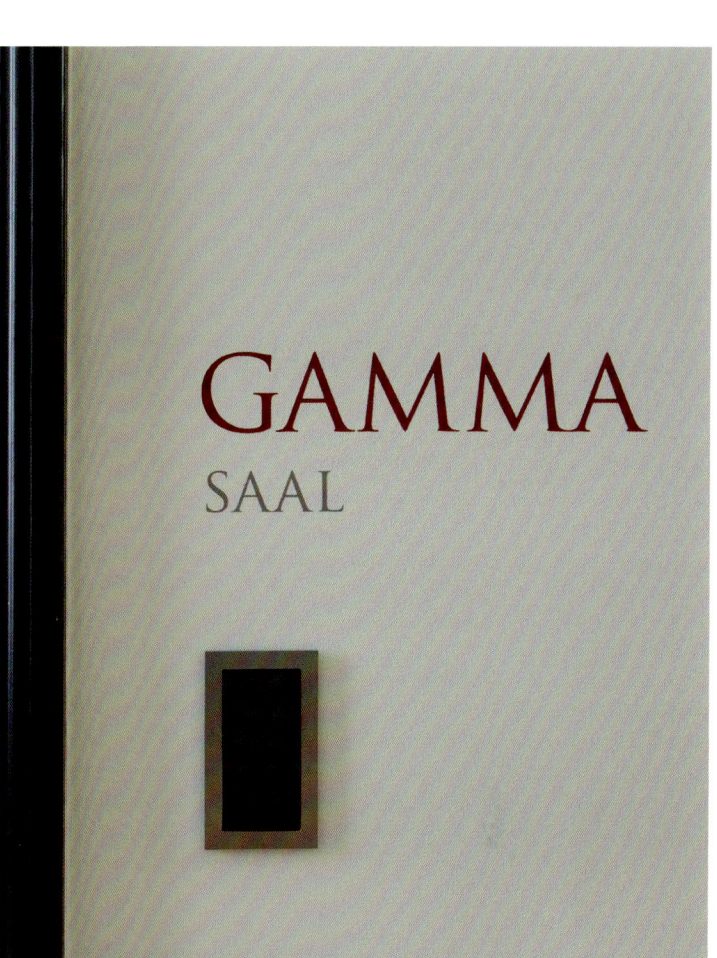

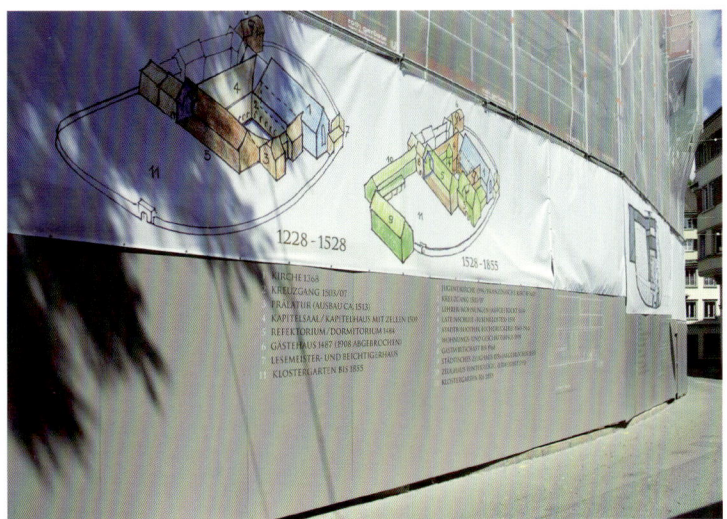

Kurhaus Medical Center Oberwaid

Design Agency:
feinform, Zurich

Client:
TKF / Oberwaid Immobilien AG / HRS, St.Gallen

Graphic Designer:
Andrea Gmünder

Photography:
Jean-Claude Jossen, St.Gallen

On the outskirts of the city of St.Gallen, with a view of Lake Constance, a new health resort with a large medical center has recently been completed. The massive structure with its curved façade is echoed in the corporate design and the signage concept. Hence, the concave and convex exterior visitor guidance signposts.

Generous, yet succinct typography and a color concept matching the interior design characterizes all information throughout the resort: situation plans, signposts, floor indicators, room numbers, spa information, privacy shield strips. Everything is easily legible, everything matches.

RUHE TAU

3 ROOMS
302-352

2 ROOMS
202-252

1 ROOMS
102-152

0 RECEPTION
RESTAURANTS

U1 MEDICAL
CENTER

TAU SPA
HALLENBAD

U2 DIAGNOSTIK
MEDICAL
CENTER

ADIPOSITAS
ZENTRUM

U3 PARKING

TAU SPA

TAU SPA   GARDEROBE HERREN

TAU SPA GARTEN

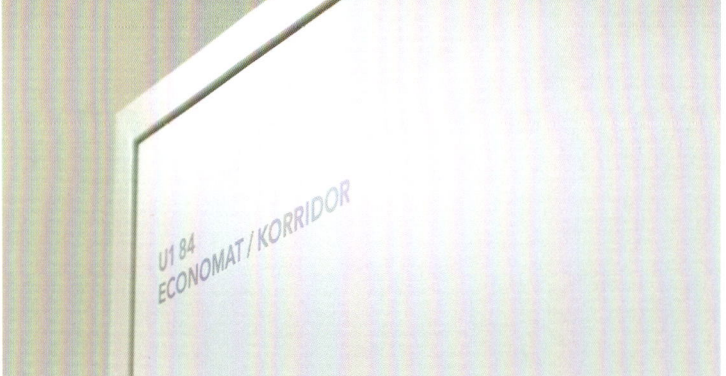

U1 84
ECONOMAT / KORRIDOR

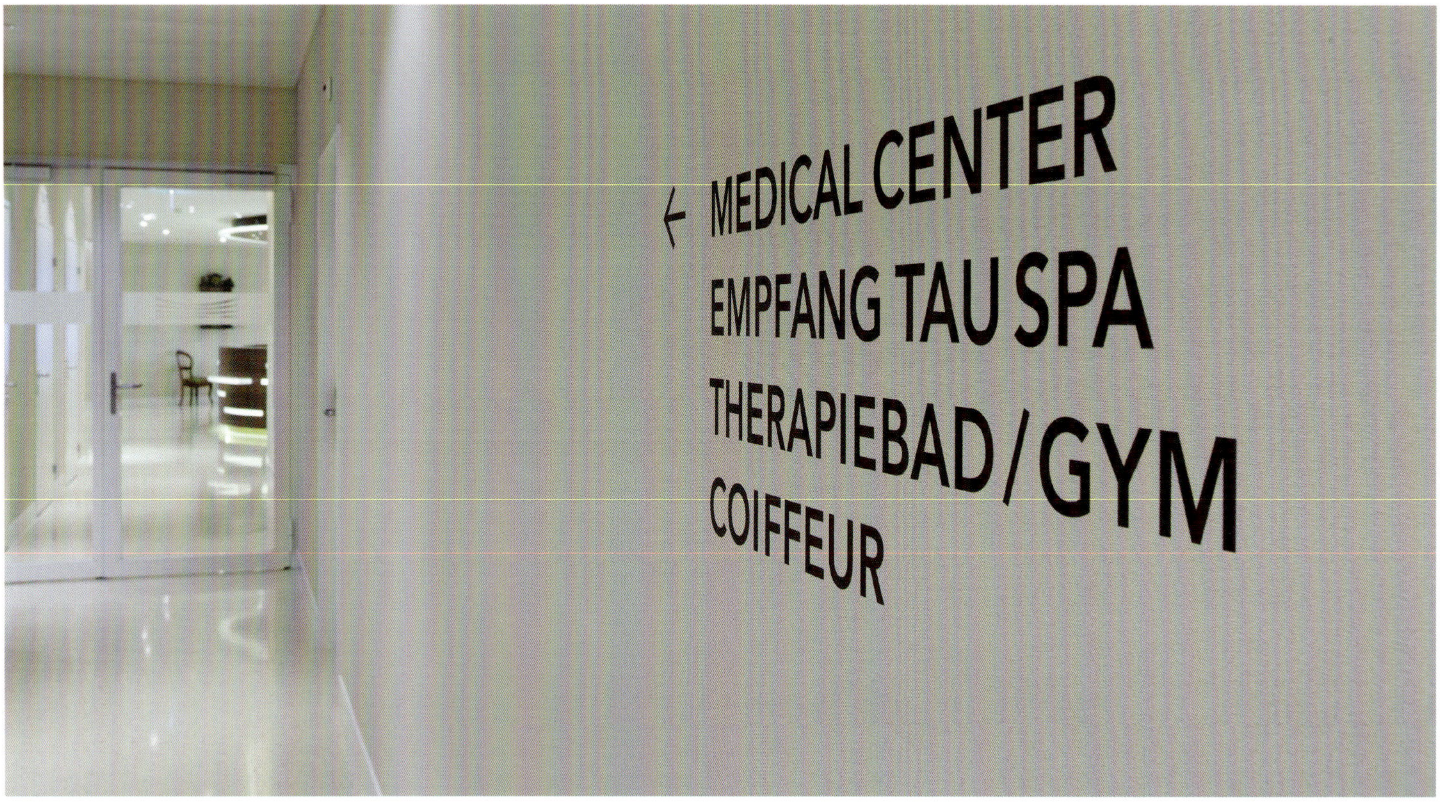

← MEDICAL CENTER
EMPFANG TAU SPA
THERAPIEBAD / GYM
COIFFEUR

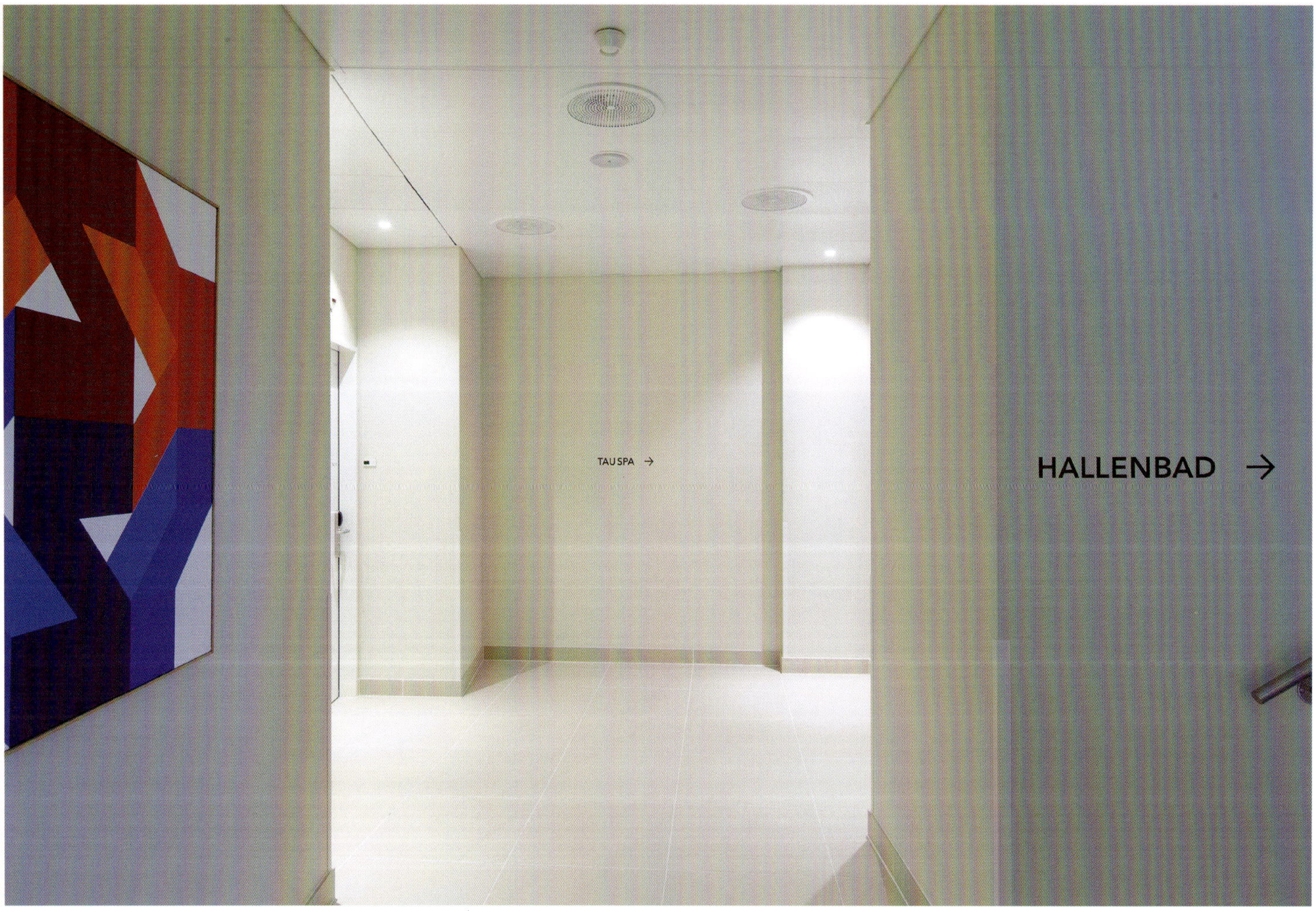

TAU SPA →

HALLENBAD →

LEHRKÜCHE/HERGER'S KITCHEN CLUB

LOUNGE

MEDIZIN/TAU SPA ADMINISTRATION

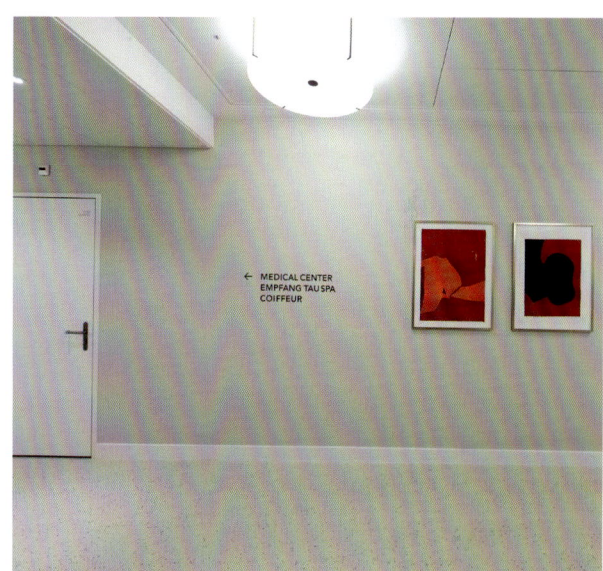

← MEDICAL CENTER
EMPFANG TAU SPA
COIFFEUR

THERAPIEBAD/GYM →

U1

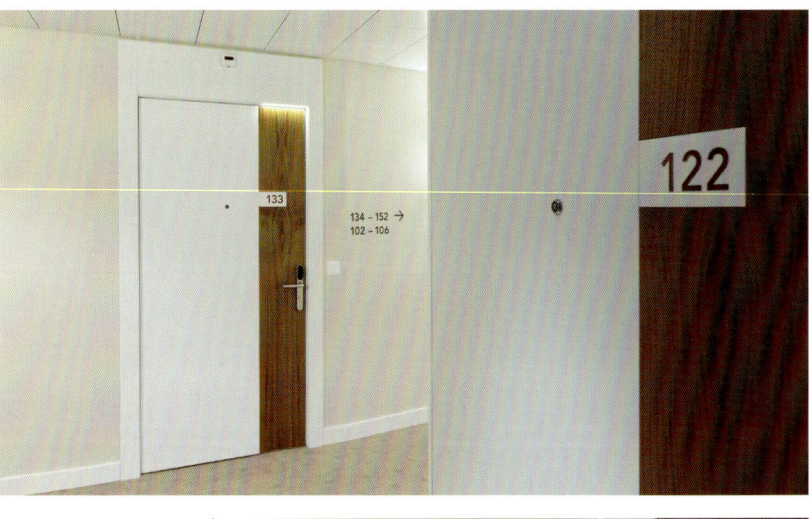

133

134 – 152 →
102 – 106

122

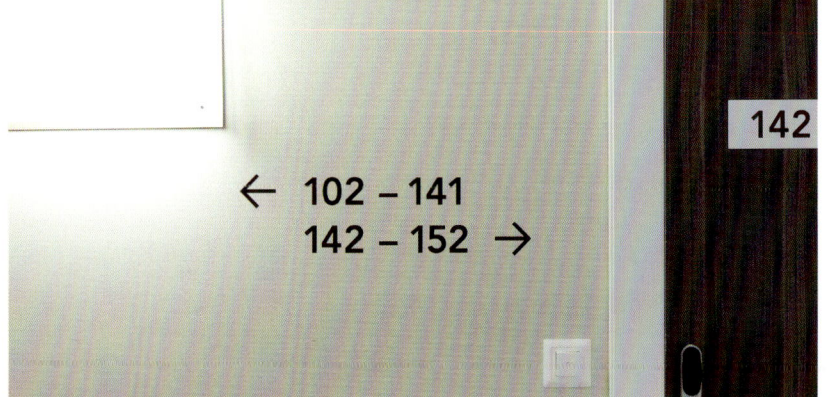

142

← 102 – 141
142 – 152 →

138

138 – 152 →

← 102 – 141

142 – 152 →

MEDICAL CENTER ←

TAU SPA GARTEN

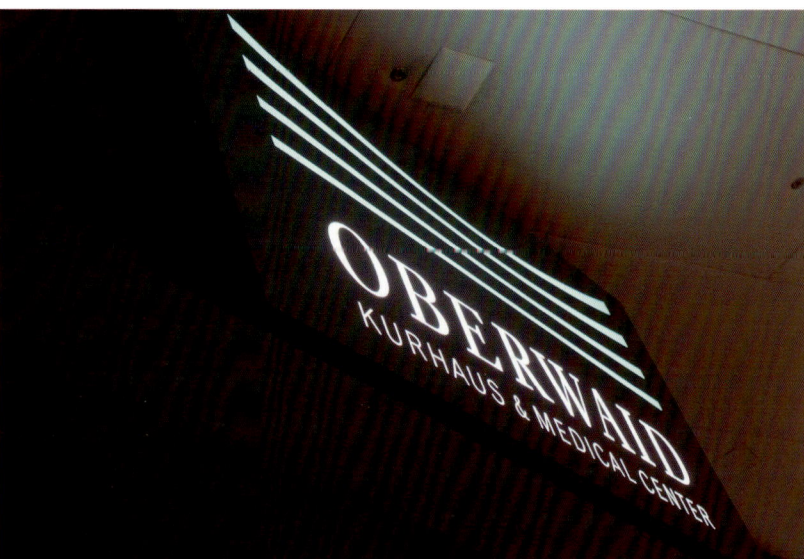

SITZUNG VR

ADMINISTRATION
BITTE ANKLOPFEN UND EINTRETEN

BBZ Biel/Bienne, Technical College

Design Agency:
feinform, Zurich

Client:
Strässler + Storck Architekten, Biel/Bienne

Graphic Designer:
Andrea Gmünder

Photography:
Andrea Gmünder, Zurich

The Biel/Bienne technical college (technische Fachschule), when given a new building – and a proper home of its own –, was open to a new customized signage concept.

The typeface selected is technical in character, following one of the types of vocational training offered by the school: sheet metal punching. Needless to say, the exterior signage is manufactured in-house by the trainees themselves.

In conjunction with the three colors, distinguishing both the school's departments and its floors, the signage concept strikingly complements the building's architecture.

The assignment also included co-designing the refectory walls, the acoustic tile ceilings, the lighting fixtures, and the stairwells' handrails, everything developed out of the basic shapes of the typeface and now acting as art in architecture.

005 ARBEITSRAUM LEHRER
SALLE DE PREPARATION ENSEIGNANTS

Commercial Building
at Blumenbergplatz 3

Design Agency:
feinform, Zurich

Client:
Quarella Architekten, St.Gallen

Graphic Designer:
Andrea Gmünder

Photography:
Büro Quarella, St.Gallen

The striking 1950s building in the heart of St.Gallen has been carefully renovated, giving it a contemporary feel while preserving its style.

The signage concept takes its pointers from the design spirit of the 1950s – using a bold Helvetica font, bleed-off digits, and the color palette typical of that era.

Coffee House Inspired Wayfinding System for NTU, School of Art, Design, Media

Designer:
Ella Han Yuhui

When I came up with a concept to redesign the wayfinding system of Nanyang Technological University, School of Art, Design, Media, I wanted the signage to capture the students' lifestyle beyond the class hours. Staying back in school is a norm, and students often creep out of their dungeons to grab a bite or coffee in the middle of the night. Hence "The Coffee House–inspired" design transpired from the need to exude life and character of the life that runs its course throughout the day.

The retro–styled coffee house design aims to enhance the students' experience while they are working late through the night. The signage becomes fully 'awakened' at night, with the light bulbs activated — giving a sense that there is creativity brewing within its doors. The colours add a warm and cosy feel to the school's concrete interior and the idea of a 'coffee house' subtly lends to the idea that life in an art school is a lot of work and sometimes very little sleep.

All together, the wayfinding system shows that the life in the School of Art, Design, Media never sleeps.

ADM

**SCHOOL OF ART,
DESIGN AND MEDIA**

Film
Product Design
Visual Communications
Photography
Animation
Interactive Media

Art - 02 - 2A
Viscomm Studio

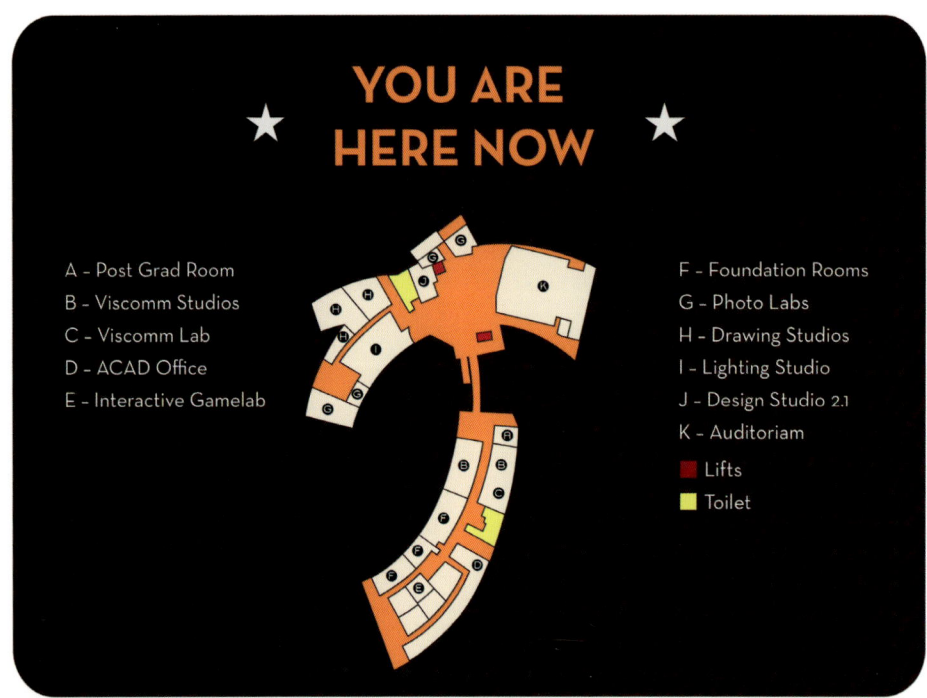

YOU ARE HERE NOW

A – Post Grad Room
B – Viscomm Studios
C – Viscomm Lab
D – ACAD Office
E – Interactive Gamelab

F – Foundation Rooms
G – Photo Labs
H – Drawing Studios
I – Lighting Studio
J – Design Studio 2.1
K – Auditoriam
■ Lifts
■ Toilet

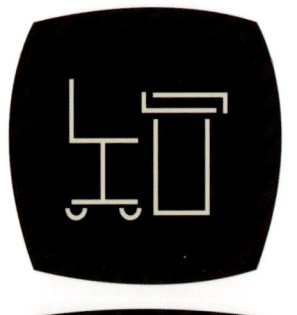

Art - 02 - 2A
Viscomm Studio

Art - 02 - 25
Photo Lab

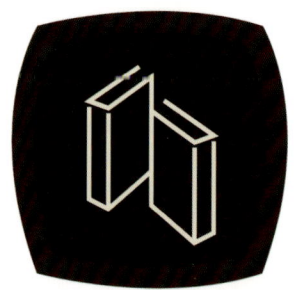

Art - 01 - 06
Gallery

Art - B1 - 02
Lecture Theatre

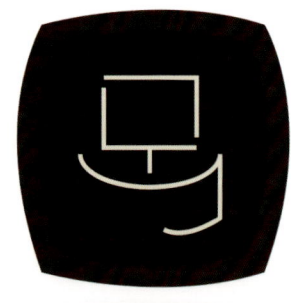

Art - B1 - 4A
Animation Lab

Art - 01 - 17
Sound Suite 1

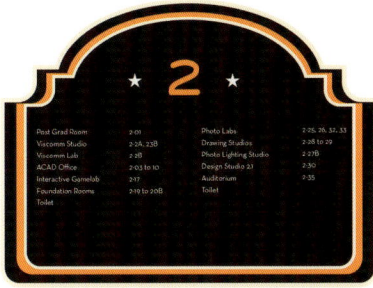

2

Post Grad Room	2-01	Photo Labs	2-25, 26, 32, 33
Viscomm Studio	2-2A, 23B	Drawing Studios	2-28 to 29
Viscomm Lab	2-2B	Photo Lighting Studio	2-27B
ACAD Office	2-03 to 10	Design Studio 23	2-30
Interactive Gamelab	2-17	Auditorium	2-35
Foundation Rooms	2-19 to 20B	Toilet	
Toilet			

3

ACAD Office	3-01 to 15	ACAD Office	3-14 to 23
Toilet		Post Grad Rooms	3-24 to 39
		Toilet	

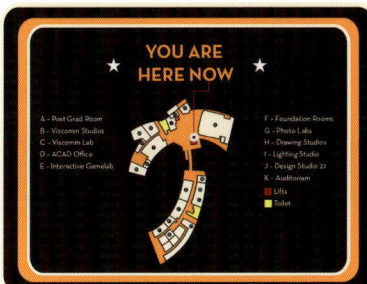

YOU ARE HERE NOW

A - Post Grad Room
B - Viscomm Studio
C - Viscomm Lab
D - ACAD Office
E - Interactive Gamelab

F - Foundation Rooms
G - Photo Labs
H - Drawing Studios
I - Lighting Studio
J - Design Studio 23
K - Auditorium

Lifts
Toilet

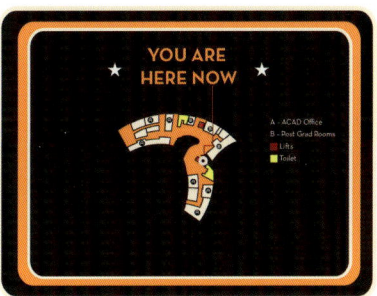

YOU ARE HERE NOW

A - ACAD Office
B - Post Grad Rooms

Lifts
Toilet

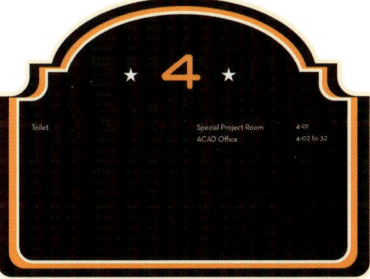

4

| Toilet | | Special Project Room | 4-01 |
| | | ACAD Office | 4-02 to 32 |

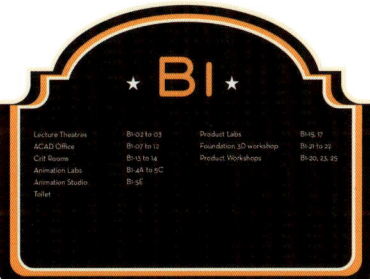

B1

Lecture Theatres	B1-02 to 03	Product Labs	B1-15, 17
ACAD Office	B1-07 to 12	Foundation 3D workshop	B1-21 to 22
Crit Rooms	B1-13 to 14	Product Workshops	B1-20, 23, 25
Animation Labs	B1-4A to 5C		
Animation Studio	B1-5E		
Toilet			

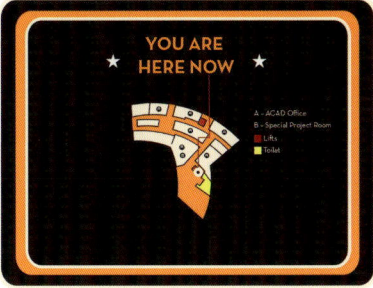

YOU ARE HERE NOW

A - ACAD Office
B - Special Project Room

Lifts
Toilet

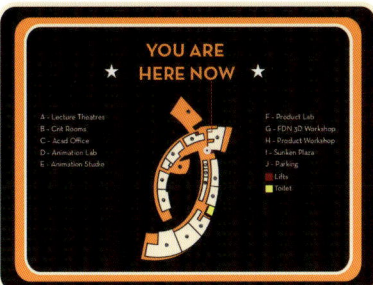

YOU ARE HERE NOW

A - Lecture Theatres
B - Crit Rooms
C - Acad Office
D - Animation Lab
E - Animation Studio

F - Product Lab
G - FDN 3D Workshop
H - Product Workshop
I - Sunken Plaza
J - Parking

Lifts
Toilet

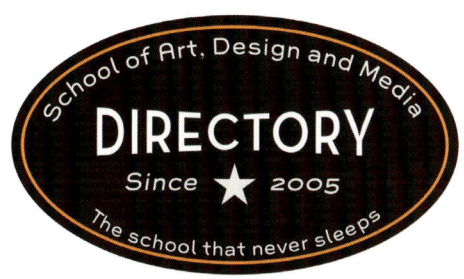

School of Art, Design and Media

DIRECTORY

Since ★ 2005

The school that never sleeps

4	Toilet		Special Project Room	4-01
			ACAD Office	4-02 to 32
3	ACAD Office	3-01 to 15	ACAD Office	3-14 to 23
	Toilet		Post Grad Rooms	3-24 to 39
			Toilet	
2	Post Grad Room	2-01	Photo Labs	2-25, 26, 32, 33
	Viscomm Studios	2-2A, 23B	Drawing Studios	2-28 to 29
	Viscomm Lab	2-2B	Photo Lighting Studio	2-27B
	ACAD Office	2-03 to 10	Design Studio 23	2-30
	Interactive Gamelab	2-17	Auditorium	2-35
	Foundation Rooms	2-19 to 20B	Toilet	
	Toilet			
1	General Office	1-01	Crit Rooms	1-17 to 9
	Gallery	1-06	IT Dept/Equipment	1-10, 14
	Library		Interactive Media Lab	1-11A
	Viscomm Workshop	1-02	Film Editing Labs	1-10, 39
	Toilet		Sound Suites	1-17 to 20
			Rehearsal Studio	1-21
			HD Editing Suites	1-23, 25, 26, 30
B1	Lecture Theatres	B1-02 to 03	Product Labs	B1-15, 17
	ACAD Office	B1-07 to 12	Foundation 3D workshop	B1-21 to 22
	Crit Rooms	B1-13 to 14	Product Workshops	B1-20, 23, 25
	Animation Labs	B1-4A to 5C		
	Animation Studio	B1-5E		
	Toilet			

YOU ARE HERE NOW

A - General Office
B - Gallery
C - Library
D - Viscomm Workshop
E - Crit Rooms
F - IT Dept
G - Interactive Media Lab
H - Film Editing Labs
I - Sound Suite
J - Rehearsal Studio
K - HD Editing Labs

Lifts
Toilet
Cafe

The Cathay Carpark

Design Agency:
Manic Design

Art Director:
Adeline Chong

Photography:
John Nursalim

Creative Director:
Karen Huang

Designers:
Wong Chee Yi

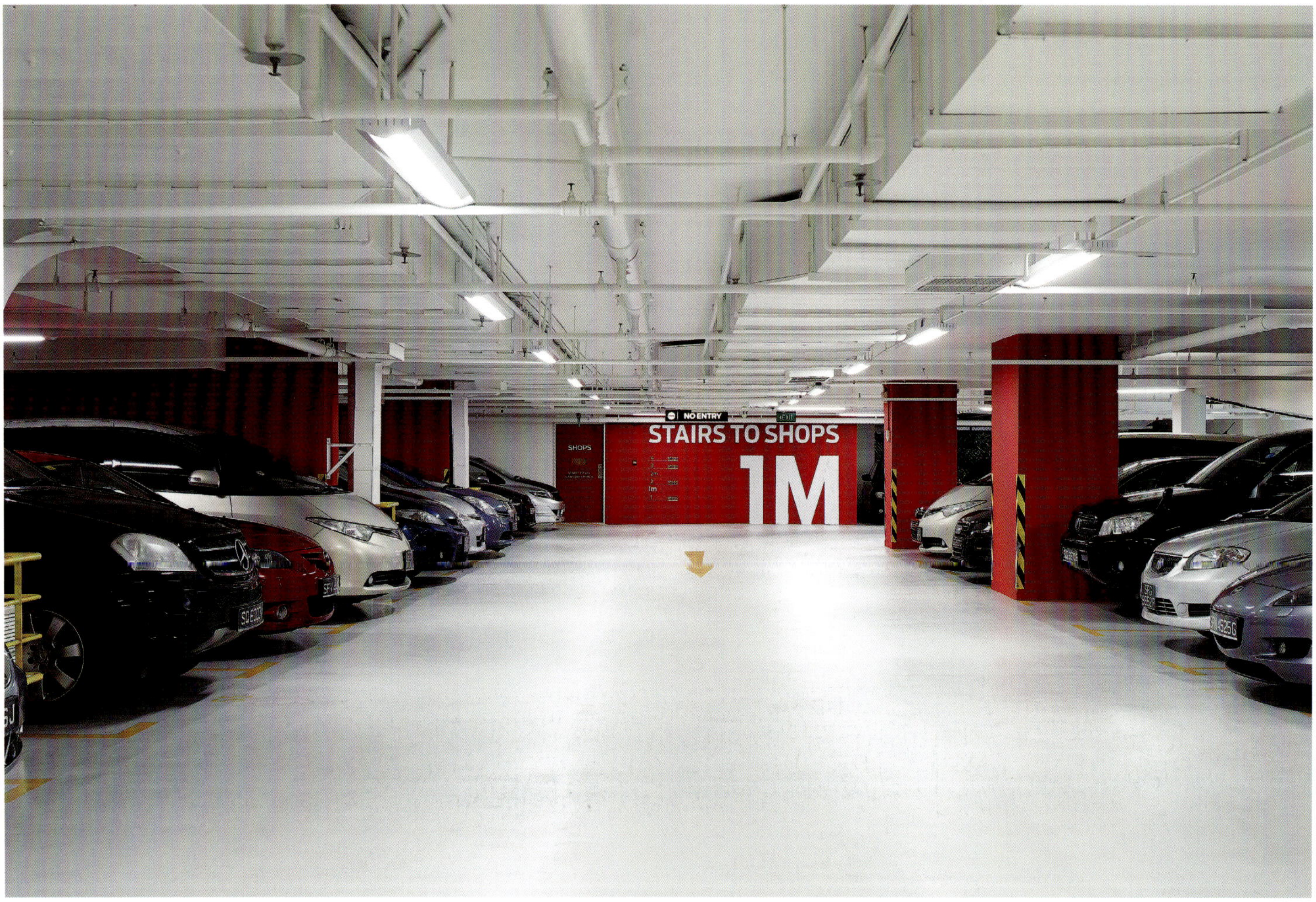

For our very first large-scale wayfinding project, we were tasked to revamp a cinema + shopping mall's carpark. A total of 6 parking floors — out of which only 4 had direct access to the shopping mall — presented us with a unique set of problems.

We solved this by carefully tweaking the language on the feature walls, stairs and doors of every floor. Coupled with bold new type and separate LED light boxes for drivers and shoppers, we are confident that people will no longer have any excuse to get lost!

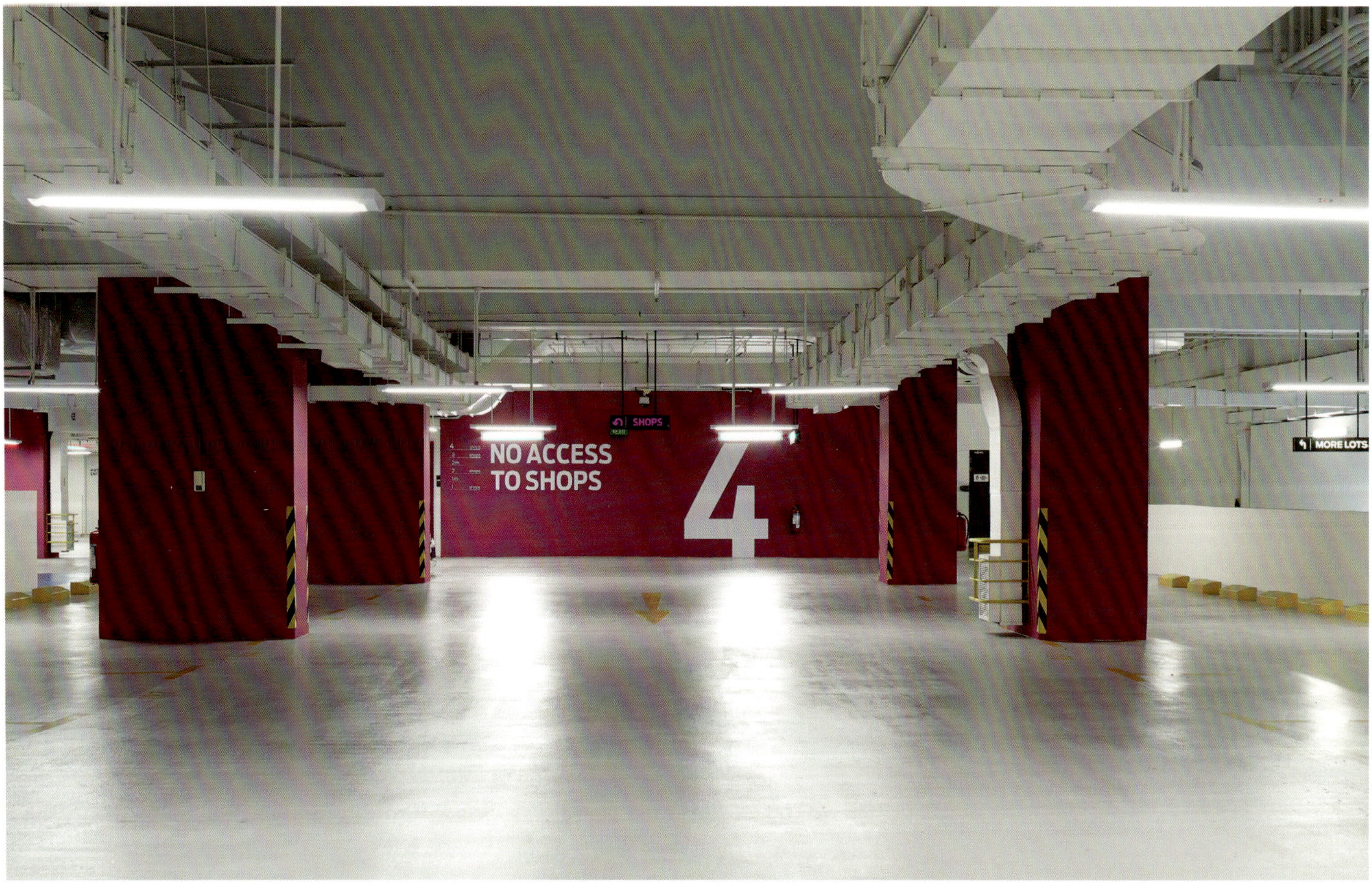

SHOPS
NO ENTRY
EXIT
SLOW
GIVE WAY
NO ACCESS
TO SHOPS
2

STAIRS TO SHOPS
2M
SHOPS

Kew Court House

Design Studio:
Nexus Designs

Designer:
Joseph Antonios

Fabrication:
Diadem

Photography:
Parallax Photography

Commissioned by the City of Boroondara (Municipal Council), the objective was to 'bring to life' this great building the Kew Court House by creating a new visual identity that could be implemented across a suite of signage and wayfinding elements. Subject to strict heritage constraints, we approached the design and placement of signage sensitively to ensure that all elements remained distinct, simple and above all easy to navigate.

We deliberately drew inspiration from the roads surrounding the Kew Court House which enabled us to explore these distinguishing lines and apply them throughout the design, resulting in a greater connection and understanding between design, the building and community.

The logotype's distinctive continuous blue line, forming the shape of the 'K', is both modern, elegant and a refreshing juxtaposition to the historical attributes of the Kew Court House precinct.

The exterior signage is further complimented with the clean lines and rounded edges of the navigational signs, which have given new life and a creative perspective to the interior space of the building. The pill-like directional signs guide you through the warren that is the court house with a friendly font, large lettering, and customised arrows. The signs are legible and clearly lead visitors to their desired destination.

KEW HISTORICAL SOCIETY
KEW COMMUNITY FESTIVAL
KEW COURT HOUSE
ARTS ASSOCIATION
E.MOTION21

Environmental Graphics and Signage for GARLAND Logistic Centre

Design Agency:
Atelier Nunes e Pã

Photography:
NeP

Client:
Garland

Ongoing graphic design project, for one of the leading international transport and logistics company in Portugal.

Interior environmental graphics for the new logistic centre.

FUNDAÇÃO
1776
THOMAS GARLAND
CRIA A EMPRESA QUE
NOS DEU ORIGEM

TRANSAÇÃO
1820
IMPRIMIMOS NOTAS
BANCÁRIAS

CRESCIMENTO
1855
FUNCIONAMOS COMO
AGÊNCIA DE NAVEGAÇÃO

CREDIBILIDADE
1822
PRESTÁMOS ASSISTÊNCIA
AO 1º VOO DE TRAVESSIA
DO ATLÂNTICO SUL

CORAGEM
1939
ENTRÁMOS NO NEGÓCIO
TRANSITÁRIO MARITÍMO
E FERROVIÁRIO

DIVERSIDADE
1963
DISTRIBUÍMOS E
COMERCIALIZAMOS
PNEUS EM PORTUGAL

TERRA E AR

sala de reuniões
meeting room

Henry Laidley (1792-1856)
foi o primeiro membro da
família Laidley a ser sócio
da Garland.
Henry Laidley (1792-1856)
was the first shareholder of
Laidley family.

Environmental Graphics and Signage for Soares da Costa

Design Agency:
Atelier Nunes e Pã

Photography:
NeP

Client:
Soares da Costa

Environmental graphics and signage system for the Soares da Costa Oporto headquarter and Lisbon office.

Exhibition design for the Oporto Headquarter Museum.

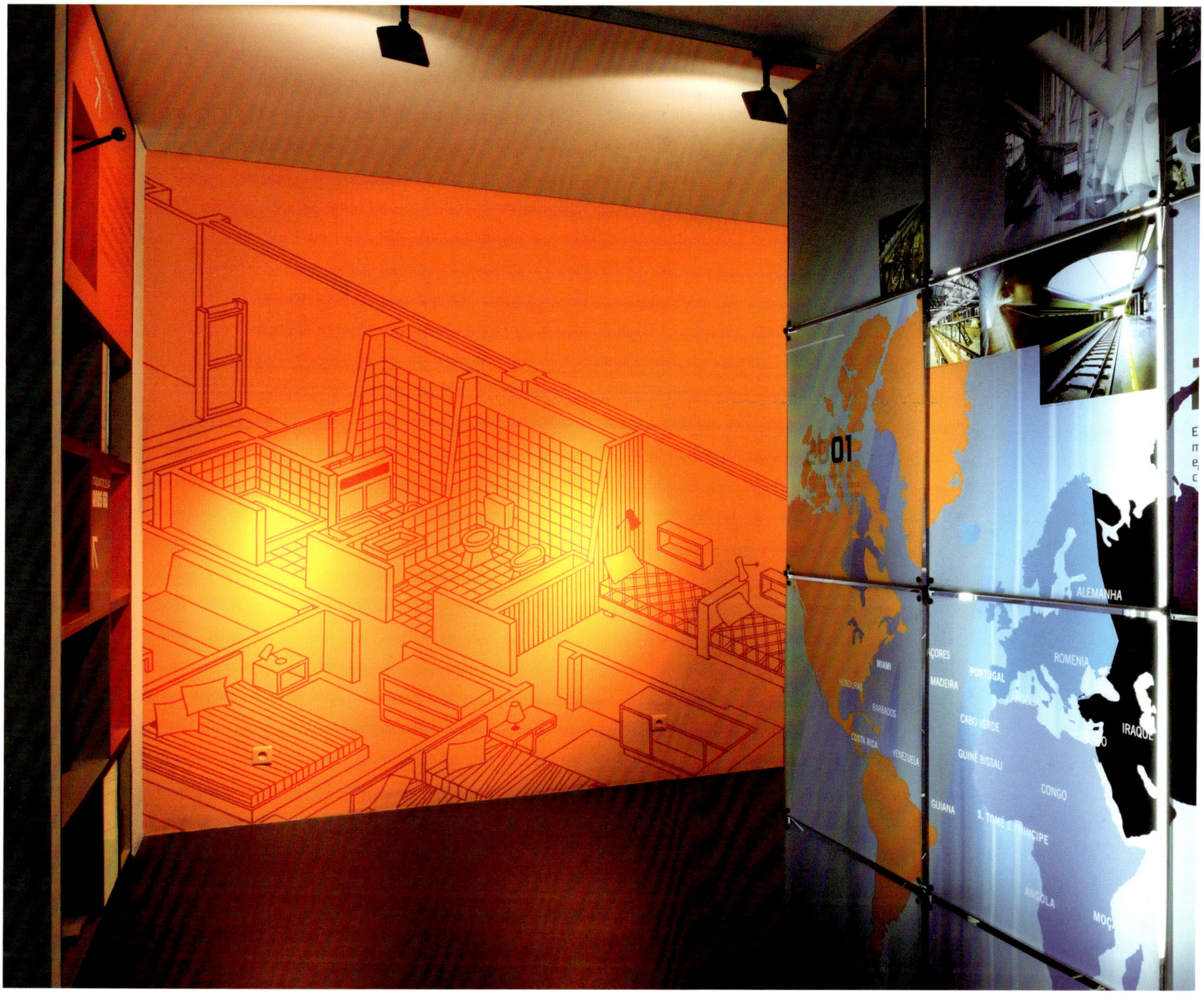

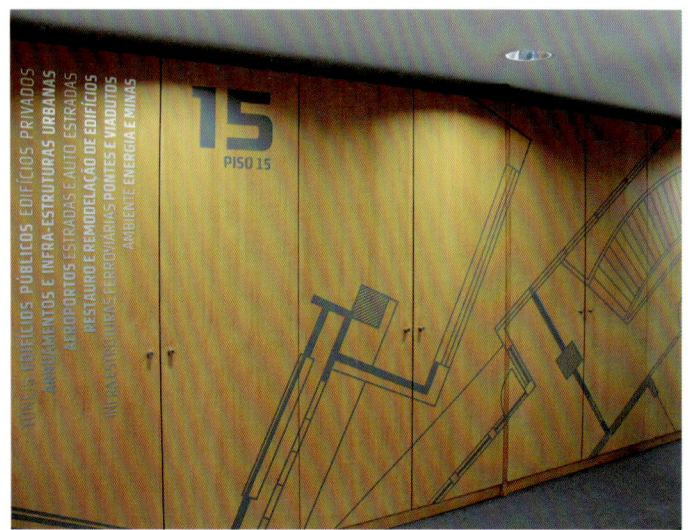

PISO 13

PISO 14

PISO 15

13 14 15

GRUPO SOARES DA COSTA, SGPS

RECEPÇÃO

SOCIEDADE DE CONSTRUÇÕES
SOARES DA COSTA

Recursos de Produção
Desenvolvimento de Negócios
Estudos e Propostas

CLEAR - INSTALAÇÕES
ELECTROMECÂNICAS

GRUPO SOARES DA COSTA, SGPS

Administração
Serviços Jurídicos

SOARES DA COSTA CONCESSÕES

SOARES DA COSTA
SERVIÇOS PARTILHADOS

CPE-COMPANHIA DE PARQUES
DE ESTACIONAMENTO

SOCIEDADE DE CONSTRUÇÕES
SOARES DA COSTA

Direcção Técnica
Direcção de Produção (área sul)
CONTACTO

MÁQUINA CALCULAR
ANOS 60

LIVRO DE CONTAS CORRENTES

15
14
SOARES DA COSTA

Federal Hospitals Lower Austria

Design Agency:
bauer – konzept & gestaltung

Client:
Lower Austrian Federal Clinics Holding

Photography:
bauer – konzept & gestaltung

1

3. Med. Kardiologie
Intensivstation

Herzkatheter

In the course of an offensive to build new hospitals in Lower Austria, all federal clinics are equipped with a specific colour and wayfinding system. A consistent nomenclature and colour systematization was developed in direct linkage with the architecture, as well as consequent route guidance from the freeway to the patients'room. A strong, distinctive colour concept separates the medical functions (ambulance: yellow, intensive care unit: turqoise), guidance colours differ the buildings of the hospital-complexes. An additional compilation of symbols was introduced at the federal hospital Donauregion Tulln, which is used to label the rooms of psychiatric patients. Psychotherapy: musical instruments; social psychiatry 1: fruits and vegetables; social psychiatry 2: plants and flowers; paedriatric psychiatry: animals; protective symbols for huge glass surfaces.

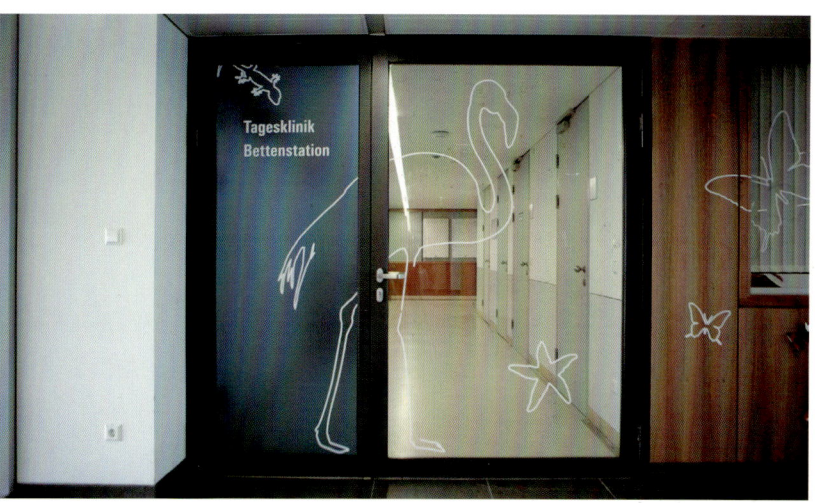

[D]iversity + [D]esign = [B]iennial

Design Agency:
Greco Design

Deisgner:
Gustavo Greco, Tidé, Ricardo Donato, João Corsino, Laura Scofield, Alexandre Fonseca

Client:
State Government of Minas Gerais

Photography:
Rafael Motta, Ricardo Donato, Mineral Image

The challenge was to create the visual identity for the 4th national design biennial in Brazil. The event, to be held in the 3rd largest state capital in the country, presented the theme "Brazilian Diversity". To do so, we decided to use our multiple diversities as a starting point: natural resources diversity, plurality and industrial/handmade production. The result should then be as flexible as the infinite possibilities for manifestations of the record of the ages of man through design. We created a variable identity, in which two letters "D" (representing Design and Diversity) featured in different types, alternating to form a "B" (representing Biennial). The variations represent the several different topics featured in the shows, such as jewelry, mobility, handmade crafts, furniture, among others, emphasizing even further the main theme of the Biennial: Brazilian cultural diversity. To promote the event around the city, urban signage equipment called "B" totems were set up. In addition to functioning as signage, the totems pointed out a path that unveiled the Biennial exhibition sites. By mingling with the urban scene, the totems restated the presence of design in people's day-to-day lives.

Mostra
Da Mão à Máquina

IV Bienal Brasileira de Design

1 Galeria Alberto da Veiga Guignard →

2 Galeria Genesco Murta

3 Prêmio Sebrae Minas Design

4 Galeria Mari'stella Tristão

5 Sala de Imprensa

W.C.

Café do Palácio

Escadas

Mostra
Da Mão à Máquina

IV Bienal Brasileira de Design

1 Galeria Alberto da Veiga Guignard

2 Galeria Genesco Murta

3 Prêmio Sebrae Minas Design

4 Galeria Mari'stella Tristão

5 Sala de Imprensa

W.C. Feminino

W.C. Masculino

Café do Palácio

Escadas

IV Biena Brasileira de Design
Belo Horizonte, MG
19 de Setembro a 31 de Outubro
mais informações **bienalbrasileiradedesign.com.br**

Eventos Culturais
Mostras
Seminários
Debates

IV Bienal Brasileira de Design
Belo Horizonte, MG
20 de Setembro a 31 de Outubro
mais informações **bienalbrasileiradedesign.com.br**

Eventos Culturais
Mostras
Seminários
Debates

205

591.6 Gruppen nichtverwandter

Upper Austrian Federal State Library

Design Agency:
bauer – konzept & gestaltung

Architecture:
Bez & Kock

Client:
Upper Austrian Federal State

Photography:
bauer – konzept & gestaltung

BUCHRÜCKGABE

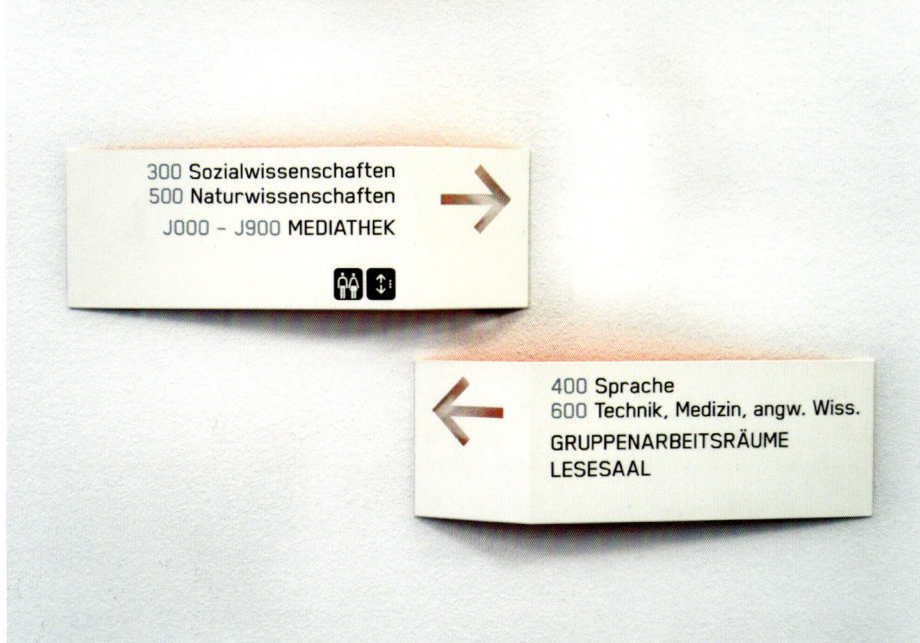

Originally built in the 1930s, Upper Austria's federal state library in Linz was renovated lately, and expanded by an additional building. The new wayfinding system merges with the historical architecture: The remaining parts of the original building signage were completed and extended. By using the typeface "Blender Western Latin" and specially built pictograms, the guidance system supports a quick and easy orientation. The information carriers – which literally arise from the walls – are referring to the 1930s themselves: the directions are indicated by the respectively longer or shorter bevel of the signboards. The label of each room follows the principle of conversing antiqua into grotesque lettering. Blending in with the historical context, this contemporary orientation system leads throughout the whole library with a clear and distinct typographical line – consequently down to the bookshelf labelling.

INTO Newcastle University Signage

Designer:
Richard Wise

Fabrication:
Signbox

Photography:
INTO

The INTO Newcastle University Centre for international students in Newcastle, UK, is a joint venture between INTO University Partnerships and Newcastle University. The signage and environmental graphics created combine elements of both brands, as well as the city itself. The way-finding is based on the University's own system and uses their dark blue as the base colour. Similarly the University logo on the exterior is made from built-up stainless-steel lettering as seen on other campus buildings. The INTO roundel can be seen as frosted-glass effect vinyl on the glazing across the entrance door panels and two storey's high on the front and back of the building.

The reception area is vast and you are greeted with an 11m high banner with the word 'welcome' in 24 languages. The floor numbers are seen running up the building interior, in their respective signature floor colours.

The manifestation on the interior glazing also uses frosted glass effect vinyl representing scenes from around the city – the Tyne bridges, the Sage Gateshead and the Angel of the North.

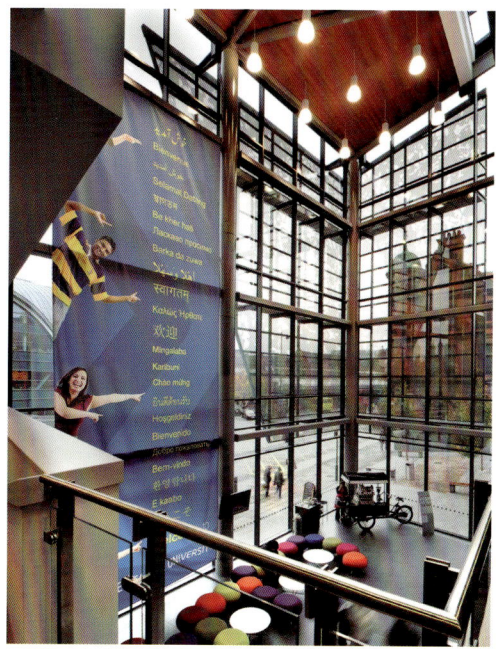

Delta Terra Wayfinding

Design Agency:
e-moebius

Designer:
DCV Sergio Smirnoff

Client:
Delta Terra

Delta Terra is a private natural wildlife reserve located in Tigre - Buenos Aires, Argentina.

In 2010 e-moebius was asked to design the global identity of its development. The job starts researching examples around the globe. Argentine and USA parks and theme parks were the inspiration to develop the strategic view.

Based on its logo, colour palette and institutional typographies were defined. All pieces are in earth tones, wood and canvas textures papers have been used for support.

Inspired by signs on buildings and organic forms, Gotham Rounded was the selected typography.

The orientation system has to be sustainable and eco friendly with the environment. So it mustn't "shout" to the visitor, but has to be clear and visible in context. To do that, the team focuses on icon design to illustrate each place. They've been divided into two groups: trails and services icons and signs.

Trails icons draw is "rustic style", according to place origins and concept. Each one of them has a particular color to identify it. By other side, services and indicative signs have simpler lines and same colours, closer to standard wayfinding systems.

Both styles work as one in the set, but with specific features to differentiate each kind of communication need.

Innsbruck Exhibition Centre, Signage System

Design Agency:
Büro Uebele

Project Team:
Carolin Himmel (Project Management), Andreas Uebele

Client:
Congress und Messe Innsbruck Gmbh

Principal Typeface:
Akzidenz Grotesk Super

Photography:
Hanspeter Schiess

Order from chaos.

Innsbruck, the characterless exhibition centre has been given a new identity: old-style cacophony has been overlaid with a new and harmonious vibe. A beautiful new hall has been added to the old buildings, and the former chaotic muddle of juxtaposed language, architecture and routes through the complex is at once echoed and resolved in a signage system that draws on the forms, colours and formats of flag design.

Wayfinding
Concept Store

Design Agency:
Adronauts

Designer:
Patrick Pichler, Wolfgang Warzilek

Photography:
Patrick Pichler, Wolfgang Warzilek

DRESS

TROUSERS

SHIRT

The idea and the proposal for our design were developed for a Concept-Store in Vienna in order to make it possible to find pieces of clothing more easily. The challenge was to design a directive system which does not depend on language and origin. It should be self-explanatory and easily understood by anybody. The directive system uses two main symbols; one for males and one for females. Each Icon shows, in addition, on which part of the body the piece of clothing is to be worn. The pictograms which were used are at the same time design elements in the shop. The wayfinding system functions without use of colour or other differentiating elements.

ACCESSORIES

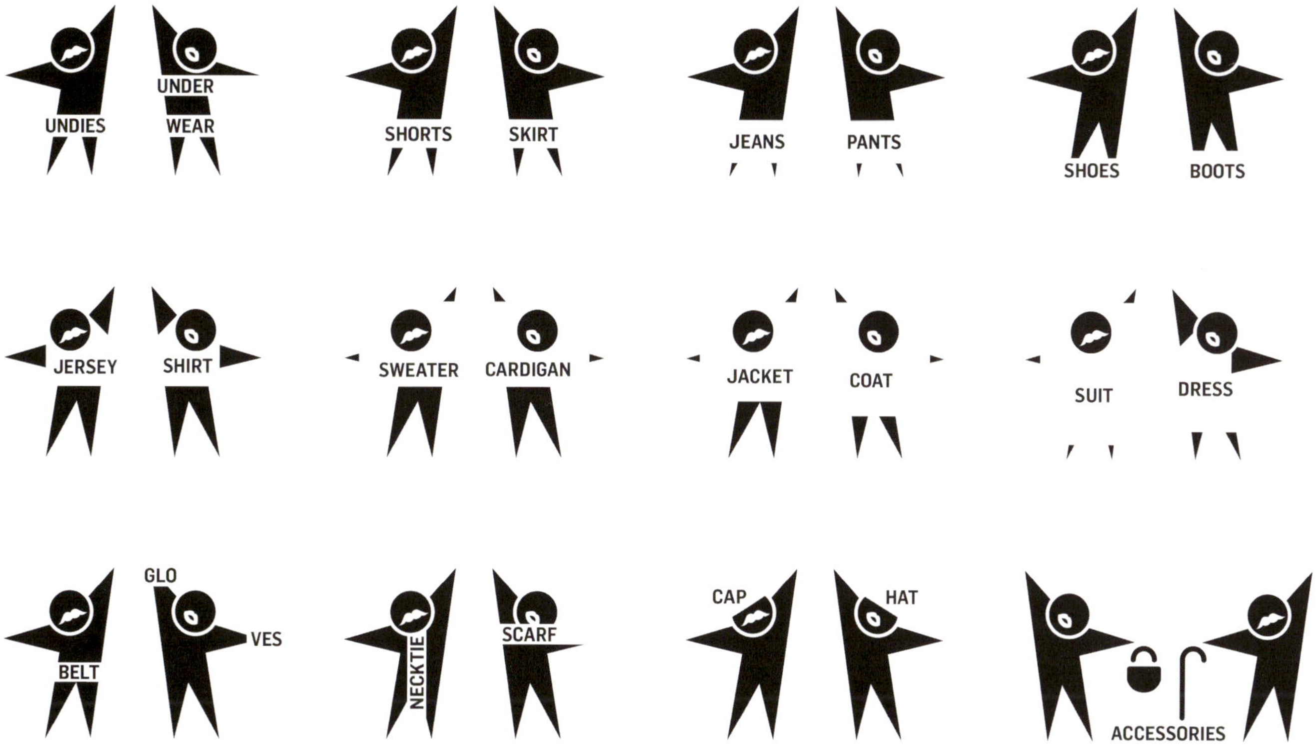

UNDIES UNDER WEAR

SHORTS SKIRT

JEANS PANTS

SHOES BOOTS

JERSEY SHIRT

SWEATER CARDIGAN

JACKET COAT

SUIT DRESS

GLO VES
BELT

NECKTIE SCARF

CAP HAT

ACCESSORIES

JACKET

JERSEY

SHIRT

CONTRIBUTOR >>

Adronauts

The name Adronauts stands at present for two creative young artists in Vienna. Patrick Pichler who comes from South Tyrol / Italy and Wolfgang Warzilek from Carinthia in Austria got to know one another in the course of their studies at the University for Applied Arts in Vienna. Both were accepted in the class for Communication Design in 2010 and work together in various projects.

Working together was not only fun for them but also brought good results. As students they pooled their resources in order to present their works. The Adronauts main focus is alongside typography and illustration, especially advertising and graphic design. In various works and projects they always attempt to follow a clear concept. For Adronauts design has to be simple and at the same time intelligent. They strive to create art which is not necessary mainstream but a work of enduring quality. In addition they want each work to have an individual design.

Albert Trulls & Javi Sastre

Albert Trulls
Before graduating, Albert had already been working as a graphic designer in a social design studio, in Barcelona, for two years. After graduating he worked for other two years in an advertising company (Shackleton), for a year in a brand design studio (Mayúscula) and in the present he works as a graphic designer at the Toormix studio, in Barcelona.

Illustration and typography really fascinate him, and this is something that stands out in his projects. Albert's work has been shown in exhibitions such as the 11th International Poster Biennial in Mexico and also in the 4th and 5th International Typography Congress of Valencia.

Recently, he has been pointed out for Creative Bloq as one of the best twenty typographers to follow on The Behance Network.

Javi Sastre
After graduating, Javi moved to London where he worked as a video editor at a fashion magazine (Tank Magazine). After a year in UK, he moved back in Barcelona and studied photography and worked as a visual designer for Hewlett-Packard. Also, he founded the online magazine Monografica.org together with the design historian and University professor Raquel Pelta. Their Magazine has been awarded by the Barcelona's City Council, the European Design Awards, the ADG-FAD Laus' Awards and by the illustration APIC Awards.

Javi has also been assistant professor in a video course in the IDEP University, in Barcelona. He has also translated into Spanish the book by Ellen Lupton 'Thinking with Type' for the Gustavo Gili's Editorial.

Javi is currently developing a new design related product with the Monografica's very same team.

Andrea Gmünder, feinform

In 2010 Andrea Gmünder founded her company, feinform, Atelier für Signaletik und Grafik (signage and graphic design studio) in Zurich – establishing herself as a freelancer with a 20-year background in her trade. At feinform, she brings exciting signage projects to fruition and develops comprehensive concepts in corporate design, visual communications and identification.

She acquired her skills at the Schule für Gestaltung (school of design) in St.Gallen, Switzerland, 1990–95, at the CMU in Pittsburgh, USA, 1993, and working for renowned graphic design and signage studios in St.Gallen and Zurich, Switzerland, 1993–2010. Enrolling in the CAS 'urban identity & design' course taught by Ruedi Baur at zHdK Zurich, she further consolidated her knowledge of designing public spaces.

Signage soon grew into feinform's core discipline. Equipped with a keen interest in architecture, a great talent for coordination and a profound knowledge of materials, workflows and advertising, Andrea Gmünder manages and coordinates public building projects – always demonstrating an extraordinary feel for the design, the location, its purpose and its users.

Alberto Corazón & Oyer Corazón

Alberto Corazón, member of the Real Academia de Bellas Artes (Royal Academy of Fine Arts) and one of the Spanish designers of international renown, as has been shown in his many well known designs: ONCE, RENFE, MAPFRE, DOMO telephone, The Zarzuela Theatre, La Casa de América... Founding member and president of the Asociación Española de Diseñadores Profesionales, (Spanish Professional Designers Association), he has won many national and international awards.

Oyer Corazón, works since 1999 in the Alberto Corazón studio as a designer and Project Director, besides being graphic designer he is also the Board of Directors and founding member of DIMAD [Madrid Designers Association], founding member of the Advisory Board of I+D+ART, founding member of GPDM (Deepening Design Management Group), member and media partner of the FEED 2010 (International Design Bloggers & Journalists Meeting).

His graphic design works have been recently exhibited in a solo exhibition in Mexico City and in numerous group exhibitions at the national level.He has given lectures and presentations throughout the national territory and has been jury in many different awards and selctions throughout this career.

Currently directs SENSIBLE DESIGN a micro space on Radio 5 Todo Noticias RNE / RTVE.

Atelier Nunes e Pã

In 2004, two of the most productive graphic ateliers in Porto decided to join forces, Atelier João Nunes and Pã Design. These two studios have had a big influence in the visual culture of the city during the eighties and nineties with an extensive body of work in the cultural area. The atelier "Nunes e Pã" is now led by Ana Menezes, Susana Nunes and Lucia Nunes.

Atelier Nunes e Pã develops work in the area of communication design: graphic, web and production. The Atelier's culture can be defined as an attitude that expresses values such as open-mindedness, experience, sharing and collaboration, the love of detail and an overall holistic vision.

The Atelier's motto is to "think globally, work passionately, create value". The multidisciplinary team develops original and customized solutions for its wide range of clients. Our team is formed by seven people.In specific projects, the team also counts with the collaboration and consultancy of the designer João Nunes.

bauer – konzept & gestaltung

The inter-disciplinarily team of bauer – konzept & gestaltung is composed of architects, branding strategists, photographers, writers, programmers and visual designers. Always concentrating on the contents, the studio is looking for surprising design solutions which are suitable for the daily use likewise. The studio works on visual and spatial identities such as for corporate designs, for museums and exhibitions, creates information design and orientation systems, as well as editorial and packaging design.

Bunch

Bunch is a leading creative design studio offering a diverse range of work, including, identity, literature, editorial, digital and motion.

Established in 2002 with an international reach, from London to Zagreb, Bunch has an in-house team of specialists to deliver intelligent and innovative cross-platform solutions of communication design.

Over the years we have been commissioned by many blue chip companies as well as younger brands and artistic industries. Building an impressive client base that covers many styles and disciplines, such as BBC, Nike, Diesel, Sony, Sky, Red Bull and others...

Bohatsch und Partner

Bohatsch und Partner develops ideas, designs and organize the realization and production of various forms of communication for business and culture. Everyone who is familiar with our work knows that we show great passion when it comes to getting to the heart of things. We enjoy coming up with aesthetic solutions that really work with a given task. Here is precisely where our activities touch success.

Büro Uebele

Büro Uebele Visuelle Kommunikation was founded 1996 by Andreas Uebele. The agency is active in all areas of visual communications, with the focus on visual identity, signage and wayfinding systems, corporate communications and exhibitions.

Büro Uebele currently has a permanent staff of nine communications designers and one assistant, as well as collaborating with an architect and a communications designer on a freelance basis.
In recent years the agency's work has been honoured with more than 300 national and international awards. In 2003 Büro Uebele won the red dot: grand prix for communication design, one of Europe's foremost design prizes, and 2009 it won Germany's top design prize, the design award of the federal republic of Germany (gold award). Büro Uebele's work is represented in Dhub Disseny Hub Barcelona, Stedelijk Museum Amsterdam, the Chicago Athenaeum und the Museum of Modern Art Toyama. One of the most important works of the office is the corporate design for the German parliament.

Claan

Claan is a creative firm based in Porto that envisions designs and builds digital products and applied communication. Claan works for startups, multinational corporations, institutional and artistic organizations of any kind and size. As visual storyteller Claan creates communication strategies, web and mobile apps, user interfaces, tangible scenarios and experimental works for clients and for itself. Claan believes in a holistic work process; designers and coders exchange ideas to tailor innovative experiences. The combination of talent and knowledge yields results that create impact in an user-centered approach. Clara Vieira and Andreas Eberharter founded Claan in 2008 in the sunny city of Porto, Portugal. The co-founders lived, worked and refined their skills in Rotterdam, Netherlands, Vienna in Austria and Santiago of Chile.

Ella Han Yuhui

Ella Han is a Visual Communication student at the Nanyang Technological University, School of Art, Design and Media with a portfolio that spans everything from branding, graphic design, photography and video. An enthusiast in diverging her interests towards moving and static images, she draws inspiration from music, culture and retrospection. She adds, "Good design surprises, and we should never lose that quality in our works and in our lives. If we do, then we will cease to live."

 ## Estúdio 196 Branding & Design

Estúdio 196 Branding & Design has created and managed brand identities since 1999.Their focus is to plan, design and implement strong brands and memorable communication projects in tune with the personality and goals of each client.Estúdio 196 Branding & Design has an enthusiastic and commited team, trained in several areas, which allows to develop complete projects of branding diagnoses, communication planning, corporate design.

 ## Foreign Policy

Foreign Policy is a design bureau and think tank based in Singapore who craft, realize and evolve brands with a creative and strategic development of ideas. Helmed by Creative Directors Yah-Leng Yu and Arthur Chin, the group of idea makers & story tellers works on a good smorgasbord of projects ranging from creative/art direction and design, branding, brand strategy, digital strategy, strategic research and marketing campaign services for luxury fashion and lifestyle brands, fast-moving consumer goods brands, arts and cultural institution as well as think tank consultancies.

 ## F1RSTDESIGN

The Cologne communication design office F1RSTDESIGN has been founded in 1999 by Christopher Ledwig. Lucid in its concepts without being ordinary – F1RSTDESIGN's design philosophy answers the needs of various fields ranging from local, national as well as international clients. F1RSTDESIGN has grown into a team of communication and industrial designers and architects performing cross-disciplinary based on international experience. F1RSTDESIGN covers the traditional skills of communication design in 2D [corporate design, graphics, interface design, editorial design] and 3D [wayfinding systems, fair trade, shop design, packaging]. The inter-disciplinary team is characterized by cross-media-solutions following an analytical design approach.

 ## Gabriele Marchi & Diego Federico & Marco Condello & Antonio di Summa

Gabriele Marchi, graphic designer / illustrator, member of 'The Doers' (interaction design, lean digital development and graphic design for start-ups). Diego Federico, born as a graffiti writer, founded in 2010 the 'Knz' Studio and 'Knz Graffiti shop'. Marco Condello, freelance graphic designer, works with 'Quattrolinee' Studio. Antonio di Summa, currently studying at ISIA Urbino.

 ## Greco Design

Greco Design was founded in 2005 as a graphic design company with a focus on visual identity, editorial projects, signage and promotional material. Leading the multidisciplinary team is creation director Gustavo Greco, the head of the company, which is based out of a spacious 1950s house. Greco embraces as its baseline the importance of enhancing interpersonal relationships, and of making information accessible by focusing on details without losing sight of the big picture. The Greco team believes in a design process that seeks stimuli that go beyond traditional project methodology procedures by means of a multi-sensorial thought process. At Greco, the work environment and work habits have built up an atmosphere that favors the creation of new formal solutions that are expressive novelties.

 ## Gen design studio

Gen design studio is a company dedicated to the development of graphic, product, environment and web design and illustration. Placing great emphasis on project methodologies, they see design as a corporative emancipation discipline. With this strategic design perspective in mind, they're constantly aware of the world around them, predicting future scenarios and programming lines of sustainable action.

 ## hat-trick

Established in 2001, hat-trick is a multi-disciplinary design company working for a wide variety of clients. Its aim is to provide the clients with the highest standard of creative design and project management. Hat-trick believes that the best way to achieve this is for the directors to be very hands-on and to lead the jobs from the front. The passion of hat-trick is to produce work that achieves its targets by creating memorable, engaging ideas that are noticed and effective. The team has a very broad experience in a wide variety of sectors: in other words they bring to all their projects fresh and objective creative thinking, not formulaic answers. They are currently ranked No. 1 in the Design Week creative survey.

Igor Skliarevsky

The "Chasopys" signage design was developed by Igor Skliarevsky, a Kyiv designer and art-director. Igor is famous throughout Ukraine for his work in the wayfinding systems industry. His works include the unofficial but very popular Kyiv Rapid Transit Map, alternative concepts of pedestrian tourist way finding systems and information panels on public transport stations in the capital of Ukraine. Igor researches the influence of the urban environment on the quality of life of the megapolis' residents and the formation of the urban culture. Igor also found a Facebook community where 2300 Kyiv people discussing issues relating to Kyiv's wayfinding systems and the urban environment design.

Kine Halland

Kine Halland is a Norwegian graphic designer with a Bachelor of Creative Arts degree from Deakin University Melbourne.

Drawing and painting has always been an important part of her life, and from her teenage years she has sold her paintings and illustrations. For a number of years she was an illustrator for a small local newspaper in Kristiansand Norway. Her skill set of analogue techniques is one of her strengths and is often incorporated in her designs.

At the Noroff Institute in Bergen Norway, where she studied for two years, the interest of photography grew and she won the award for best first year student work for a photo essay in 2010. Kine brings her Canon everywhere she goes and she has sold several photo prints. She now works as a freelance graphic designer, illustrator and photographer.

Kittaya Treseangrat

Kittaya Treseangrat spent the first thirteen years of her life navigating the mean streets of Bangkok, Thailand. After moving to the United States by herself, she made her home on the sunny slopes of Southern California's beautiful San Fernando Valley. Kittaya always had artistic inclinations, but wasn't sure how to apply them. After taking a graphic design course during her first year at University, however, she never looked back. Today, Kittaya makes a living as a successful freelance designer, and hopes to one day establish her own studio. She misses her fat dog, who lives in Pattaya Beach now.

KS Design Studio

KS Design Studio is a small firm with big ideas. Led by Principal Karin Seja, our experienced team has a vast array of award winning projects under their belt ranging from one person consultancies to large multinational corporations. Every project, client and market is unique and our ideas and experience make a difference.

KSD is highly proficient in all areas of communication design but is arguably best known for its achievements in corporate branding, packaging, literature and signage.

The firm consistently demonstrates an ability to address client problems with skilled and professional behaviour, sound strategies and visually arresting creative excellence.

Manic Design

Manic Design is an award-winning creative agency with a portfolio of work that ranges from websites and online campaigns to advertising and branding.

The studio was founded in 1999 with the belief that good design always includes both creativity and communication. A piece of work that looks great but fails to speak to its audience is not good design. We have embraced this and cemented it into our culture and our work.

Mohammad Hamed Zeinali

For the past 12 years, Mohammad Hamed Zeinali, aka Emech, has developed his creative skills and pursued his graphic design career. He does not consider himself a graphic designer, but an ambitious visual communicator and his passion lies on creating and developing beautiful designs & brandings. His major skill sets lie in the world of graphic design, brand identity design, typography and packaging design. Previous to joining ESADORE International, he worked as publisher, senior editor & creative director.

Nexus Designs

A design process driven by research and strategy propels our studios commitment to providing enduring brands and active environments. Our collaborative approach to design and visual communication is informed by an acute awareness of our social and cultural surroundings and the influence of art, design, interiors and architecture. With clear dialogue and simple executions we aim to transcend client expectations and deliver outcomes that are carefully considered, unique and always memorable.

Joseph Antonios is the Art Director of Graphic Design. With over twelve years experience in the industry, Joseph designs and directs graphic design projects from inception to their completion. He leads an award winning creative team and delivers solutions that are both highly engaging and effective in their communication outcomes.

Osmond Tshuma

Osmond Tshuma is a twenty four year old (Zimbabwean born and raised) illustrator & graphic designer. Inspired by all forms of design whether it is architecture or industrial design, he always rises up to the occasion to try and create inspirational work for others. He is currently doing his BTech degree at the University of Johannesburg; he is also a tutor for the Graphic Design department. Other Zimbabwean designers like Sindiso Nyoni, Saki Mafundikwa and Chaz Maviyane-Davies have inspired some of his works.

P-06 Atelier

P-06 Atelier is an international award-winning firm specializing in communication and environmental design on a wide range of scales. Bacod in Lisbon, Portugal, the studio was founded in 2006 by partners Nuno Gusmão, Estela Estanislau, Pedro Anjos and Catarina Carreira. It has since undertaken a variety of projects from complex, large scale wayfinding systems, museum and exhibition design, to communication and editorial design for the printed page, with a bold, striking style that has garnered a number of distinctions. P-06 Atelier actively engages in collaborations with architects, urbanists, landscape designers and engineers, in a continuous, seamless workflow with complementing disciplines, enriching the firm's scope of work and amplifying every intervention's outcomes.

Richard Wise

With many years of design experience including Creative Director at Brand Blue and Senior Designer at the University of Oxford, Richard Wise is now the Visual Brand Director for INTO University Partnerships, based in Brighton, UK, and has been working within the communications and design team for the last six years. One aspect of the company's brand is the way-finding and environmental graphics for the educational centres that INTO create with their partner universities around the world. Richard's signage design includes both brands and more to help create stimulating, unique and inspirational environments for both students and staff.

Sergio Smirno

Sergio Smirno is a visual communication designer. After getting his degree in Fine Arts University of La Plata, he had more than 15 years experience in many design fields. He begun working in a newspaper called Hoy Journal, then for an Apple reseller, designing AppleNet Magazine. Later he worked for a .com and multimedia developer company. In 2001 Sergio founded e-moebius with a team of friends. Since then he worked for very different markets with al kinds of communication elements. Also he teaches Graphic Design course in UADE, Argentine University of Enterprise.

Simen Strøm Braaten

After studying two years in Norway, where he was born and raised, Simen Strøm Braaten finished off his final year in Melbourne, where he graduated from Deakin University. Here he received a bachelor's degree in Visual Communication. To him, graphic design is more than an education, more than a profession; it's an entire way of thinking. It sets the grid for a creative lifestyle, and encourages curiosity as you explore the details of day-to-day interactions.

As with packaging, typography, and lettering, wayfinding is just another piece of the puzzle. This puzzle largely consists of graphic design, photography and filmmaking, and with all these pieces at hand two days rarely look the same.

As in life it's the diversity of the pieces that makes the final outcome exciting. And in return, having the ability to explore and combine different techniques, and skill-sets, is what inspires him in the first place. This is what separates one piece of work from another.

Stephanie Demeter

Stephanie Demeter is a graduate of Ball State University, and has a Bachelor of Fine Arts degree in Visual Communication. Stephanie interned at Sweetwater Sound Inc. in Fort Wayne, Indiana. She was born in Cincinnati, Ohio, and currently lives in Fishers, Indiana. She is currently available for freelance work and is pursuing a full time position.

Syaza Za'ba

Syaza Za'ba is a Diploma graduate student from Limkokwing University of Creative Technology, Malaysia. She is into Graphic Design and now discovering her passion in illustration and branding. She is looking forward in continuing her degree course in Graphic Design. Her interest and inspirations are mostly on illustrated cartoons and cute designs. She loves drawing and painting. While waiting for the degree intake in Graphic design, she is doing freelance to gain more experience as a designer.

250 gramm

250 gramm is an independent graphic design studio specializing in editorial design, corporate identity and visual communication for the creative industry. Founded in 2006 by Dutch graphic designer Nivard Thoes (creative director) in partnership with Ma Yin Kwan (project coordinator), 250 gramm is currently based in Guangzhou, China.

We strongly believe in a content-driven design approach, achieved by rigorous research on the specific characteristics and context of a project in close collaboration with our clients. Our ultimate aim is to deliver authentic and progressive concepts and to craft unique, intelligent design solutions that adapt to the particular needs of each client and do not go unnoticed. Besides a strong dedication to craftsmanship and a commitment to experimentation, we always aim to create appropriate and sincere design solutions that are impactful and multilayered...

Besides executing commissioned projects for clients we regularly initiate autonomous projects, implementing a down to earth design mentality combined with playful anarchy. Our passion lies in (co-) authorship and editorialism, giving birth to inventive heavyweight food-for-thought with high nutritional value.

Tomatdesign

Tomatdesign is branding agency from Moscow, Russia. In 2012 Tomatdesign was recognized as #1 branding agency in Russia by AKAR creativity ranking. Tomatdesign has over 80 international awards for design and branding and is the only Russian agency that was awarded at ADC*E.

Visual Communications Studio

Faculty of Visual Arts - Visual Communications Studio.

Tomas Bata University in Zlin.

Students at the Department of Visual Arts are systematically taught to deal with design in the field of advertising production.

The Visual Communications Studio deals with the graphic aspect of electronic publishing, particularly with web presentations with multimedia overlap. The Department aims to educate graduates who are fully equipped with sufficient knowledge and skills and are able to quickly adapt to concrete activity in the course of pursuance of their profession, particularly in the field of advertising production.

Students gain such a level of competence in the sphere of multimedia and design that will enable them to perform their tasks in advertising and communication agencies, marketing departments of big companies, design studios, etc.

About ARTPOWER

BOOK PUBLISHING

Independent plan, solicit contribution, printing, sales of books covering architecture, interior, graphic, landscape and property development.

BOOK DISTRIBUTION

Publishing and acting agency for various art design books. We support in-city call order, door to door service, mail and online order etc.

COPYRIGHT COOPERATION

To further expand international cooperation, enrich publication varieties and meet readers' multi-level needs, we stick to seeking and pioneering spirit all the way and positively seek copyright trade cooperation with excellent publishing organizations both at home and abroad.

PORTFOLIO

We can edit and publish magazine/portfolio for enterprises or design studios according to their needs.

BOOKS OF PROPERTY DEVELOPMENT AND OPERATION

We organize the publication of books about property development, providing models of property project planning and operation management for real estate developer, real estate consulting company, etc.

INTRODUCTION OF ACS MAGAZINE

ACS is a professional magazine specializing on high-end space design. It is a color printing bi-monthly with 168 pages and 245*325mm format. There are six issues every year which are released in the even months. Featured in both Chinese and English ACS is distributed nation-wide and overseas. As the most cutting-edge counseling magazine ACS provides readers with the novelist works of the very best architects and interior designers and leads the new fashion in space design. "Present the best whole-heartedly with books as a media" is always our slogan. ACS will be dedicated to build the bridge between art and design and create the platform for within-industry communication.

Artpower International Publishing Co., Ltd.

Add: G009, Floor 7th, Yimao Centre, Meiyuan Road, Luohu District, Shenzhen, China
Contact: Ms. Wang
Tel: +86 755 8291 3355
Web: www.artpower.com.cn
E-mail: rainly@artpower.com.cn

QR (Quick Response) Code of ACS Official Wechat Account

Acknowledgements

We would like to thank all the designers and companies who made significant contributions to the compilation of this book. Without them, this project would not have been possible. We would also like to thank many others whose names did not appear on the credits, but made specific input and support for the project from beginning to end.

Future Editions

If you would like to contribute to the next edition of Artpower, please email us your details to: artpower@artpower.com.cn

WAY OF THE
SIGN | IV >> VOL. 2

ARTPOWER

WAY OF THE SIGN IV
Copyright © Artpower International Publishing Co., Ltd.

CARTPOWER™

Designer: Wang Anlei
Chief Editor: Mo Tingli

Address: Room C, 9/F., Sun House, 181 Des Voeux Road Central, Hong
Kong, China
Tel: 852-31840676
Fax: 852-25432396

Editorial Department
Address: G009, Floor 7th, Yimao Centre, Meiyuan Road, Luohu District,
Shenzhen, China
Tel: 86-755-82913355
Fax: 86-755-82020029

Web: www.artpower.com.cn
E-mail: artpower@artpower.com.cn

ISBN 978-988-12616-5-6

Printed in China

PREFACE

Finding the Way

Going down the steps of a subway in an unfamiliar city without knowing where to start looking for the way to go to reach your destination can be as bad as going up the escalator of an office building and encountering a huge hall with many corridors. Getting lost and with no direction is always a frustrating experience. At these times signage systems are immediate remedies for our anxiety and give us reliable clues to deciding which way to go.

A signage design basically consists of organizing information and displaying it with words and images. Information must be legible, visible and in the right place. The main aim of signage is to accurately and clearly direct people who have no mastery of the space to the place or direction wished for. A good signage design is one that orientates users in the space, regardless of the willingness of the people who work there to tell them which way to go.

Creating an effective signage system requires understanding of how the place is organized, how it works and is used, the needs of the people to whom information will be directed and also the kind of environment.

Some assumptions are fundamental to drawing up this type of design: maximum visibility, easily interpretable messages, information hierarchy, accessibility, universally understood pictograms, appropriate use of colors and typography and adjustment to the space/architecture.

But the design can go farther. In some cases, when you have a definite brand or identity strategy, the signage system helps strengthen it. It is well known that frustration caused by guidance difficulties affects not only the perception of the space in question but also the image of the corporation and the services it offers.

There are various ways, but when the brand strategy and the signage project are coherent, the outcome is a greater reach of the strategy and the resulting understanding with its audience. Helping the user find his way it can be a shortcut for him to reach out to your brand. After all, design is what makes the brand tangible.

Gustavo Greco – Greco Design, Brazil

CONTENTS »

Siège ATC Groupe

Design Agency:
Drive Design

Photography:
G. Bourdon

Client:
ATC Groupe

Created in 1991 by Christophe Aussenac and Robert Combes, ATC Groups is the French leader of the marking of vehicles and the signage system large format. The construction of their future site to Rillieux-La-Pape, near Lyon, allows gathering in summer, 2009 the teams of ATC and Goss Sérigraphie.

Contacted at the end of 2008 to realize the outside and internal signage system of the site, the agency made it a point of honor to give a soul to premises with an objective: use at most techniques and know-how of the group ATC.

Client:
Ackermannshof AG, Basel

Design Agency:
Notice Kommunikation & Design

Photography:
Helen Hüsser

Designer:
Helen Hüsser, Gilles Bachmann

Signage System Zentrum Ackermannshof, Basel (Switzerland)

Oversized words have been "stamped" on the walls of the courtyard in reference to the historic use of the building. The removable metal lettering was developed by Notice and is made from laser-cut cast iron plates and screwed directly into the wall on a perforated grid.

The Zentrum Ackermannshof in Basel is home to culture, business and science, and houses offices, an events hall and a restaurant with bar. The historic building dates back to the 12th century; the house was re-opened after extensive renovation in autumn 2011.

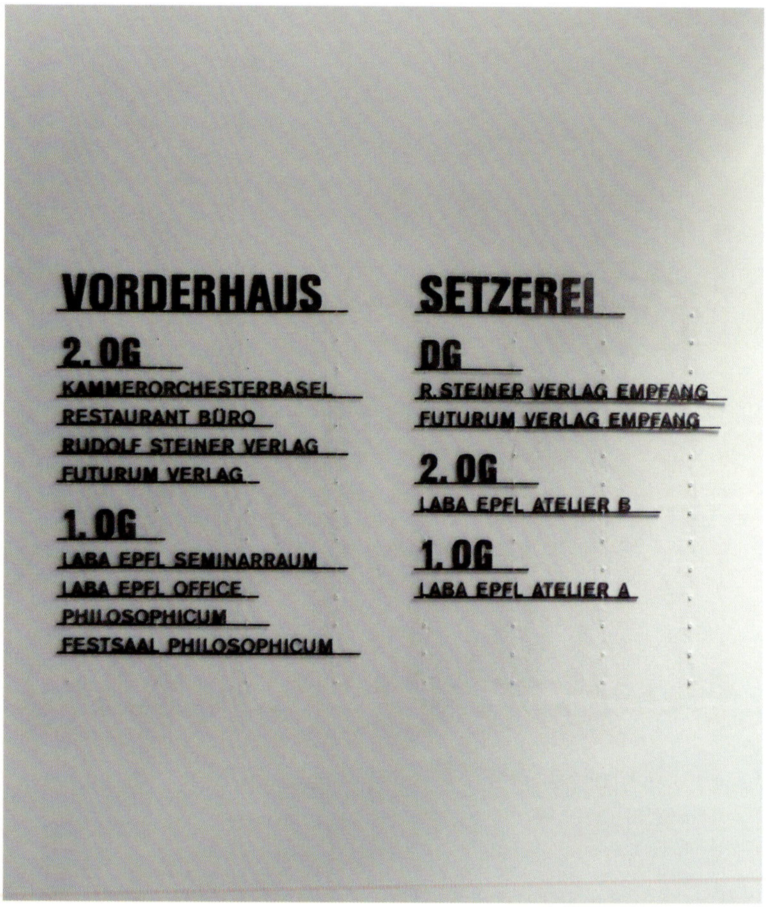

VORDERHAUS

2. OG
KAMMERORCHESTERBASEL
RESTAURANT BÜRO
RUDOLF STEINER VERLAG
FUTURUM VERLAG

1. OG
LABA EPFL SEMINARRAUM
LABA EPFL OFFICE
PHILOSOPHICUM
FESTSAAL PHILOSOPHICUM

SETZEREI

DG
R.STEINER VERLAG EMPFANG
FUTURUM VERLAG EMPFANG

2. OG
LABA EPFL ATELIER B

1. OG
LABA EPFL ATELIER A

Client:
Züblin Immobilien AG, Zurich

Photography:
Michael Egloff, Hannes Henz

Design Agency:
Notice Kommunikation & Design

Designer:
Helen Hüsser, Gilles Bachmann

Signage System Office Building in Egg/Zurich (Switzerland)

Contrasting lighting and colours characterise the signage for this office building complex. The main lettering in bright yellow guides visitors in the right direction, while the posts made of folded sheet steel in the outdoor space are illuminated from the inside. A detailed guide in the building uses replaceable white vinyl lettering that can be produced inexpensively.

Employees and visitors travel mainly by car, so particular emphasis has been placed on the ground markings on the driveway and parking spaces. The arrows direct traffic around the building and a prominent numbering system guides motorists safely to their parking space.

> Dardelet GmbH
Landschaftsarchitektur

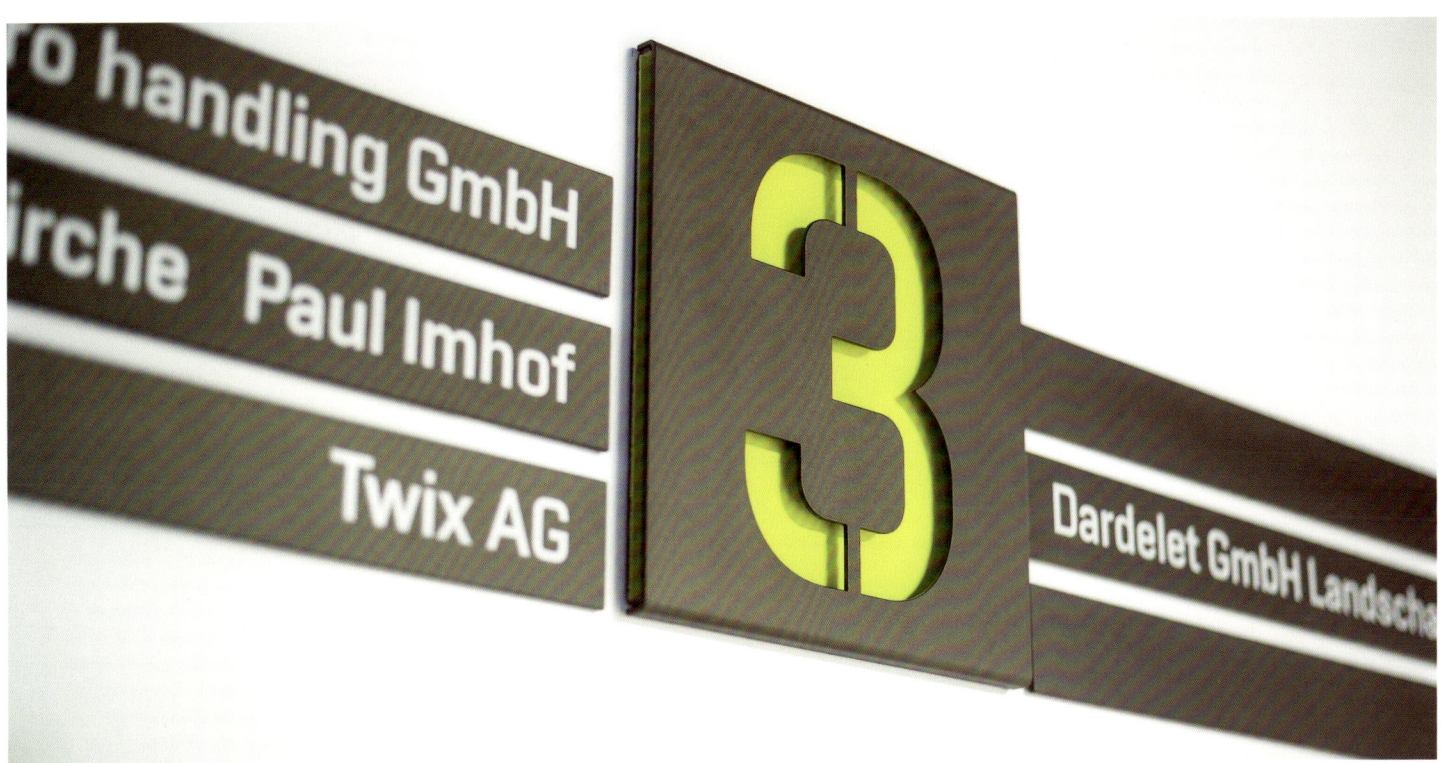

Signage for a Residential Building in Barcelona

Design Agency:
Roseta y Oihana

Designer:
Roseta Mus Pons
Oihana Herrera Erneta

Client:
José Luis Bonet, architect

Photography:
Xavier Carreras, Haut Touch

We really enjoyed designing this project, as we had the opportunity to work together with the architect of the building, a brand new building with a few number of residential flats. The architect, José Luis Bonet, asked us for a signage system that followed the style and the characteristics of the building. For the flats doors numbers we designed signs made of iroko wood covered with a thin aluminum enameled in white color, the aim of this signs is to follow the perception created by the materials and colors used by the architect in that area of the building. Watched from one side, one can see the wood, but watched from the front each number is transformed in a more subtle and special sign, integrated with the wall. For the main door of the building we designed some big numbers made of aluminum enameled in dark grey, the same color of the façade, visible but at the same time integrated with the building. In the parking, the signs, made in row aluminum, light automatically when the cars enter to park.

Designer:
Roseta Mus Pons, Oihana Herrera
Erneta, in collaboration with Marina
Hoyos, Javier Sastre, Cristina Solé,
Albert Trulls, Oscar Viñas

Design Agency:
Roseta y Oihana

Client:
Elisava, Barcelona School
of Design and Engineering

Signage for Elisava, Barcelona School of Design and Engineering

The particular needs of this signage system, commissioned by a design school of Barcelona, were to create a signage system that would fit with the characteristics of the building and also to design some of the signs that would allow to be done by the academic staff themselves (the signs with academic information related to the class schedule and lecturers). To solve these needs, on the one hand, we created a system visually quite sober and simple (Helvetica typeface and dark grey and white colors) and we transformed some parts of the building (mainly doors and panels) into signs themselves, resulting a collection of divers format signs that integrate with the building. On the other hand, for the signs containing the academic information, we created a system that allows to holding Din A4 and Din A3 papers, easily printable and placeable for the academic stuff.

4 Aules 411 a 414
Taller de maquetes i prototips
Direcció
Estudis
Coordinació acadèmica
Administració
Sales de reunions

**3 Aules 301 a 314
Gestió de postgrau
Comunicació i màrqueting
Taller de disseny**

2 Aules 201 a 218
Informàtica
Sala de professors

1 Aules 104 a 114
Sala d'actes
Gestió acadèmica
Copisteria
Àgora
Bar i terrassa
Sala d'estudiants
Sala de professors

0 Vestíbul principal
Consigna
(Accés a Taller de moda i
Laboratori de ciències i tecnologia
per planta 1)

-1 Laboratori de fotografia
Biblioteca
Gestió de treballs
Magatzem de publicacions

301 302

3

‹ Aules 301 a 306
Taller de disseny

› Aules 307 i 308
Gestió de postgrau
Comunicació i màrqueting
Aules 311 a 314
Lavabos ♿

> Aules 207 i 208
Sala de professors
Lavabos

< Aules 209 a 218
Lavabos

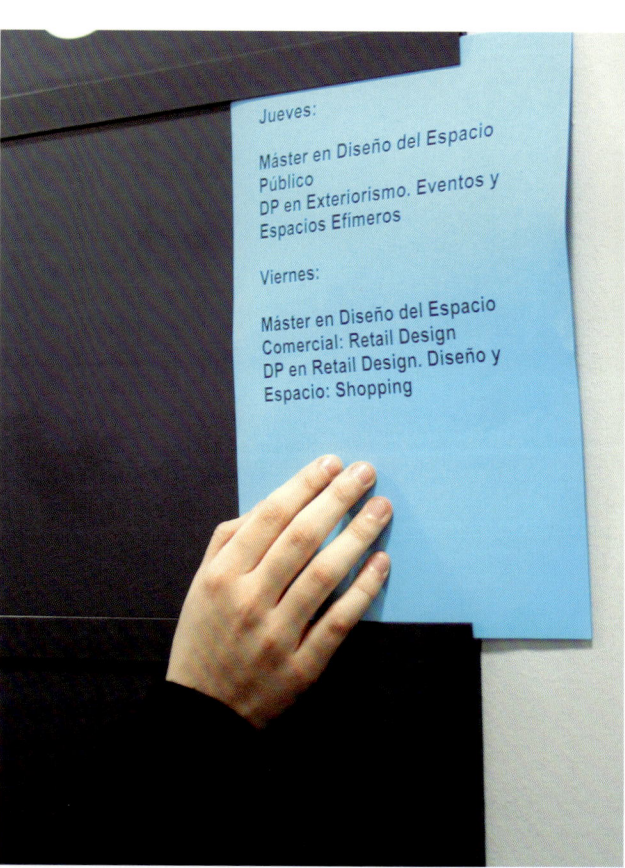

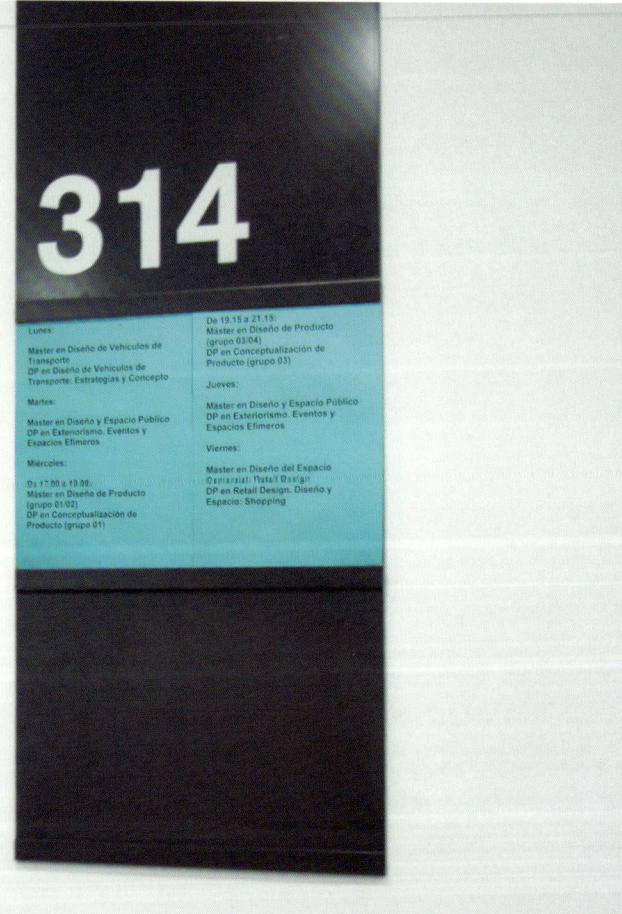

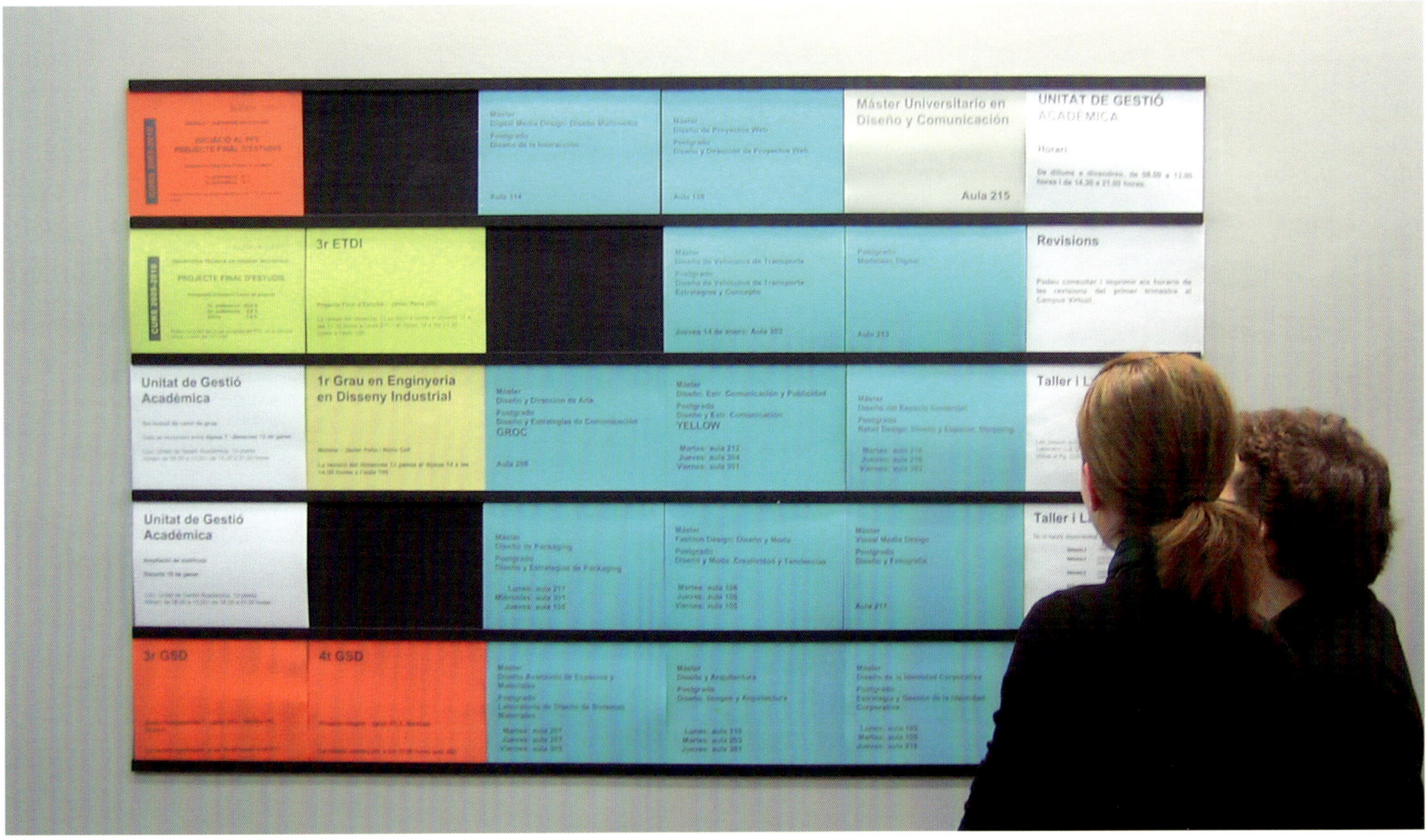

Signage for FAD (Fostering Arts and Design)

Design Agency:
Roseta y Oihana

Designer:
Roseta Mus Pons,
Oihana Herrera Erneta

Client:
FAD (Fostering
Arts and Design)

Photography:
Xavi Padrós and Roseta y Oihana

This project was commissioned by FAD (Fostering Arts and Design), an association that promotes design and architecture in Spain. We decided to design the signage for their offices starting from their corporate graphic identity (designed by Base) not only to maintain coherence in the organization‚Äôs communication but also because their system (made up of squares and triangles) seemed to be a good fit, as the square can be converted into an identifying sign and together with the triangle, makes up a directional sign in the shape of an arrow.

In order to resolve the specific necessity or directing visitors to the activities that take place in the different rooms, it was necessary to find supports that could be set up and taken down comfortably. With this goal it was decided to use magnetic film for the signs located on iron (the reception desk and the access door to the stairwell), make the directional signs located in the lobbies out of iron in order to be able to add information to them with magnets. Cover part of the wall in the entryway to the rooms with a thin sheet of iron that, painted grey, was camouflaged with the rest of the wall. In this way large format posters could be hung with magnets to announce the activity taking place in the room and, in addition, the support would be , "invisible" when not in use.

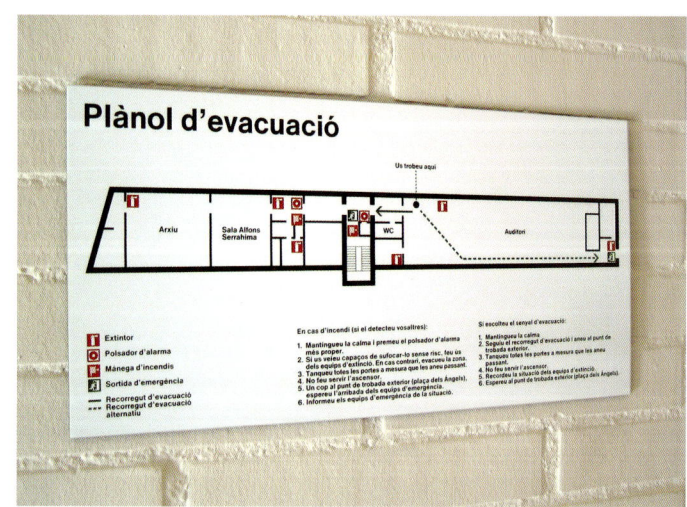

Avui al FAD

L

3 Mater

2 Oficines FAD
Oficines Associacions
Sala Santiago Marco
Sala Antoni Moragas
Sala Guinovart
Copoteca
WC

1 Sala Alfons Serrahima
Auditori
WC

0 Recepció
Bar Restaurant
Cripta
Sala Fòrum
Sala exposicions
Terrassa
WC

Auditori

LAUS 09

L

Auditori

L

Recepció
Cripta
Bar
Restaurant
Sala Fòrum
WC

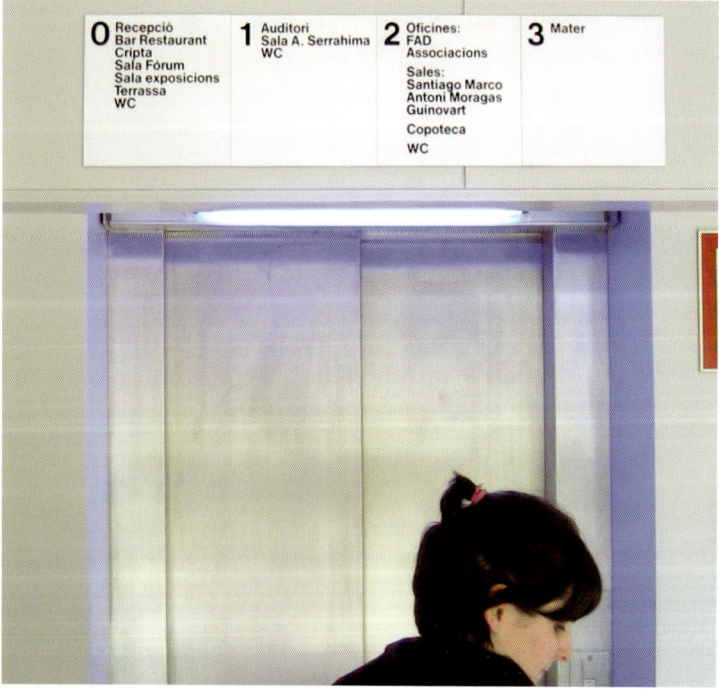

0 Recepció
Bar Restaurant
Cripta
Sala Fòrum
Sala exposicions
Terrassa
WC

1 Auditori
Sala A. Serrahima
WC

2 Oficines:
FAD
Associacions

Sales:
Santiago Marco
Antoni Moragas
Guinovart

Copoteca

WC

3 Mater

1

Auditori
Sala Alfons Serrahima
WC

L

Signage System for Stadtwerk Lehen

Design Agency:
Christian Salic, Werbe- und Designagentur

Designer:
Hans Renzler, Christian Salic, Alexander Rothbacher, Katharina Kronberger

Client:
Verein Stadtwerk Lehen,
Raimund Gutmann, Sarah Untner

Photography:
Alexander Rothbacher

Stadtwerk Lehen is the biggest construction site in the city of Salzburg, Austria. The site is divided into two areas: the northern area is dedicated to social housing. The southern area will be used as a science park and for offices.

The signage system is based upon the basic form of a cube. All the cubes are made from dark grey concrete. The signage information and the orientation maps are painted on the cubes with fluorescent paint. At day the paint looks plain white. After sunrise the paint starts to glow in a greenish yellow.

The Stadtwerk Lehen Logo is the Letter »L«. The Letter »L« is engraved into each cube and painted with fluorescent paint, either.

Cabot Circus

**Product Design Partner &
Wayfinding Consultant:**
Fwdesign

Manufacture:
Woodhouse

Client:
Bristol Alliance

A key part of fwdesign's philosophy is to try, where possible, to integrate signage with the environment. The most demanding example of this philosophy is the series of 13 free- standing information points, in stainless steel with vitreous enamel infill's in cyan blue, lime green and purple to give each precinct a visual distinction. Positioned at key points around the site, the highly sculptural 3.3m signs have two sloping 'legs', linked by a tight upper loop of steel. A further detail is the street name sign, laser cut and pushed 2mm proud of the surface on each stainless steel foot. While half the signs have inline legs, the others are offset from the centre line – but in all cases their curved steel 'feet' have to run perfectly flush with the ground.

A combination of this complex design with sloping floors and undulating ground (only two out of 13 are truly horizontal) means that each individual unit has a different geometry and had to be designed to the millimetre by CAD. 'This degree of precision would frighten all but one or two manufacturers in the country,' says Roger Crabtree, 'but we were delighted with the results we got from Woodhouse... they are always prepared to go the extra mile to deliver what you intended.' The folded 'ribbon' theme is repeated on a grand scale in the large-format graphics on the walls of the car park. Screen-printed on 1.5m by 2.4m aluminium panels, mounted on three-quarter inch ply, for rigidity, they provide a dynamic splash of colour as visitors enter the centre from the car-park.

Perhaps the most prominent piece of signage for visitors arriving by car to the centre is a large, internally illuminated 'Cabot Circus' brand sign mounted on the wall of the centre's multi-storey car-park. The circular sign, custom-made by Woodhouse, is 4.8 metres (16 feet) in diameter and houses 100 x LED panels, each with 144 LEDs, which backlight the stretched PVC skin bearing the 'Cabot Circus' brand-name.

New Signage for Tourists by the Metz City Council

Design Agency:
Intégral Ruedi Baur

Client:
the Metz City Council

To mark the opening of the Metz Pompidou Centre in 2010, Ruedi Baur and staff produced temporary signage linking the museum with the city centre. Further to this initial project, the Metz City Council then entrusted Intégral Ruedi Baur with designing the signage for the entire city. Based on an analysis of needs, it emerged that the response to information and direction issues would not be solved satisfactorily by a set of mass-produced information points repeated throughout the city. It was more a matter of responding to a variety of issues, in various contexts, some of which posed quite a challenge given the need to blend in visually in order to preserve the historic dimension.

Starting with a concept of messages written in space, the typographic composition is laid on horizontal lines that both link the letters and hold them up. The whole can stand in its own right, adorn an existing feature or actually mark a building. The Irma font appears to thread over the stretched clear frames, in order not to conceal the city's pre-existing architecture.

Unlike the temporary signage, which was decked out in pastel hues, this permanent signage is white, enhanced with touches of bright and even fluorescent tints. The single or double posts are white, with colour painted on the edges and inside the lettering, the colour being chosen to fit the environment. Each directional sign is water-jet cut in a single piece from an aluminium block, meaning that there are no soldering marks or joins to mar the beautiful precision in the use of colour painted within each letter and on the edge of each word.

There are eight separate tourist circuits, starting at the railway station and fanning out towards the city centre, neighbourhoods and the Metz Pompidou Centre. As from 2013, there will be signs denoting the entrance to pedestrian districts, signage to identify the entrances to covered markets, like typographic canopies, or over-hanging lines announcing the various neighbourhoods. The concept of this new informational and directional signage system is to depict the city as it is, slipping into the context, revealing it and endeavouring to promote it.

A poetic approach for a fresh twist on the city of Metz and its riches.

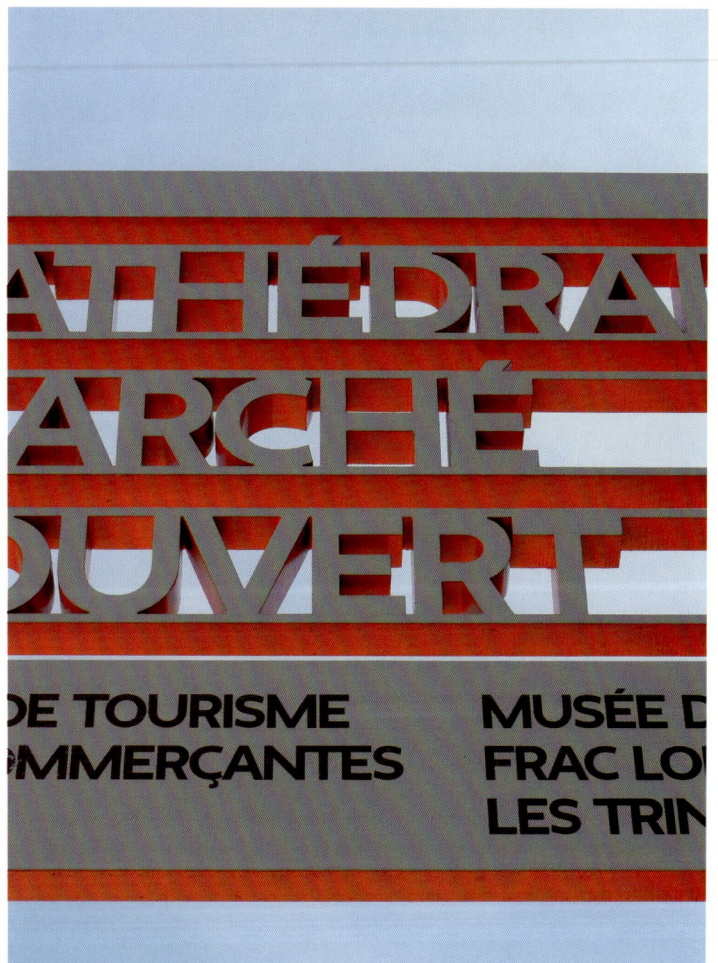

CATHÉDRALE,
OFFICE
DE TOURISME
RUES COMMERÇANTES
MUSÉE DE LA COUR D'OR
MARCHÉ COUVERT
QUARTIER
OUTRE-SEILLE
PORTE DES ALLEMANDS
RUES COMMERÇANTES
ÉGLISE SAINT-MAXIMIN
ÉGLISE SAINT-EUCAIRE

ESPLANADE,
ARSENAL
RUES COMMERÇANTES
OFFICE DU COMMERCE
SAINT-PIERRE-AUX-NONNAINS
PLAN D'EAU
PORT DE PLAISANCE
LAC AUX CYGNES
OPÉRA-
THÉÂTRE
RUES COMMERÇANTES
LES ÎLES, TEMPLE NEUF
BASILIQUE SAINT-VINCENT

The Style Outlets
Wayfinding System

Design Agency:
Mayúscula Brands

Design Direction:
Rocío Martinavarro

Client:
Neinver

Corporate wayfinding system for Neinver's shopping centers The Style Outlets. Based on an existing visual identity, consisting of triangles strips and a corporate color for each center, Mayúscula has worked a solution that highlights the information on a black background for optimum visualization, relegating colors to a second level on bevels and sign sides. The wayfinding system is corporate, bilingual and modular. The triangle is enhanced as the main element and transferred to all sign typologies: in bevels for positional and directional ceiling and wall signs, in a triangular prism for corporate totems, on the coronation of floor totems to call immediate attention, in custom pictograms or in the parking lot to identify zones and floors.

SALIDA

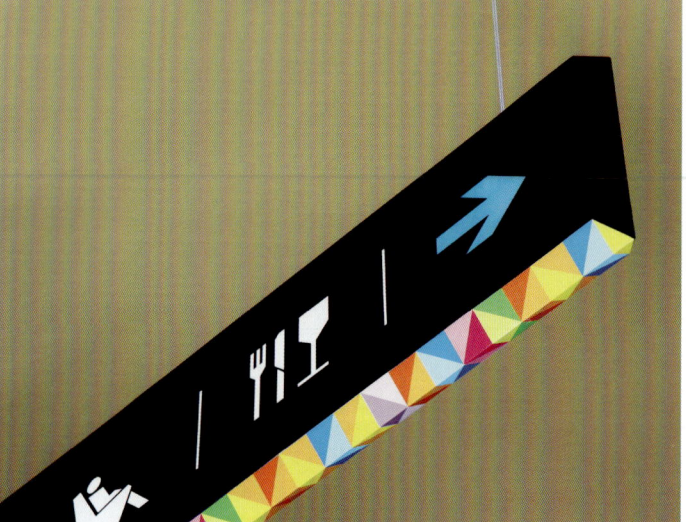

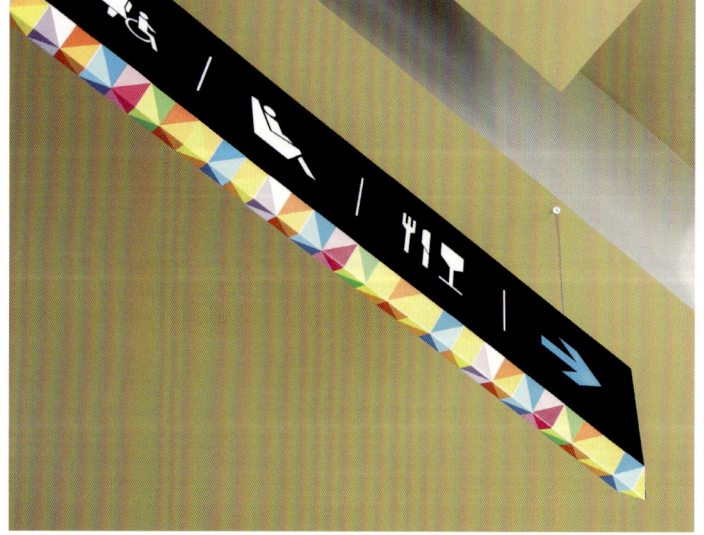

Prince Alfred Park Pool

Design Agency / Consultants:
Frost*

Client:
Neeson Murcutt Architects for the City of Sydney

Frost* have created the identity, wayfinding system and signage for the newly reopened Prince Alfred Park Pool, part of one of the largest public works projects from the City of Sydney in recent years.

The work was unveiled with the opening of the refurbished pool last week, which is amongst the final stages of Council's extensive, multi million dollar upgrade to the parkland and recreation facilities at the 7.5 hectare Prince Alfred Park, Surry Hills' largest open space. We were engaged by award winning Neeson Murcutt Architects, the lead consultants overseeing the entire project.

Prince Alfred Park Pool, located next to Central railway station in Sydney, is the city's first pool that is fully trigeneration ready, has an accessible pool ramp and an accessible kids splash deck with water toys. The amenity incorporates the best in sustainable practices and is physically embedded into the park landscape by Sue Barnsley Design, under a green 'meadow' of native grasses.

We created a circular, azure-hued identity for the pool referencing the heritage of the location, which is the former site of a seasonal circus once famous throughout Sydney. The mark and visual language is also a representation of the playfulness of water, realised through a series of dots and concentric bands of aquatic colour, with accents of red and yellow.

In keeping with the architectural language of integration, we designed a minimal, unobtrusive signage and wayfinding system. Signage is in-ground and materials and colours were chosen that are sympathetic and complementary to the surrounding landscape. Statutory Royal Life Saving signage was applied to the concrete concourse or glazed onto tiles, whilst the site's sustainable initiatives were communicated through a series of discs embedded around the site.

Creating environmental graphics that integrated seamlessly into the site was not always easy to achieve, and called for a diverse range of materials and techniques to be employed. The result is signage that ranges from traditional, hand-painted graphics on timber paneling, through to designs kiln-fired onto the pool's tiled interiors and exteriors. All in-ground signage also underwent a rigorous testing process to ensure signage embedded into the new landscape was anti-slip and compliant for a high-profile public environment.

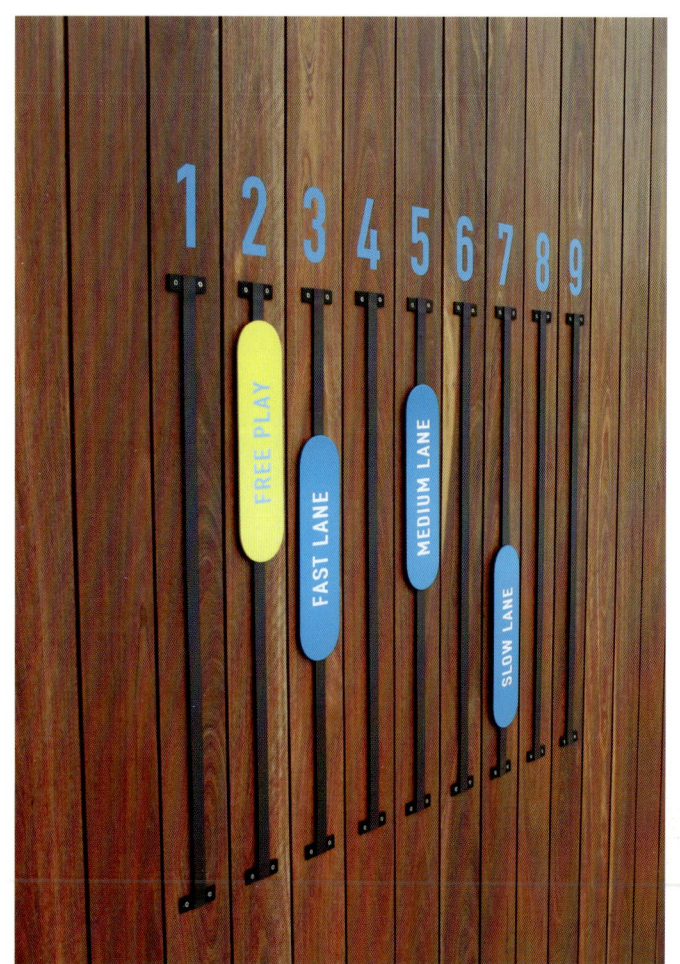

Primary School Gamprin

Location:
Liechtenstein

Designer:
Tom Seger

Photography:
Tom Seger

Design Agency:
Screenlounge, Zurich,
Switzerland

Client:
Gemeinde Gamprin

For the new primary school and kindergarten in Liechtenstein, Screenlounge created this signage system which is highly customized and, therefore, unique. In a very close working process with the architects they sought the right balance between contrast and conformity with the building itself. As a result, there is no substrate or other elements necessary than the pure wayfinding information and functional illustration.

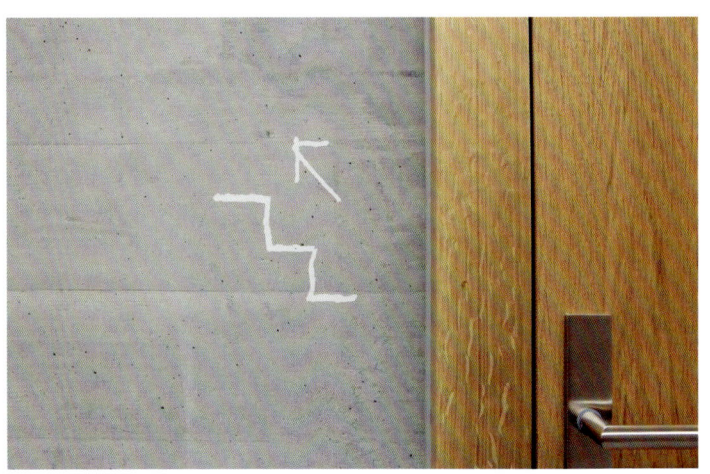

kindergärtherinnen

Ørestad Bibliotek (Ørestad Library)

Design Agency:
Rama Studio

Client:
City of Copenhagen

The design consists of a line of sculptural signs that are visible from several angles and levels of the library's main hall. The signs are constructed in plywood with acrylic cut-out letters painted in different colors that match the visual profile of the library.

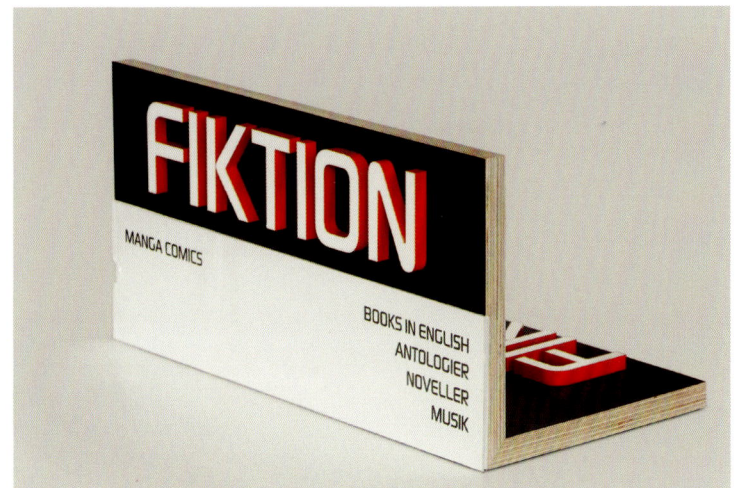

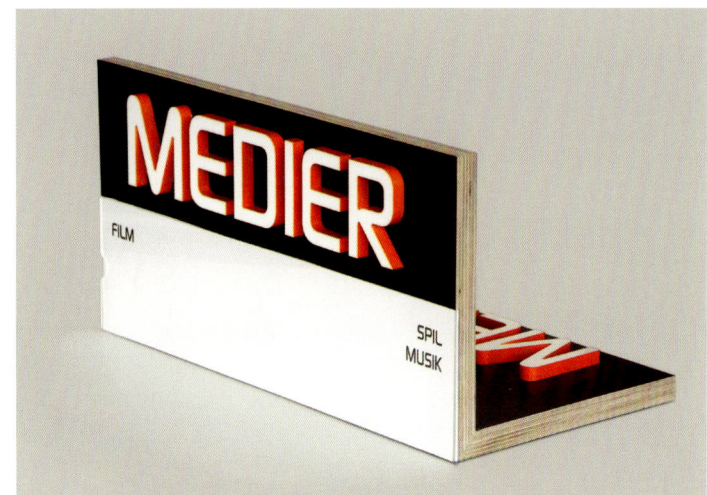

| Client: | Design Agency: |
| Firmenich | [sic] |

| Photography: | Designer: |
| Beatriz Sá | Beatriz Sá, Debora Barbieri, Juliana Garcias, Ana Carolina Aipp, Fabio Kassai |

Signage at Firmenich Brasil

Firmenich Brasil is a Swiss multinational company branch in Cotia, São Paulo.

The signage project respected the visual identity manual created by the Swiss designers using the pre-determined typography and color palette. Within these parameters, three colors were chosen to identify each of the buildings of the Brazilian branch of the company.

Flavors: orange. Firmenich Brasil develops citric flavors. In Addition, orange is a color related to food;
Fragrances: purple. The color is related to spirituality and intuition. It was attributed to the perfume area due to the association of the sense of smell with sensory stimuli, which is a great concern of perfumers while developing new products;

Central: Firmenich blue, which represents the multinational company.

Besides the colors, an identifier was created for each building in the form of a pictogram. Every floor and meeting room also had its identifying pictogram. To that end, extensive research was carried out in order to determine the main elements used by perfumers and flavorists in their job. It was decided that the flavor building should be identified by fruits and seasonings. The perfume building, by flowers and plants. Finally, the central building, by Brazilian trees, the perfect representatives of the national branch.

The plaques were designed with three rounded corners and one straight, alluding to an organic shape, after all a great deal of the raw material used by perfumers and flavorists comes from flowers, fruits, roots and other organic matter. The materials chosen for the plaques were aluminum and acrylic for the internal areas and aluminum and glass for the external areas. These were the same materials used in the finishing of the tower façade.

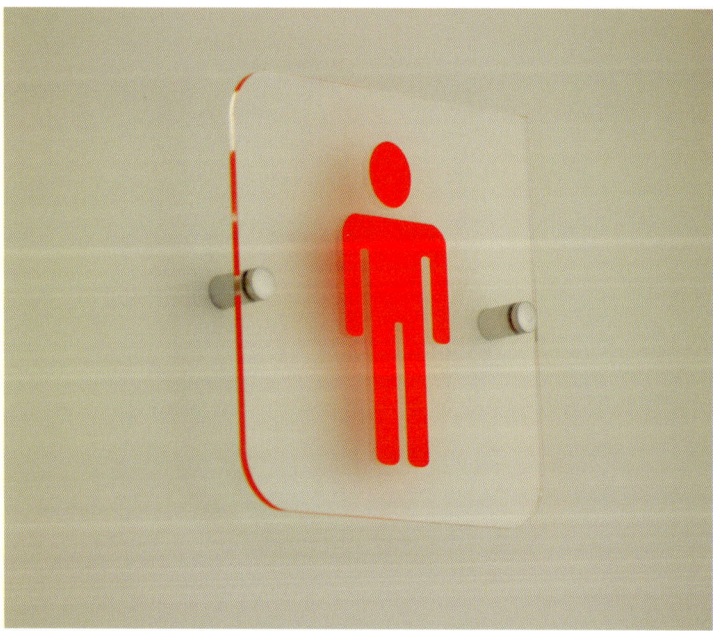

2° andar ↑

Ed. Central

Área Técnica Salgados →
Aplicação/Plantas piloto ←

CMS Estúdios

Sala Oliva

Meeting Room

PERFUMES
fragances

Perfumaria Fina

Sensorium

Sala Spicy

2°andar

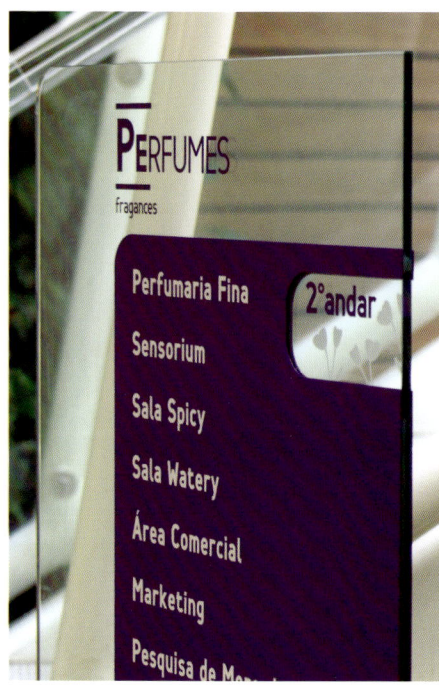

PERFUMES
fragances

Perfumaria Fina

Sensorium

Sala Spicy

Sala Watery

Área Comercial

Marketing

Pesquisa de Mercado

2°andar

Térreo

Ed. Central/Recepção

Biblioteca Técnica

Área Técnica Laboratórios

Avaliação Sensorial

em Consumidor

Toilettes

Toilettes

Signage at Prime Office Park

Design Agency:
[sic]

Designer:
Beatriz Sá, Debora Barbieri, Juliana Garcias,
Ana Carolina Aipp, Fabio Kassai

Photographer:
Juliana Garcias

Client:
TPA Empreendimentos e Construções

This project was made for TPA Empreendimentos e Construções, a business venture located in a three-block building complex in Cotia, São Paulo.

The project seized the geometric forms of the building architecture to create rectangular plaques with volumes that could create a harmonic composition with the buildings. The lettering orientation, sometimes vertical, others horizontal, reinforces the geometric style. At the same time, elegance and discretion were elected key features, considering the characteristics of the business.

The choice of materials took into consideration three main aspects, low-cost production, materials that could contrast with the finishing of the buildings and materials that added a sense of refinement to the minimalist design of the plaques. Therefore, an option was made for the use of dark and opaque wood on white acrylic, the latter giving evidence to the plaques. The façade was signposted in white box lettering and the remaining plaques produced in tobacco-colored laminated MDF and white acrylic. The lettering was applied in adhesive vinyl cut.

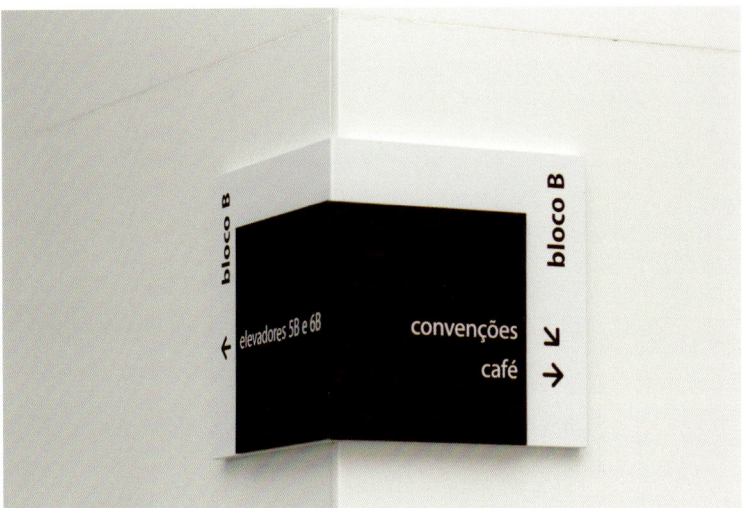

bloco B

↖ ↑ ↖

bloco A

elevador 1A e 2A

elevador 3A e 4A

bloco B

térreo

ELEVADORES
01B e 02B

É vedada sob pena de multa, qualquer forma
de discriminação em virtude de raça, sexo, cor,
origem, condição social, idade, porte ou
presença de deficiência e doença não
contagiosa por contato social no acesso
aos elevadores deste edifício.

Lei nº 91.120 de 10/10/1980

Antes de entrar no elevador verifique se o
mesmo encontra-se parado neste andar.

Lei nº 12.722 de 04/09/1998

Em caso de incêndio, não use o elevador.

Signage at Torre Z

Design Agency:
[sic]

Client:
Hines

Designer:
Beatriz Sá, Ana Carolina Aippi

Photography:
Debora Barbieri

Dinheiro em penca
Pilea nummularifolia

20-story commercial building and a floor area of 87.000m², located in one of the most prestigious areas in São Paulo, the project for Tower Z was developed based on sustainability concepts, following the LEED U.S. Green Building Council standards, aiming at a Gold certification, which is awarded only to buildings that are committed to the environment.

The signing followed the same green building standards. That way, it was determined that recycled PET bottles were to be used as raw material for the manufacturing of the plaques. The layout took into account the contrast of the architectural design – which is contemporary and uses high-tech finishes – with the simplicity of the material chosen for the plaques. That is why it was preferred a clean design that at the same time referred to the main concept: the commitment to the environment. The plaques have three round edges and one straight, evoking the shape of a leaf, and the colors chosen were green (which is natural color of PET bottles) and white. The idea behind the pictograms in box lettering is to instill refinement to the plaques and enhance them, since most of the icons chosen are related to the environment.

Barba de serpente
Ophiopogon jaburan

Pandanus
Pandanus utilis

Bromélia gigante
Vriesea imperialis

Barba de serpente
Ophiopogon jaburan

depósito de lixo

depósito de lixo reciclável

bicicletário

água **não** potável

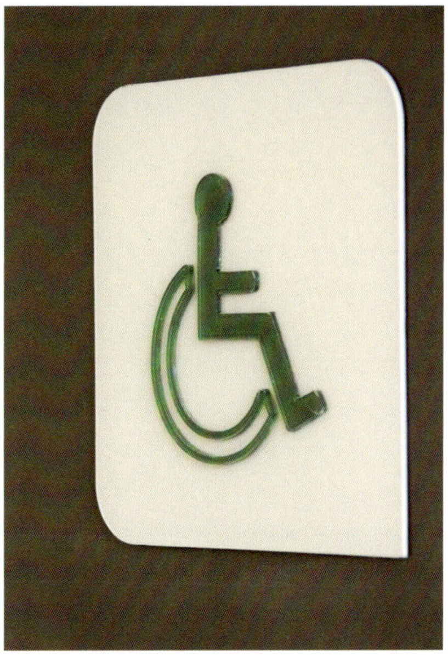

Piala-City

Design Agency:
ujidesign

Architect:
Nishikura Architectural Design Office

Client:
Misato City

The Misato City Piala-City Community Center is a cultural exchange center based on the theme of "food education."

In order to clearly convey this theme, we made all of the sign plates in the shapes of foods. Foods all have unique shapes, such as eggs, onions, beans, and apples, and these shapes have great beauty of form. In this facility, many spaces have been made for children, and we thought that fun, easy-to-understand sign layouts would match the character of this building.

The plates are not simply flat, but rather are given 3D, semi-protuberant shapes, and this makes it easier to identify them as foods. We designed these infographic-type sign plates based on the idea of generating new value by using shapes that support the objectives of the building.

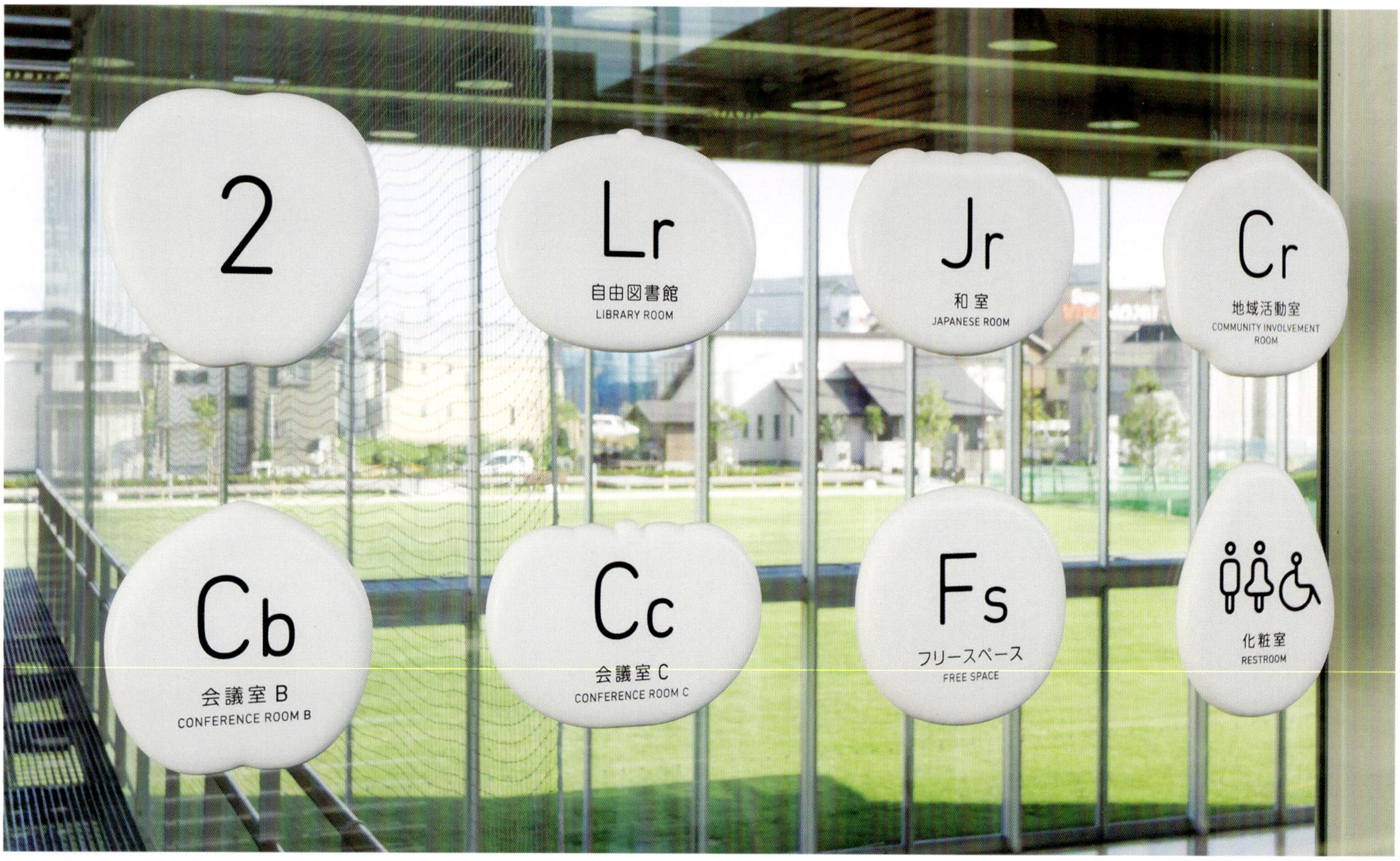

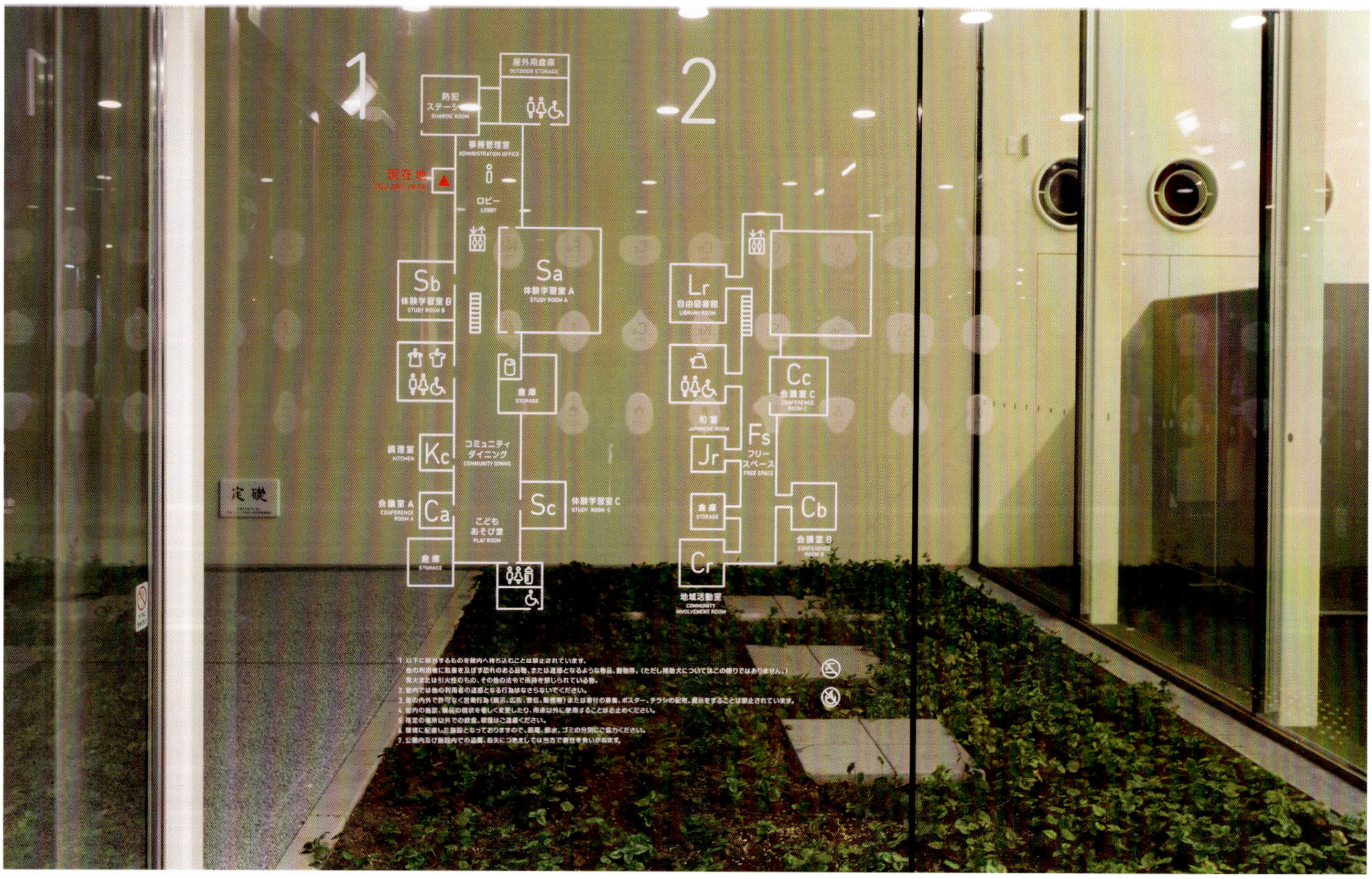

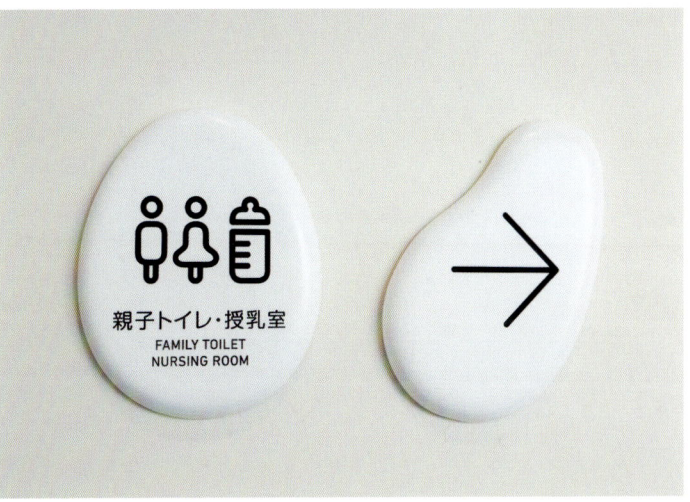

ABC

Design Agency:
api(+)

Photography:
Mark Steele

Designer:
Juan Romero, Tom Henken,
John Scheffel, Heidi Garcia

Over the course of its 70 year and more than 150 store history, the ABC image has evolved from the corner liquor store with a bar to a purveyor of fine wine and spirits. ABC tasked api(+) with developing a new approximately 12,000 to 15,000 square foot prototype store concept better aligned with the modern ABC brand and shifting customer base which had become more upscale and increased from 30% female to 55%. The new design combines logo redesign, store planning, interior design, fixture design, in-store signage, brand communications, and in-store communications.

The design goals were to appeal to a more female friendly customer, organize and de-clutter the store, enhance the wine offering, and make the entire store easily shoppable. This was largely accomplished with signage. A key design element is separation of the store into four distinct departments that can be viewed upon entry. Architectural features were created for the cigars, fine wines, and wine vault. The cluttered environment has been simplified through displaying fewer but more effective signs, creating hierarchy with the space, and clearly identifying each area through color, graphics, merchandising and floor finish. The new system is simple, clean, and categorized to direct, inform, and educate the customer.

Another key design element is the introduction of an educational communications system that informs customers about wine varieties and pairings. This is a direct result of ABC's brand promise to be helpful, welcoming, and a source for everyday celebrations.

Each department is identified clearly and simply with individual slab-serif letters. All signage components were fabricated in-house by ABC and were designed in conjunction with ABC's fabrication capabilities.

The new design is modern, simplified, aesthetically appealing, and has facilitated the shift in customer demographic to a more upscale base.

Photography:
Mark Steele

Design Agency:
api(+)

Super 1 Foods

Designer:
Juan Romero, Tom Henken, Michael
Northcutt, Judy Norlin, Ryan Martin

Super 1 Foods is debuted a new, branded 57,600-square-foot concept designed by api(+) to provide a customer-friendly warehouse environment featuring excellent produce and low prices in a colorful product-centric experience highlighted by an intuitive layout and inspired merchandising. Durable architectural finishes and materials such as concrete and metal panel have been lightened through a refreshing blend of tonal banded colors and solid forms.

Bold graphics and colors make this warehouse anything but monolithic. Customers enjoy a shopping trip visually broken into bite-size vignettes through material and finish changes as well as interruptions of color that are both fresh and energizing.

Shoppers entering the store are welcomed into a spacious area replete with daylight-harvesting skylights, galvanized roof decking and exposed gray primed structure. The Wall of Values department utilizes three bay-high warehouse racking clad with pine slats emulating the bulk shipping pallets they hold.

A palette of bright, energetic colors in carefully measured doses balances with the cool polished concrete floors and industrial warehouse racking. Merchandisers and fixtures communicate value to the customer while retaining core operational principles.

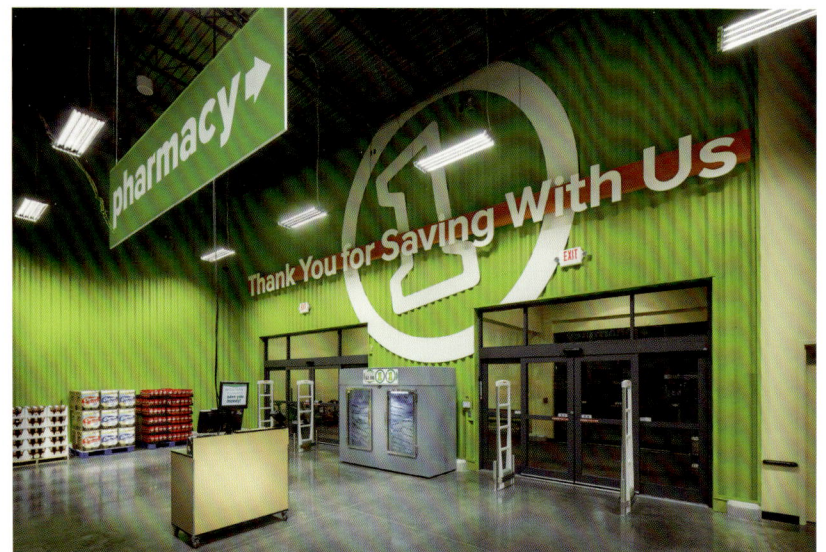

Photography:
Anthony Gomez

Design Agency:
api(+)

Designer:
Juan Romero, Tom Henken,
Ryan Martin, Judy Norlin

Yummy Market

A EUROPEAN FOOD EXPERIENCE

Yummy Market was founded in 2002 to fill a need for familiar foods desired by the growing number of Europeans living in the Toronto area and by adventurous foodies seeking new experiences.

When owners Alexei and Ana Tsvetkov saw demand for a second Yummy Market location, they sought api(+)'s food retail design expertise and holistic approach to achieve their vision and bring their new store to life. From the beginning, the design goal was to create a fully branded European-style environment and to define the Yummy Market brand essence, focusing on brand personality, brand promise, point-of-difference, and tone-of-voice.

Prominent design features include images of European landmarks, curved bulkheads featuring colorful tiles and signage, and an open layout. In the frozen department, an overhead Tetris-shaped floating trellis creates an intimate feel. Hints of European culture, such as the Cyrillic 'Я' in the dairy department signage, can be seen throughout the store.

Enjoy the unique flavours of our quality hot and cold smoked fish

Our chefs are trained in traditional Eu

Photography:
John Bosio, Glen Swantak,
John Scheffel

Design Agency:
Merje, api(+)

Designer:
John Bosio, Glen Swantak,
Amy Rees, John Scheffel

Tampa Wayfinding Images

api(+) teamed with MERJE and the Downtown Tampa Partnership on a civic wayfinding program for downtown Tampa, an area evolving to include a mix of business, culture and residentialuses. The new wayfinding system highlights cultural areas and guides pedestrian and vehicle traffic to its destination. Downtown Tampa is currently experiencing a resurgence of development interest including a continuous pedestrian walkway along its waterfront (Tampa Riverwalk), residential towers, new museums, larger conventions and more activities designed to attract people downtown on nights and weekends. Tampa Downtown Partnership has been joined by local, county and state agencies to develop a unified wayfinding and identity systemto connect the clusters of the downtown urban core. The project's Steering Committee selected the team of MERJE and api(+) to design a wayfinding program that projects a consistent image, eases vehicular congestion, promotes walking and mass transit and is sustainable as well as expandable. Wayfinding issues included the creation of districts, clear direction and wayfinding to parking and large events, and adopting the new regulations enacted by the Federal Department of Transportation. The design team created three options, each focusing on different potential themes for the system. The Steering Committee did not want imagery typical of Florida concepts such as palm trees, flamingos and beaches. The selected theme of "light" was inspired by the "Lights on Tampa" program that creates permanent and temporary light installations throughout Downtown Tampa. Gateways are approached as public art, and directional signage placement alternates between freestanding and traffic signal-mounted. Unique parking symbols guide visitors to the nearest parking facility, and pedestrian signage establishes walking corridors.

The system of vehicular, pedestrian and parking signs creates a sense of place and connects visitors and residents to downtown attractions, government buildings and parking garages by providing clear direction, consistent terminology and a unique graphic identity.

Client:
Gewerblich-industrielle Berufsschule
Bern gibb, Berne (industrial school)

Photography:
Beat Schweizer, Berne

Design Agency:
Bloom Identity

Designer:
Rahel Grünig

Steel Tube Signage System for the Industrial School

The signage system uses the same concept as a traditional signpost to guide visitors. Short, concise arrows and lettering on steel tubes 35cm thick form the link to the signpost, directing people. The information is written on both sides to reflect the dynamics of the visitor flows. (Red Dot design award 2011)

3b 150m

Berufs-, Fach- und
Fortbildungsschule BFF/BVS

Client:
Biennale of Sydney

Design Agency:
Collider

Collaboration:
Clemens Habicht,
Sarah Nguyen, Mitchell Brown

Creative Direction:
Andrew van der
Westhuyzen

18th Biennale of Sydney 2012:
All Our Relations - Campaign

The 18th Biennale of Sydney: all our relations (27 June – 16 September 2012) was one of Australia's largest and most exciting contemporary visual arts events. The Biennale staged a three month exhibition including a program of artist talks, performances, forums, film screenings, family events, guided tours and other special events across multiple Sydney venues.

The third oldest biennale in the world, the Biennale of Sydney continues to be recognised for showcasing the freshest and most provocative contemporary art from Australia and around the world.

Collider was engaged to visualise the complete campaign for 2012. In collaboration with Biennale artist, Zoe Keramea, a full suite of elements was created including the identity system, all printed collateral, merchandise, event signage and wayfinding, press advertising and the exhibition catalogue.

Cockatoo Island Wayfinding

Design Agency:
Collider

Lead Designer:
Sarah Nguyen

Creative Director:
Andrew van der
Westhuyzen

Client:
Sydney Harbour
Federation Trust

In addition to rebranding Cockatoo Island, Collider implemented a new signage and wayfinding strategy across the island. The strategy, consisting of over 200 signs, aimed to both improve visitor navigation through the vast island, and also provide more concise information, mapping and changeable systems for events.

The signage needed to clearly sit apart from the visually busy industrial context whilst being sensitive to the historical nature of the space. We approached the system as though it was an annotation, using clear open panels of type with faded teal (reminiscent in many of the old internal spaces) to sit clearly removed from the setting.

One of the reasons the key typeface was chosen was for its ability to be laser cut out of metal panels providing interesting detail in keeping with the nuances of the architecture and industrial machinery found across the island.

An important component of the project was redeveloping a new mapping system to help people traverse the island and overcome challenges relating to the island's varying relief. Traditional 2D maps were less successful at communication so we modeled a 3D relief map using master plans of the site to give visitors a more illustrative understanding.

With a highly detailed model of the island, we were able to reduce the key features to clear and simplified forms of distinctive landmarks such as cranes, escarpments, buildings and grassed areas. Through re-orienting the renders of the mapping according to the context of the view, each sign gives a context-aware view of a visitor's current position.

Eastern Apron

Dog-Le Tunnel

Tunnel 1

Dog-Leg Tunnel

Surry Hills Library & Community Centre

Design Agency:
Collider

Creative Direction & Design:
Andrew van der Westhuyzen,
Clemens Habicht

Client:
City of Sydney

Consulting Architects:
Akin Creative

Designed by FJMT Architects and City of Sydney, the new Surry Hills Library and Community Centre is an eco-sustainable building with the highest efficiency rating of any government building in Australia.

Collider was asked to create the principle signage for the centre, which was a great opportunity to make something permanent and lasting. The design work included four elements - the main entrance and the three floor directories. The directories, in sympathy to the materials they exist within, are designed to feel like large tilted switches or books roughly stacked.

Each module not only holds the description of the destination but also tilts towards that destination. The proximity of the destination determines the angle of the tilt. The angularity of the tilted entrance type bows to the entering public while mimicking the angle of the internal glass facade.

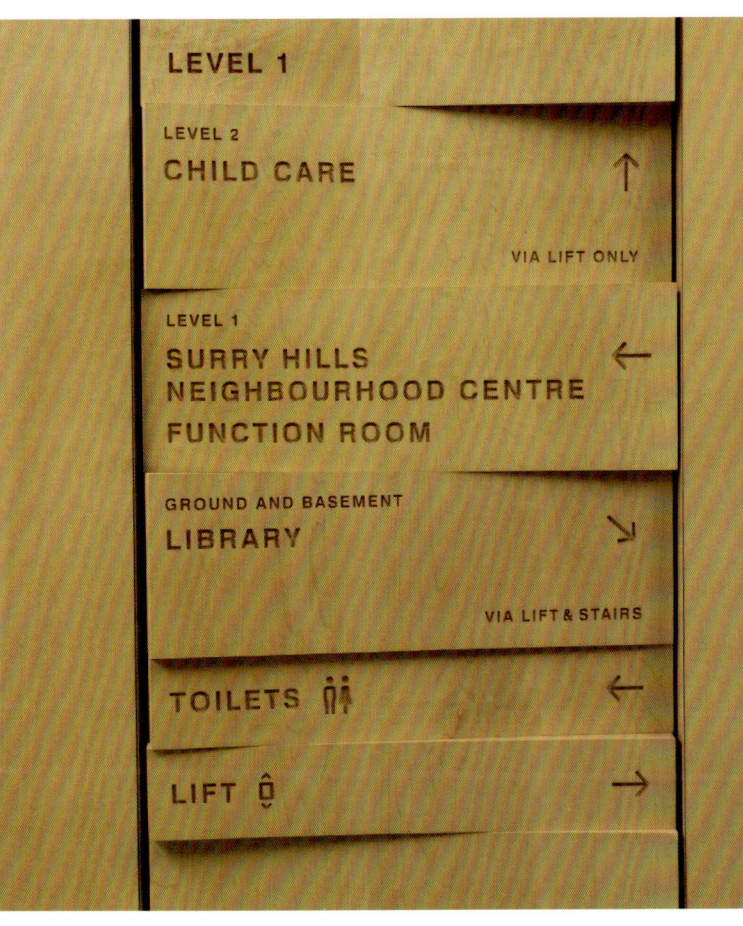

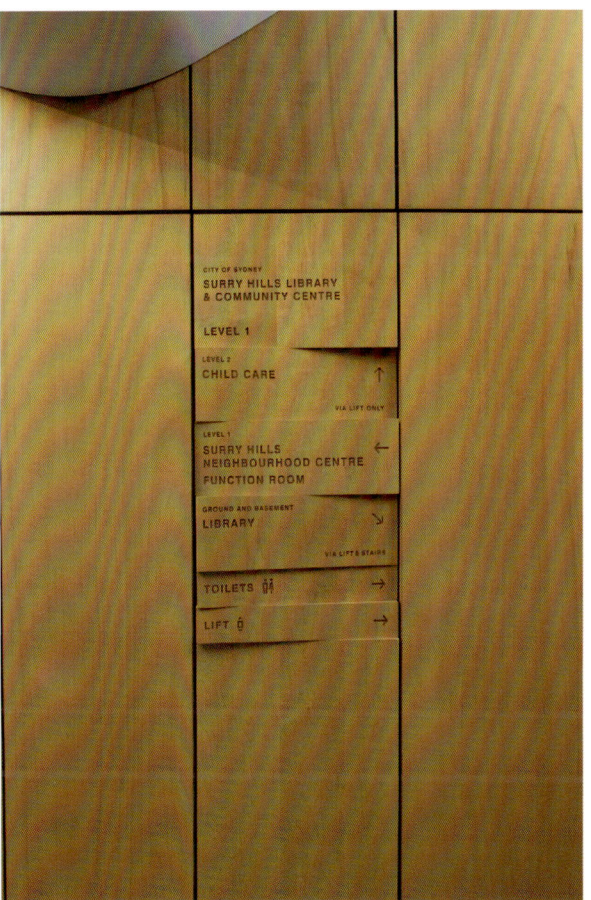

JA Minds

Design Agency:
6D-K Co., Ltd.

Designer:
Shogo Kishino, Nozomi Tagami

Photography:
Shingo Fujimoto

Art Direction:
Shogo Kishino

Client:
Minds Agriculture Cooperatives

JA stands for Japan Agricultural Cooperatives; the nation's largest cooperative in its category; and JA minds is an agricultural union responsible for the Tama district in Tokyo.

JA is currently views as massive and conservative, somewhat like a government body.

With plans of remodeling the Tama branch to commemorate the 20th anniversary of JA minds, we proposed a new visual identity with pictograms that would enable communication with customers and capable of building affinity and instantly communicating its various services to wide generations from children to senior citizens, as well as people engaging in agriculture.

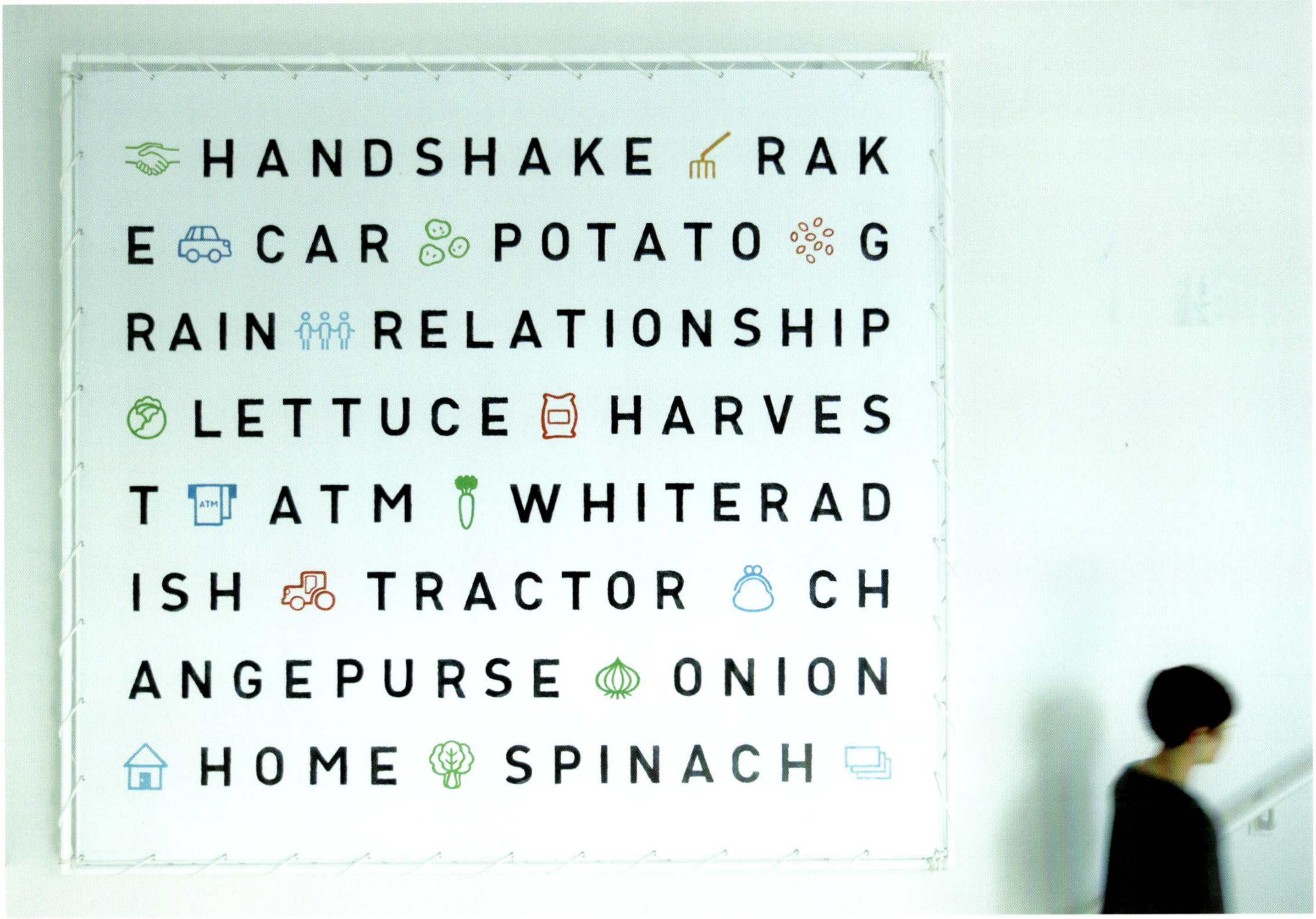

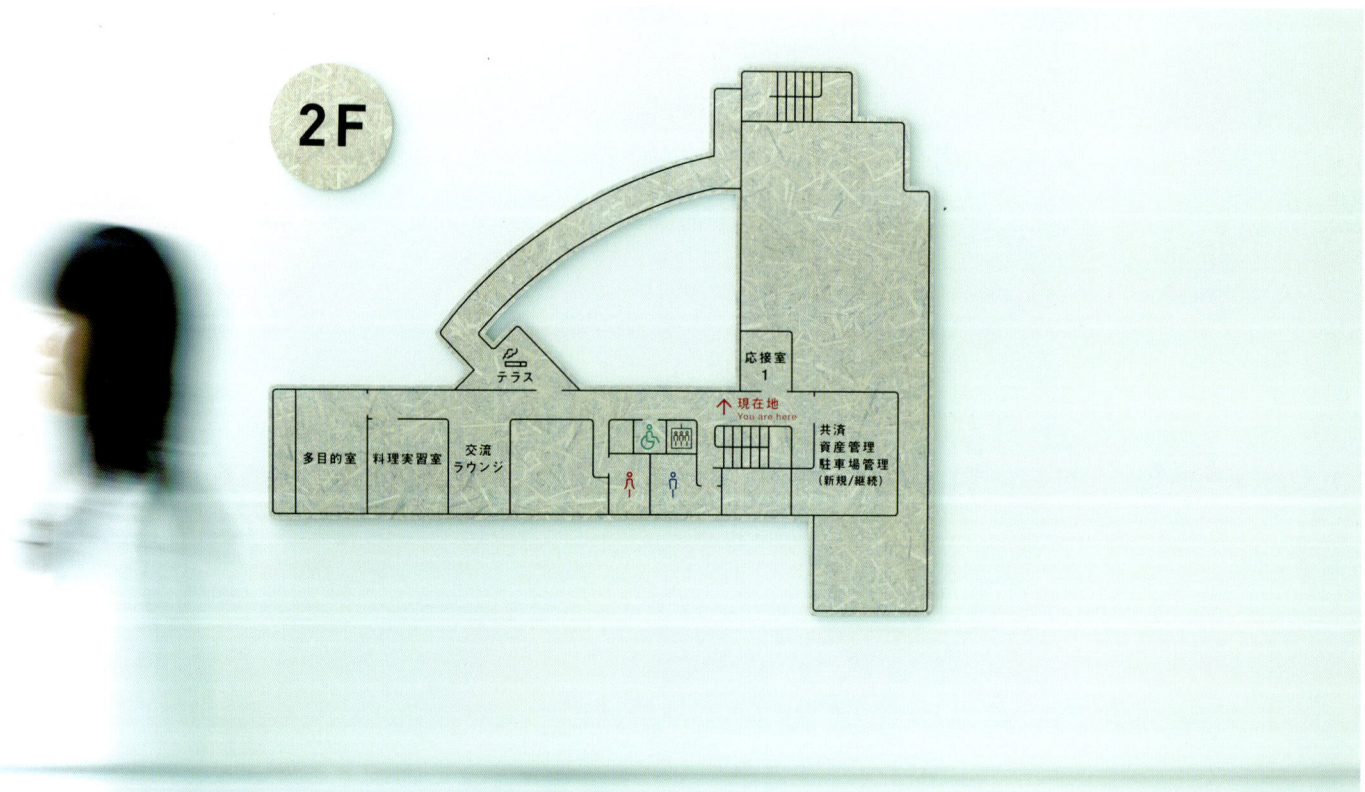

JA MINDS SHOP   JA MINDS FRESH

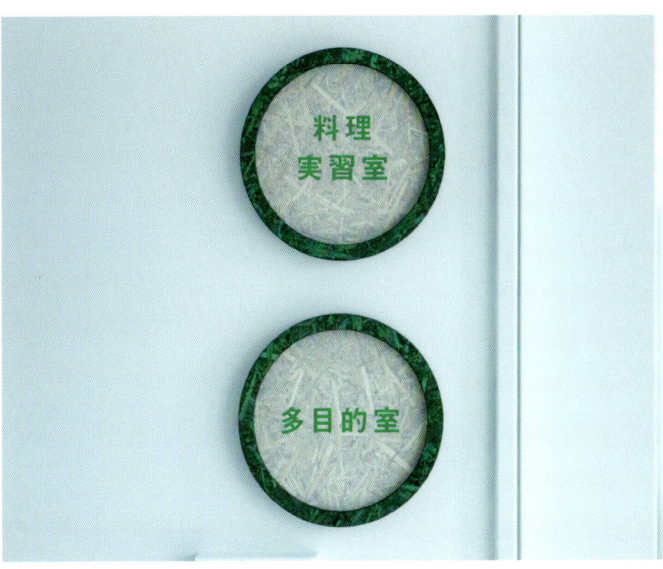

料理
実習室

多目的室

2F

Signage for the Sports Center Science City of ETH Zurich

Design Agency:
TGG Hafen Senn Stieger, St. Gallen

Architect:
Dietrich Untertrifaller Stäheli
Architekten, Bregenz

Production:
Jank + Blatter AG, Rotheburg

The extreme reduction of the bright color interior makes the red signage clearly visible. The signage system works with visual elements, which are inspired by the world of sports and which are taken from the visual systems of ball game fields. These are for example lines leading through the system in the function of a red thread.

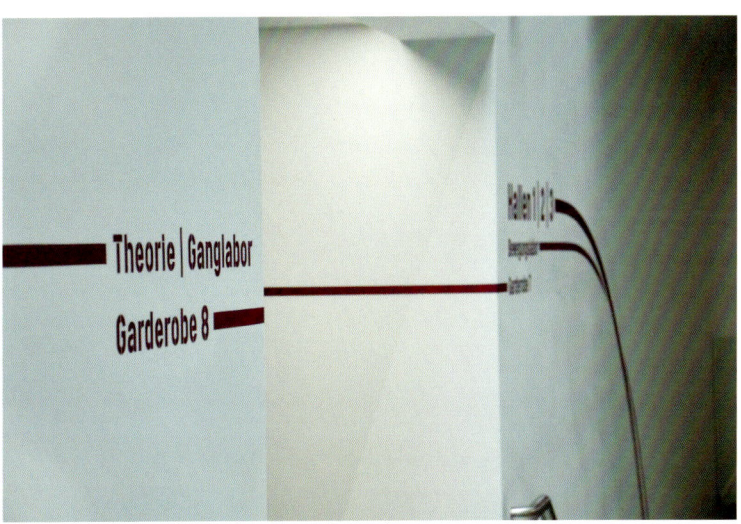

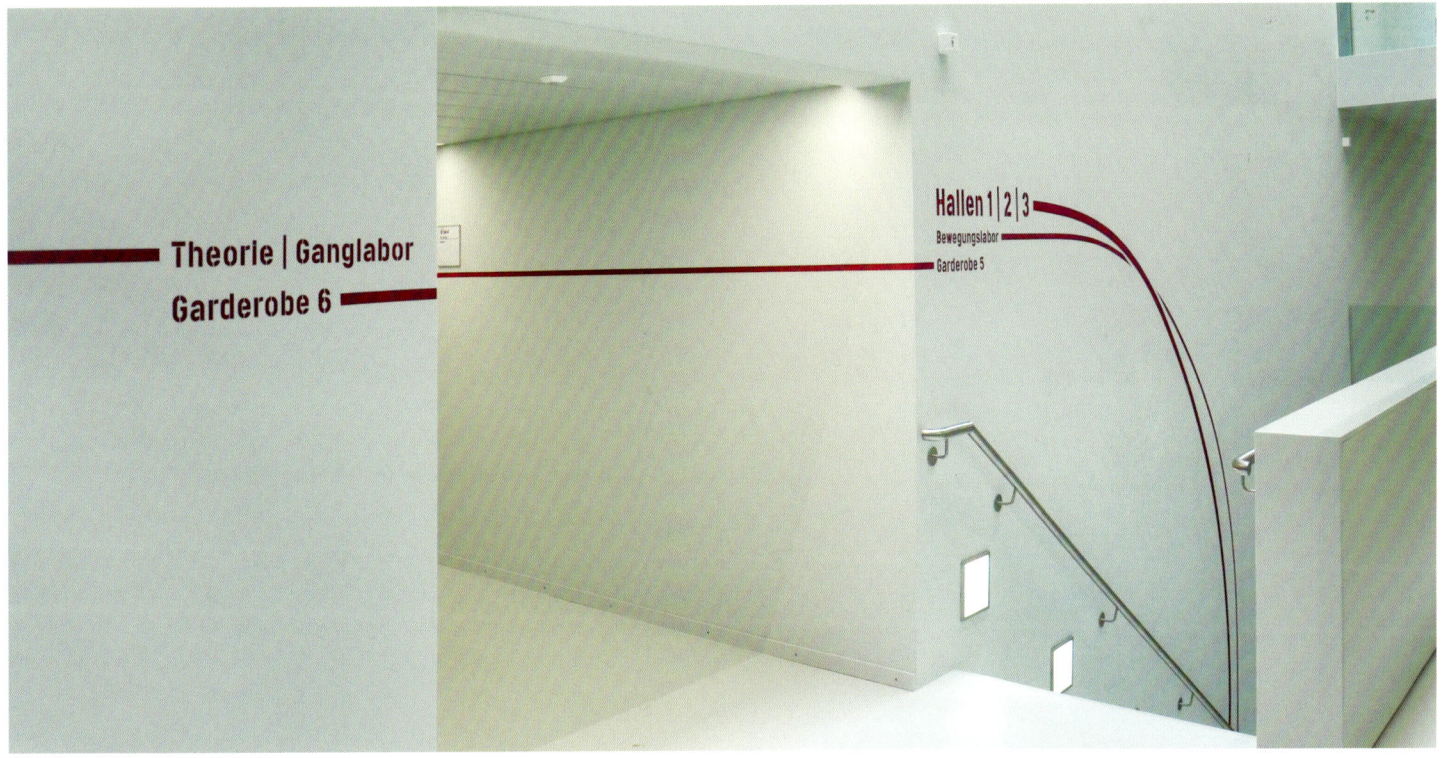

Kawagoe Red Cross Blood Donation Room

Design Agency:
6D-K Co., Ltd.

Art Direction:
Shogo Kishino

Designer:
Shogo Kishino, Nozomi Tagami

Client:
Japanese Red Cross Society

Located in the front of the Kawagoe station, Saitama Prefecture, it is a sign system for Red Cross blood donation room.

It is easy to understand and aim with familiarity.

Signs are mounted in different ways for each location, in the configuration with a combination of single stroke line of red and grain-based, which makes the final result united.

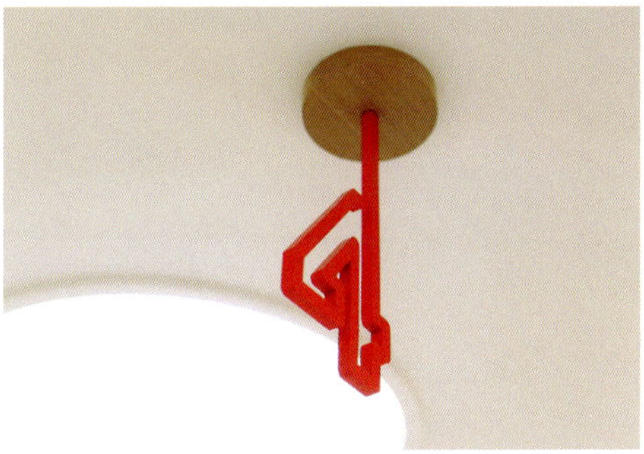

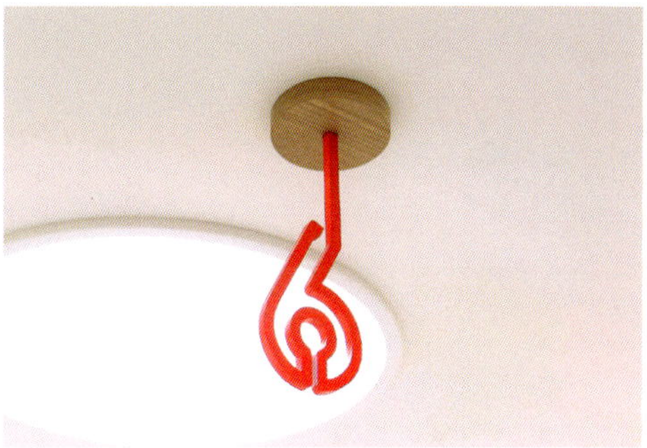

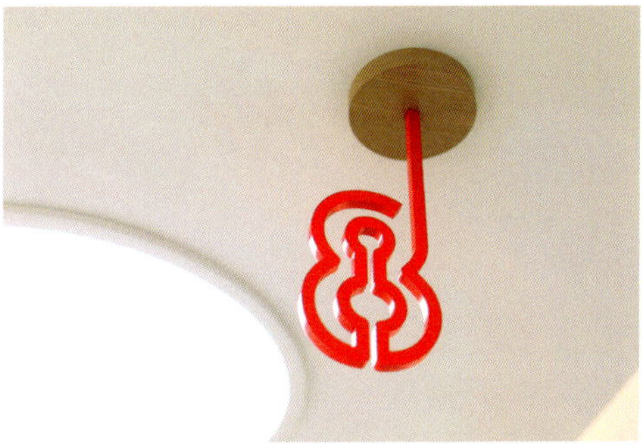

The Galeries Victoria

The signage system for The Galeries Victoria consists of everything from shop front signage to external & internal wayfinding. Drawing inspiration from the new Galeries identity, with angled cut letters, we proposed using folded metal & protruding acrylic lettering for the signage to become tactile, evocative & eye-catching whilst remaining functional & practical.

The GreenWay

Design Agency:
Deuce Design

Designer:
Shogo Kishino, Nozomi Tagami

Client:
Ashfield Council

Client:
Japanese Red Cross Society

We were engaged by Ashfield Council to create a complete signage & wayfinding system throughout the GreenWay, an urban green corridor that stretches from Iron Cove to Cooks River in Sydney's Inner West.

It is a bush corridor and a hub for community arts and groups, bushcare, walking and cycling. A campaign is currently underway to see the GreenWay shared pathway completed as part of the light rail extension from Lilyfield to Dulwich Hill. As the majority of the corridor is surrounded by nature, the signage is deliberately subtle in its colour & shape to blend into its surroundings.

Waverley Library

Design Agency:
Deuce Design

Client:
Waverley Council

Typographic and dynamic, the bright and bold Deuce graphics energise Waverley Library's main children's' dept. and main public spaces. Waverley Library commissioned the studio to provide schematic and spatial design for the Waverley Library foyer and two customer service areas within the adult and children's library adjacent to the foyer area on the ground floor, stairwell and gallery. In conjunction with RDO Architecture, the studio gave the library a much-needed facelift to invigorate the spaces, print collateral and super graphics. The result is a highly activated library, new and engaging print collateral and a library that is tech savvy.

Photography:
Denis Riou /
Rennes

Design Agency:
Drive Design

Client:
Cap l'Orient

BSM

The conception of the signage system for this site, both from the point of view of the graphics and of the furniture, had to join within the universe of the sail, and lean on an activity: navigating.

Inspired from graphic and informative codes used in the past and contemporary marine mapping, the signage system of the site develops a strong identity, in adequacy with the character of the site.

All the information gets organized on a very specific contrived bottom: the latter gives the effect of a changeable and unstable surface to the user who moves - a kinetic effect based on the retinal vibration, evoking the surface of the ocean.

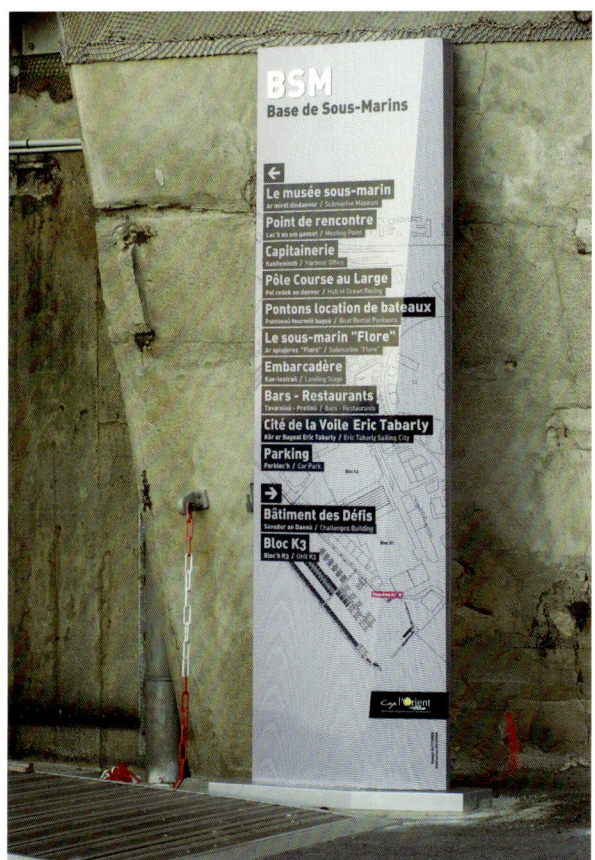

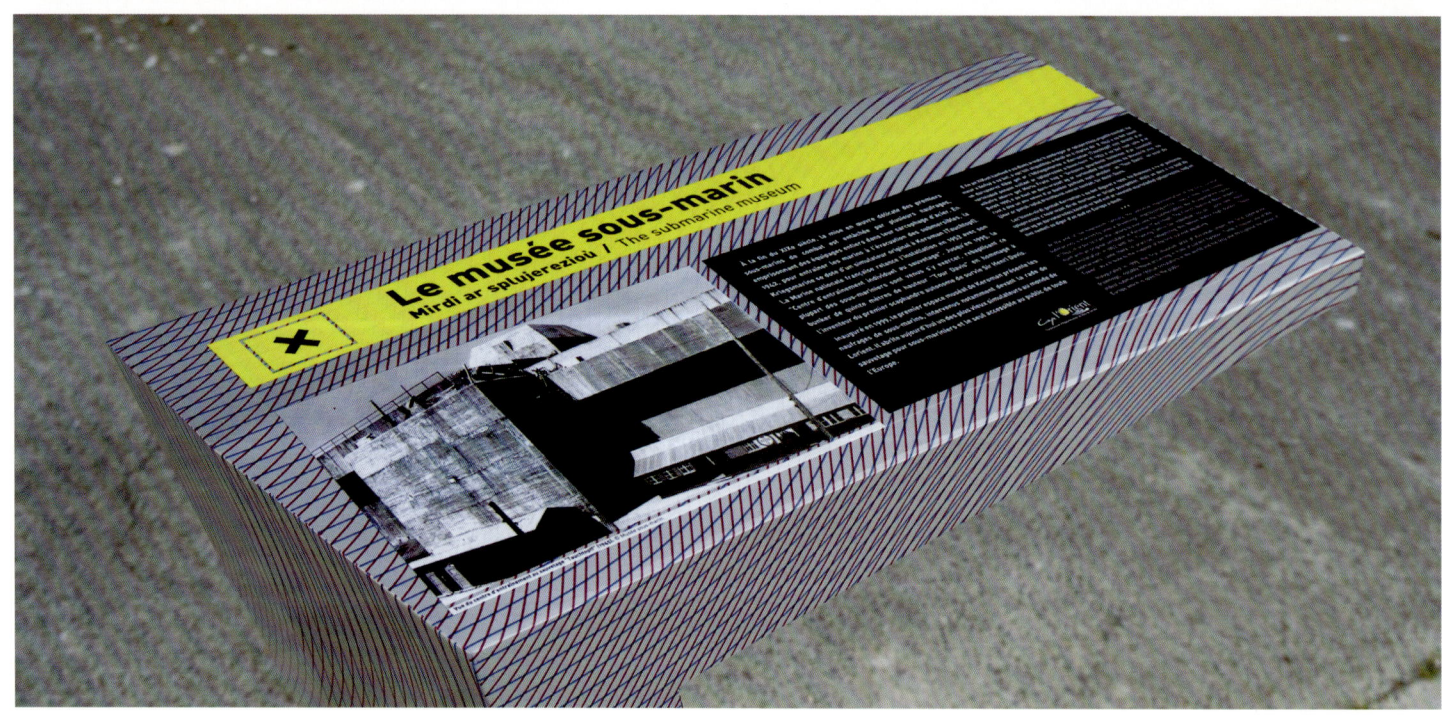

Saint-Cyr

Design Agency:
Drive Design

Designer:
G. Bourdon

Client:
Mairie de St
Cyr au Mt D'or

Photography:
G. Bourdon

The city hall of Saint-Cyr (French military academy) wishes to position itself as a "village of his time" and give an image and brand identity of generating closeness and contacts between the inhabitants.

The signage concept which we have established answers several objectives:

to identify the Saint Cyr 's territory in its entirely, to make it readable by asserting its vocation to return the set homogeneous and to direct the public and the professionals visitors on the site, to add value in Saint-Cyr identity thanks their new logo and the overall policy of communication, to create a specific atmosphere arouse the curiosity and the desire to penetrate on the site.

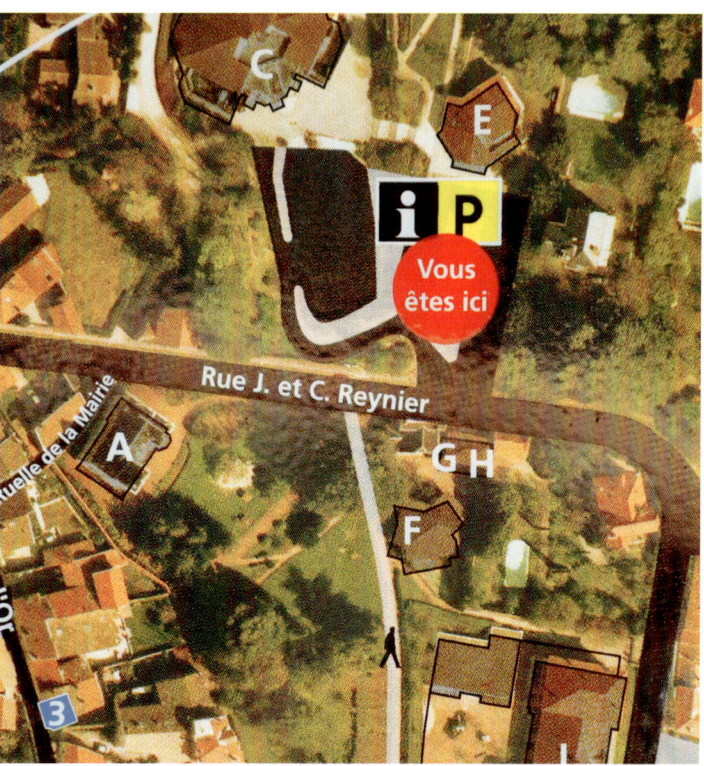

Signage for the Montjuic Cemetery Cultural Routes

Design Agency:
Roseta y Oihana

Designer:
Roseta Mus Pons,
Oihana Herrera Erneta

Client:
Cementiris de
Barcelona s.a.

Photography:
Xavier Carreras

One of the most beautiful cemeteries of Barcelona, the Cemetery of Montjuic, holds a cultural route formed by three itineraries: artistic, historical and combined. Some of the sepultures belong to one, two or three of the itineraries, having a different number in each itinerary. This, together with the fact that the cemetery is an open and complex space, was one of the challenges of the project. Also, the client main request was that the signage system should not be funeral, so we decided to differentiate each itinerary using blue, yellow and green, colors that are quite environmental (sky-sea, sunshine and vegetation) and fit with the graveyard, placed by the sea and with Mediterranean vegetation. The colors at the same time are visually respectful with the sepultures. Regarding the typeface we wanted it to be both classical and modern, so we choose the New Johnston typeface, considered one of the first typefaces without serifs. The material used in the signs resembles the one used in the decorated doors of some of the mausoleums.

BSL Garage

Design Agency:
Studio 360

Art Direction and Dseign:
Vladan Srdic

Creative Direction:
Vladan Srdic

Client:
BSL

The task was to deliver a way-finding system which is easy to use and to create more pleasant, friendly public space. The garage interior was pretty degraded due to the long and heavy usage, so it needed a wide-range renovation. Because of the budget-limits, we had to find an inexpensive, but effective solution. The idea was to "neutralize" the vast interior, so we could "highlight" the complex poles system in the variations of bright yellow colors (making a stunning visual effect). The direction-signs were divided into two user-groups — for pedestrians and the vehicles, some of them using LED diodes for a better visibility.

Creative Direction:
Toni Tomasek (Mayer McCann)

Client:
Mayer McCann

Design Agency:
Studio 360

Art Direction and Design:
Vladan Srdic

Signage System for Citypark Shopping Mall

The signage system for Citypark Shopping Mall is in Ljubljana, Slovenia. It is based on minimalist redesign of an old logo, dynamic interpretation of primary colors (red, blue) and clever usage of the interior space. Regardless to the limitations of this strictly commercial project, we wanted to add some creative flavor and make the Citypark way-finding interface not only user-friendly, but more compelling and recognizable.

Fenway South

Design Agency:
Ashton Design

Designer:
Ronald Younts, Jonathan Han,
AngeloAlcasabas, Alison Grissinger

Client:
Boston Red Sox

In 2011, Ashton Design was engaged to infuse the Fenway aesthetic into a new, modern ballpark- the Red Sox's Spring Training Facility in Fort Meyers, Florida. JetBlue Park at Fenway South, which debuted in 2012, was conceived as a modern version of Fenway park- replicating the original's dimensions, and re-creating or re-using a number of iconic elements of its 100-year-old inspiration in a setting appropriate to the climate, landscape, and energy of its Southwest Florida location.

The Fitzgerald

Design Agency:
Ashton Design

Client:
The Fitzgerald

Designer:
Danny Jones

Inspired by F. Scott Fitzgerald, this community of Baltimore apartments is completed with stunning features including exotic amenities and breathtaking details. Ashton Design had the task of updating The Fitzgerald logo along with both interior and exterior signage that can be seen throughout the entire complex as well as the parking garage.

Wayfinding System
for Korona Kielce Mall

Design Agency:
dodoplan

Wayfinding Graphics:
Robert Mieniok

Client:
MGC Invest

Women are key customers for shopping centers around the world. For them a trip to the mall should be a pleasant experience associated with a relaxing walk, not an exhausting marathon. The space of the Korona Kielce center was designed to satisfy their needs and to make shopping enjoyable.

The project created by Dodoplan studio included a complete visual information system along with 3D media, info graphics, multimedia elements and a parking information system.

The visual information system and the information counters were designed with the use of Corian. Owing to the unique construction properties of this material, the elements created are light and self-supporting, referring to the architecture of the building in shape.

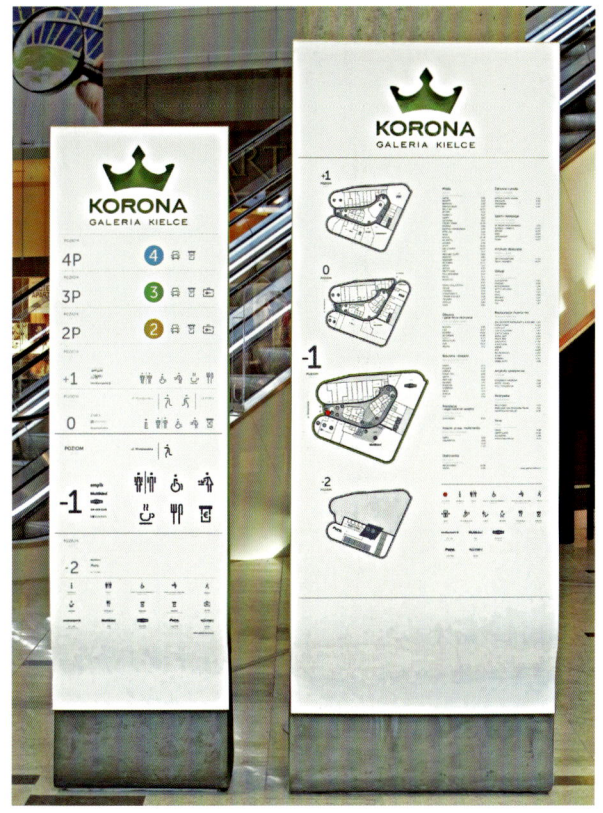

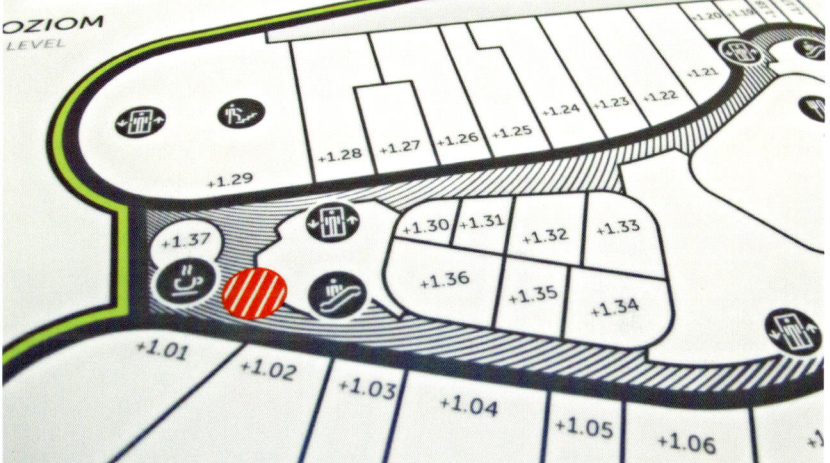

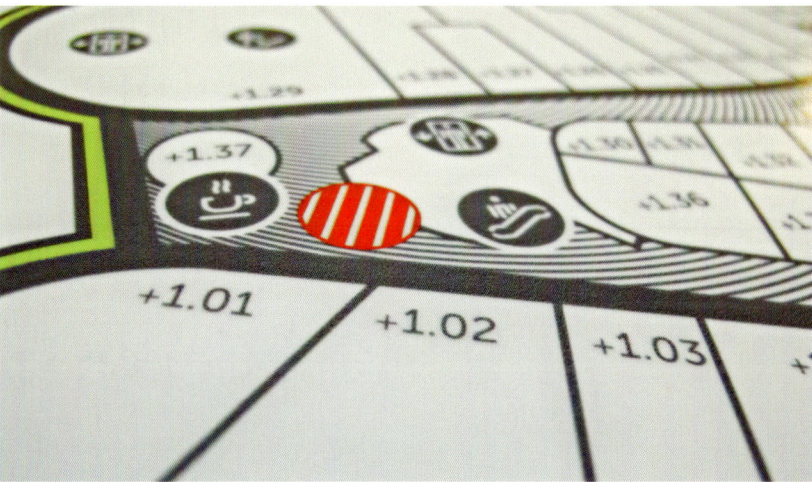

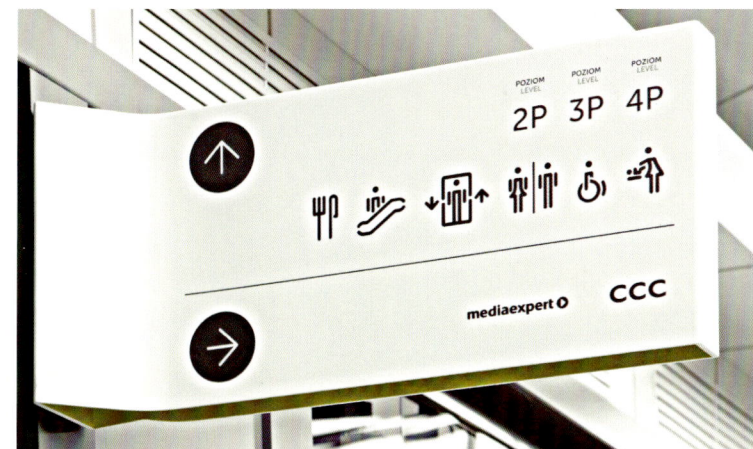

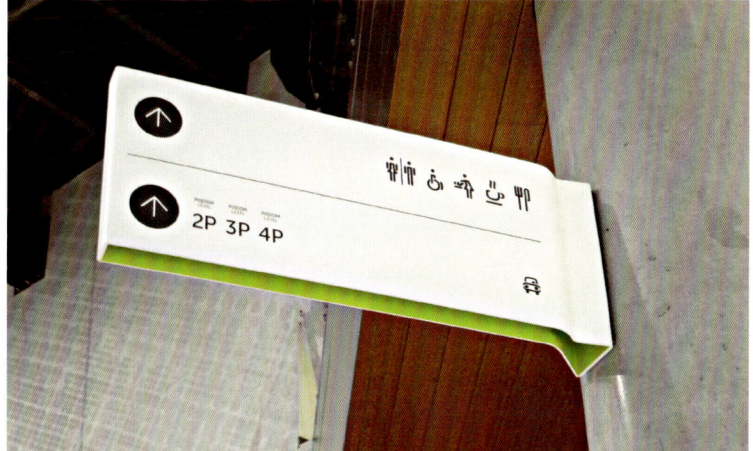

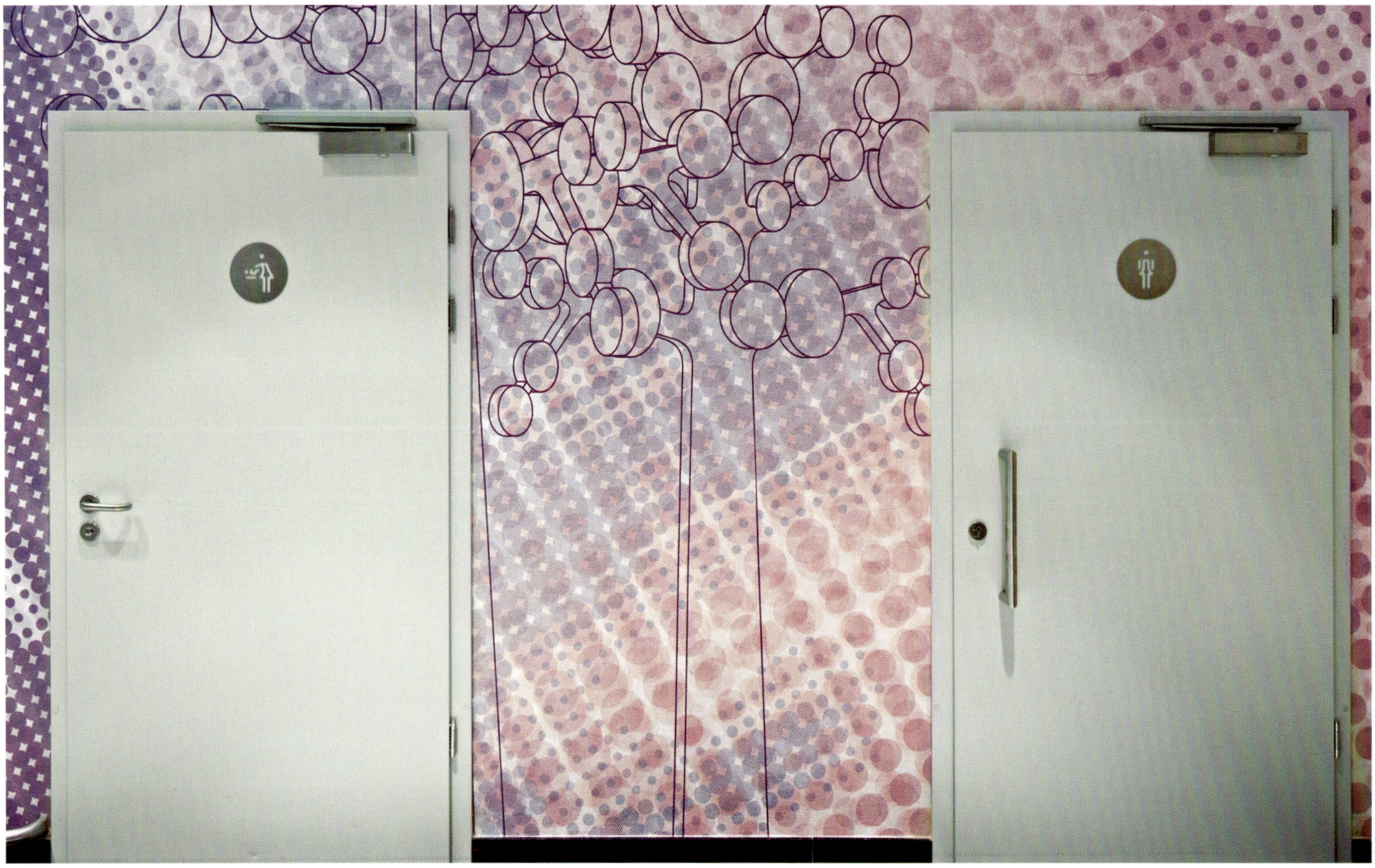

The Garden of Barco

Designer:
Filippo Partesotti

Client:
Children School San Domenico
Savio Barco di Bibbiano (RE)

Photography:
Filippo Partesotti

Logo, wayfinding signage and visual renewal of an old nursery-kindergarten school of 1920 in Barco (Italy).

On the original facade there was writing which is still readable as the ancient name that formed from the pedagogical theories of these times: "GIARDINO D'INFANZIA", (Children Garden) or, better, as they call that type of school in Norther Europe KINDERGARTEN.

So we decided to respect it, and we renamed the school IL GIARDINO DI BARCO (The Garden of Barco).

And, by the way, we decided that everything will have to remember a garden, so we choose to have a lot of flowers all over the school. And the logo and the wayfinding signals too are surrounded by flowers.

We draw the flowers, and print them on forex slabs, cut by digital cutter. Every class of the school is indicated by a different color and by the image of garden insects (ladybug, butterfly, bee…) drawned in a child way.
But the most important choice we did was to persuade the adults (teachers, partents) that everything, and mostly the wayfinding system, had to be placed at the children height. We did and the result was wonderful!

Herdade do Esporão Signage

Design Agency:
White Studio

The project for outdoor signage at Herdade do Esporão was born out of a need to integrate clear information in the property, without disturbing the landscape.

We chose to use the big rocks already found in the area to contain the information. These rocks were then treated and properly cut to receive the white ink.

We believe we have achieved a good balance between man made intervention and the natural feel we were looking for.

The City of London Signage

Design Agency:
Woodhouse

The City of London may be home to many globe-spanning businesses and some of the most cutting edge architecture in Europe, but it still essentially retains what its original, medieval street plan. The complex, tight grained layout has resulted in what is now considered an excessive amount of signage in the form of finger posts, which are now outdated and inflexible. This creates a unique challenge for and led to the development of a new coherent wayfinding strategy for the whole of the City of London. The wayfinding design for the City has involved a detailed analysis of the historical make up and identity of the place which has established recognisable districts and character areas, along with a study of the location and distribution of landmarks and places of interest. Key routes are chosen to provide easy navigation and orientation.

This project started with a comprehensive design study for a complete new wayfinding system for the City of London. Placemarque included the design of a new map for the City of London which then had to incorporate appropriate materials into the design of a bespoke new structure for the map, node points and finger posts. The project has also involved developing prototypes for illuminated dot matrix and dynamic information signage. These prototypes of the main arrival point maps have been installed at St Paul's Cathedral and Fenchurch Street Station, with nodal prototypes at Guildhall and on the River walk.

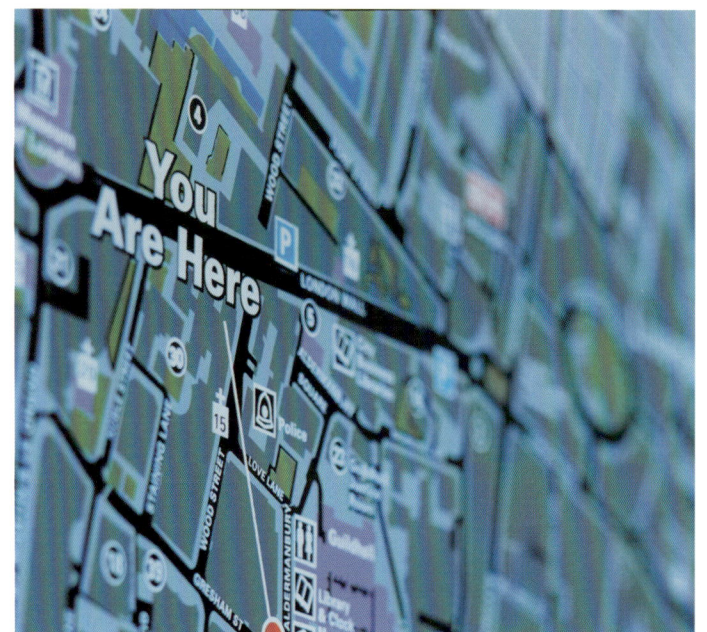

Legible Brighton Wayfinding System

Architect:
Applied Information Group (AIG)

Bespoke:
Woodhouse

Client:
Brighton and Hove City Council

It might not be such a bad thing getting lost in one of the UK's premier's seaside resorts, but Woodhouse made this far more difficult thanks to their contemporary and customised wayfinding system.

Research has shown that people are more likely to return to a city if they have found it easy to navigate their way around. This inspired Brighton & Hove City Council, to commission a series wayfinding units, as part of a programme for the city designed by Applied Information Group (AIG). Woodhouse created a highly functional and legible way-finding system, with coloured detail that effectively highlights Brighton & Hove City Council's 'Royal Pavilion' logo.

A combination of highly durable 'Node' signs, special adaptations of the 'Legible City' range, were designed and manufactured for AIG by Woodhouse. These take the form of either wider monoliths or narrower 'minilith' signs. The stainless steel paving plates also include a North indicator for those who have truly lost their sense of direction. Woodhouse also provided conventional finger-post signs located around the town.

One of the unique features is the innovative base plate and 'manhole frame', which means that the signage units can then be rapidly de/reinstalled later, with no further disruption to the ground finishes or pedestrian circulation routes. This intelligent detail reduces installation costs, accommodates slopes and facilitates easy removal, for maintenance or temporary street clearance.

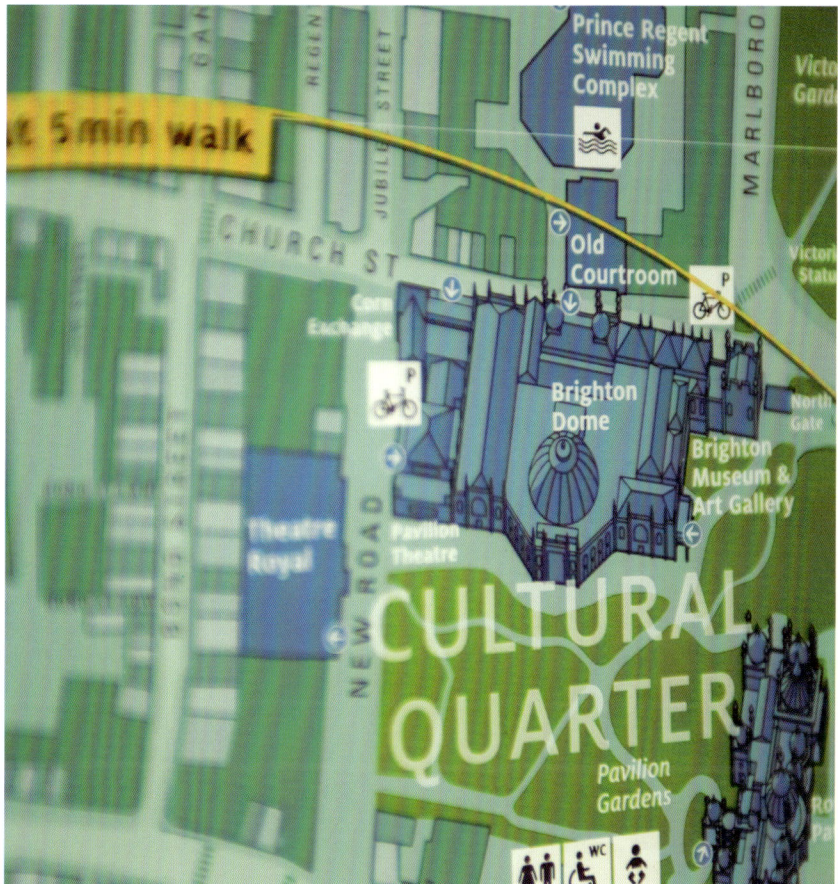

North Laine 4min

Churchill Square 5min

Brighton Station 13min

3min Coach Station

4min Visitor Information

4min Royal Pavilion

The Lanes

cocoti SHIBUYA

Design Agency:
ujidesign

Direction:
Contemporary Planning Center

Client:
Tokyu Corporation

Accompanying the renewal of "cocoti," a commercial complex in Shibuya, we redesigned all of the signage of the building.

The building has a very complex structure, so it was necessary to improve the flow created by the signs. We sought to make the sign layouts large and easy-to-follow, and at the same time, we kept in mind that they would be placed inside a cultural commercial building in central Shibuya.

First of all, in order to give the impression that 2F and 3F — the main floors — are important floors, we installed floor number signs that are around 2 meters in height, to serve as icons. We also used large sizes for the guidance signs and other floor number signs in order to lead people along vertically-structured pedestrian flows. By portraying the maps stereoscopically, we made it possible for people to take in the layout of the entire building using an overhead view.

We used classic stencil lettering that matches the mellow wood-based interior design, and created original fonts and pictograms, fine-tuning them so that they would look natural and modern. By installing these signs on each floor, we succeeded in enhancing the identity of the building overall.

MUSEE PLATINUM

3	3-1	レストラン GREEN GRILL
	3-2	カフェ & ダイニング 347Cafe
	3-3	メンズ & レディス ファッション マーノガーメントコンプレックス

2	2-1	レディス ファッション Anthubute
	2-2	美容室 資生堂ビューティーサルーン
	2-3	レディス ファッション WEEKEND by Little New York
	2-4	レディス ファッション Little New York

Casa Gracia Boutique Hostel

Design Agency:
Mayúscula Brands

Art Direction:
Mayúscula Brands

Client:
Casa Gracia

Creative Direction:
Mayúscula Brands

Illustration:
Klas Ernflo

Casa Gracia is a boutique hostel in a modernist building in Paseo de Gracia (Barcelona). For the branding, we defined the concept for this hotel as a continuous mix and balance of opposites: low cost with premium customer service, homey but elegant, in a vintage Catalan modernist setting with a young and cool social atmosphere. These opposites are enhanced by a visual identity taking formal references from Modernism, using vintage colors and manual looking illustrations that connect very well with young travelers.

The visual identity in the space lacks the typical formality and signage icons, to endow spaces with special warmth, which is much more memorable to an audience always eager to recommend what they enjoyed.

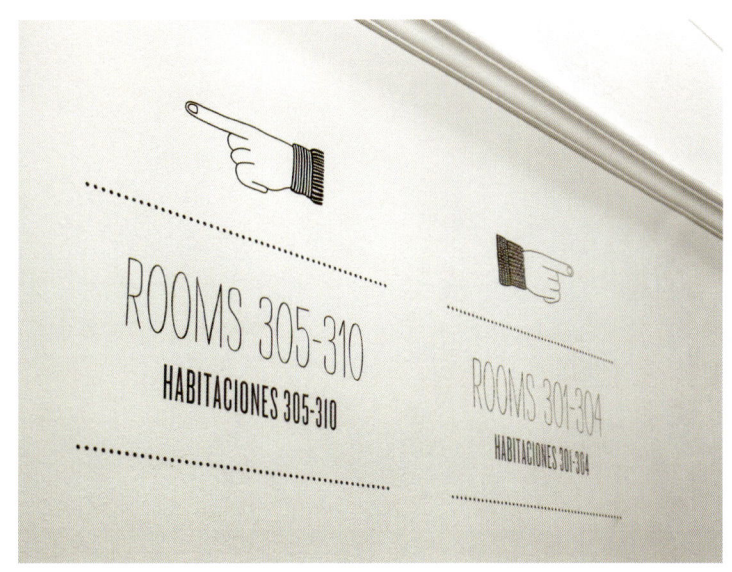

ROOMS 305-310
HABITACIONES 305-310

ROOMS 301-304
HABITACIONES 301-304

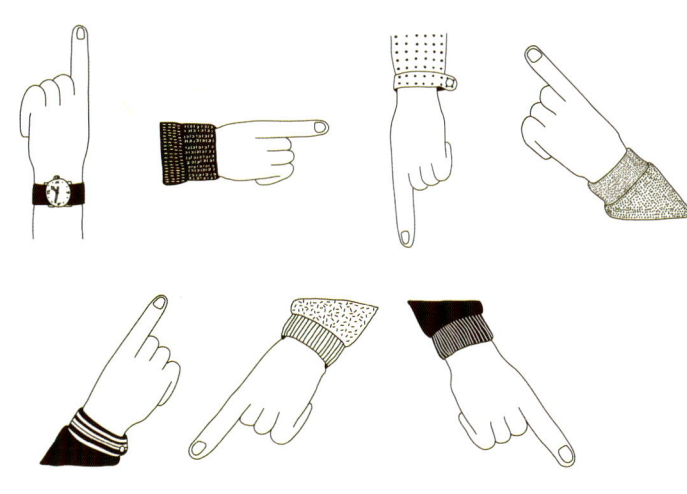

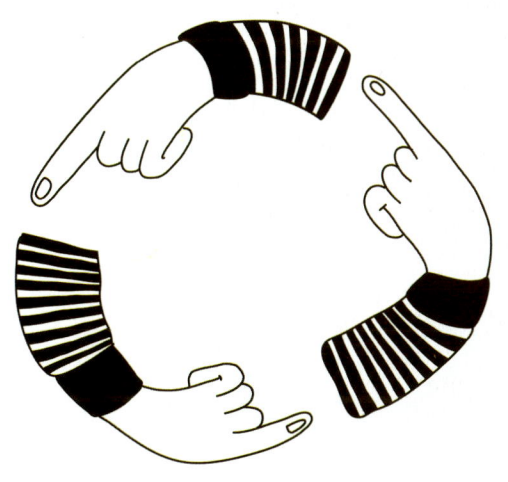

RECYCLING AREA
ÁREA DE RECICLAJE

WC

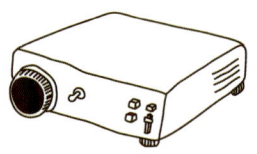

LIVING ROOM
SALÓN

TERRACE
TERRAZA

BAR
BAR

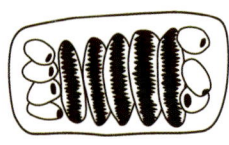

DINING
COMEDOR

TOUR DESK
INFO TURÍSTICA

INTERNET
INTERNET

LIBRARY
BIBLIOTECA

KITCHEN
COCINA

405

LIBRARY
BIBLIOTECA

CASA GRACIA

THE SAGRADA FAMILIA
MORE THAN 400 STEPS ON
A SPIRAL STAIRCASE.
THE BREAKFAST YOU WILL NEED
TO FACE THEM, HERE 8 TILL 10AM.

CASA GRACIA

AMATEUR CHEFS
AND MICROWAVE FANS.
ALL WELCOME
FROM 7AM TILL 23PM.

CASA GRACIA

THESE GAMES ARE
HERE FOR YOU!
ENJOY AND SUERTE!

CASA GRACIA

PLEASE, WRITE ROOM #
AND CHECK-OUT DATE
ON THINGS IN THE FRIDGE!

SALAS DE ESTAR LIVING ROOMS

TOUR DESK

INTERNET

INFORMACIÓN TURÍSTICA

LIBRARY BIBLIOTECA

Scotts Square Car Park Signage & Wayfinding Program

Design Agency:
Calori & Vanden-Eynden / Design Consultants

Design Team:
David Vanden-Eynden, Chris Calori, Ana Rosales-Boujnah, Marissa Dessanti

Architects:
Aedas Singapore, Architects 61, Singapore

Photography:
Tim Nolan, Singapore

The car park provides three levels of private parking and one below grade level for public use. Floor level identification graphics are a delightful balance of bold numerals paired with a script pattern of the initials for Scotts Square. The pure and simple black on white sign program blends with the pristine all-white car park interior. Signs along Scotts Road direct visitors to the residential entrance signal if the car park is full, and alert taxi drivers of a pick-up. The asymmetrical forms and materials palette of the exterior signs are derived from the architectural composition of the buildings and also feature a graphic flourish of a script numeral 8, the address on Scotts Road.

Architects:
Aedas Singapore, Architects 61, Singapore

Photography:
Tim Nolan, Singapore

Design Agency:
Calori & Vanden-Eynden / Design Consultants

Design Team:
David Vanden-Eynden, Chris Calori, Ana Rosales-Boujnah, Marissa Dessanti

Scotts Square Residential Tower Signage & Wayfinding Program

↑
CONCIERGE

THE DRAWING ROOM

LIFTS TO THE FITNESS ROOM

SKY POOL

Poised above the Scotts Square Mall, the 43-story twin residential towers at 8 Scotts Road are the epitome of luxury and refinement. Reinforcing the upscale quality of the development, the towers feature artworks and sculptures by Bernar Venet, Salvador Dali, Henry Moore, and Dale Chihuly among others. To capture the elegant personality of the residences, C&VE combined decorative flourishes and refined typography with a rich materials palette of bronze and stone. The finely detailed and elegantly crafted signage program includes room and lift bank identification, directional signs, residence unit numbers, and even the recycling stations.

Mathematisch-Physikalischer Salon, Dresden

Design Agency:
Gourdin & Müller

Project Participants:
Nathanaël Gourdin, Katy Müller,
Friederike Kühne, Felix Wissing

Client:
Saxon state real estate and
construction management,
Dresden branch

The collection of the Mathematisch-Physikalischer Salon (Royal Cabinet of Mathematical and Physical Instruments) dates back to the art collection established by Elector Augustus of Saxony in 1560. In 1728 Augustus the Strong transformed the collection into a museum – the "Royal Cabinet of Mathematical and Physical Instruments" – which has been located at the Dresden Zwinger ever since. Since 1746 it has borne the name "Mathematisch-Physikalischer Salon".In the course of the renovation of the Mathematisch-Physikalischer Salon and the presentation developed by HolzerKobler Gourdin & Müller was assigned with the design and planning of the signage system. The cabinet reopened in April 2013.

Both the colour and the materials of the signs correspond to the instruments in the exhibition on the one hand and on the surfaces of the furniture (cash desk, benches, lockers etc.) on the other hand. The combination of black surfaces with copper coloured edges gives a precious effect to the signs.

KAKAO Game
Partners Forum
Brand eXperience Design

Design Agency:
Plus X

Project Directing:
Myungsup Shin

"KAKAO Game Partners Forum Brand eXperience design" was an experience design project for game forum of KAKAO which is a well-known IT company in South Korea. The forum was held in Seoul, South Korea in May 2013. Plus X, the total experience design and marketing company directed all design for the forum. The design concept and identity was inspired from the elements of a game for expressing the character of game forum. Also overlapped images with a solid color mean a core value of connecting with game developers and co-existing together. The identity was widely used in all applications such as space design, banners, leaflets, souvenirs, and it created unified visual experience.

Design Agency:
Frost*

Client:
Commonwealth Bank Australia

Commonwealth Bank Australia, Melbourne Call Centre

The Frost* Environments team recently completed an exciting new project for employees at Commonwealth Bank's Melbourne call centre. Working in collaboration with Interior Designers Davenport Campbell, the agency was commissioned to animate the newly refurbished activity-based workplace, whilst inspiring and engaging staff who are often working on intense, monotonous tasks.

The scope of work included signage and way-finding for the 7 level development, alongside super-sized environmental graphic backdrops that added a distinctly Melbourne identity to the inner-city office.
The concept involved visually breaking up the building's floor plate by referencing urban-laneway culture in work zones and parklands and nature in the break-out spaces.

Working closely with New York based illustrator James Gulliver Hancock, they established sub-themes of work, rest and play to tell the everyday stories of the city's inhabitants, with a fantastical twist. Hidden pockets of quirky detail were incorporated at a micro-scale, as a cheeky nod to the city's laneways where there is always something new to discover. A graphic language formed from iconic Melbourne architecture also helped embed the signage firmly into its location.

Nitka Lake Lodge

Design Agency:
John Peachey & Associates

Nestled next to tranquil Nita Lake with a contrasting backdrop of the rugged Coastal Mountains of Whistler, British Columbia, Nita Lake Lodge required a complete identification package to blend with this environment.

Incorporating the surrounding natural elements of wood and stone and the industrial look of railroad metal, this majestic lodge required the signage to be an extension of the architecture and indigenous materials.

We were responsible for design, manufacture and installation of the entire signage package.

Nankun Mountain Hot Spring Valley

Design Agency:
SIDO DESIGN

Nankun Mountain hot spring valley is located in a national 4A level scenic spot. Architecture there is built along with the water and mountain; inherited natural resource is its biggest advantage. The site covers 2,177,000 sqm, on which there are the buildings in different styles and different functions. A scientific and functional signage system can well unite all the architecture space as a whole.

Besides the practical function, an excellent wayfinding system can dramatically improve the brand profile. The system should be in harmony with the environment and respect the overall feeling of the project. SIDO inspires from the natural environment and uses wood and stone as its raw materials, which illustrate the valley's ecological profile and original aesthetics. The wood is processed by the special technology, elegant, graceful and at the same time erosion resistant.

Tsangning Mansion Signage Design

Design Agency:
SIDO DESIGN

This site enjoys a new British style with the slope roof and royal garden, which create a dense charming of British feelings.

The signage for Tsangning Mansion is emphasized on the stylish aesthetics, visualizing, functionalizing and branding its low-key but luxurious architecture style.

Royal emblem, fancy handwriting, all these elements demonstrate the nature of British royal demeanor. The elaborated and high qualified design helps improve the overall environment.

A good signage design not only needs to carry the functions of orientation and explanation, but also to highlight the brand culture and position accordingly. By selecting the form, material and technology, the signage system for Tsangning Mansion infuses the brand core so as to improve the user's recognition for the brand profile.

Wuyuan Jiangwan Scenic Spot Wayfinding

Design Agency:
Sinyu Signage Design

This project was designed as a part to assist Wuyuan Jiangwan in achieving AAAAAA level as a scenic spot. At the same year, it was awarded the 5A level by China National Tourism Administration.

The design is based on the local culture, history and environment color style of Jiangwan, and chooses the plan of traditional Chinese ink painting, the ancient painting scroll, archaized bluestone and heavy archaized aluminium to unite the project and the conception of the environment as a whole.

建于新中国成立初期，人民公社时期曾是江湾村公共食堂，如今这里还留存着当年的一些记忆。

It is founded in the early days of P.R.C and used to be canteen in the period of people's commune. Some memories at that time are still preserved here now.

新中国の成立初期に建てられ、人民公社時期には江湾村の公共食堂でした。今も当時の記憶が残っています。

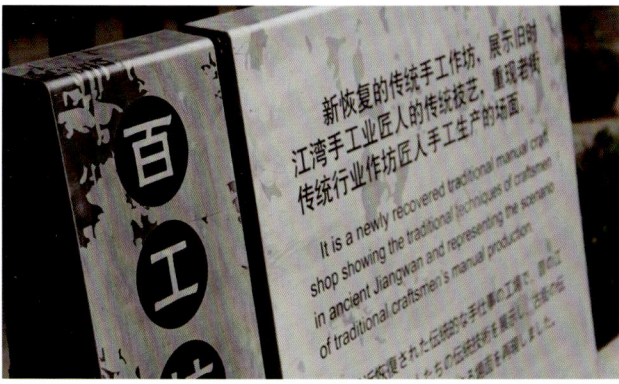

203

Design Agency:
Sinyu Signage Design

Shanhai Pass Scenic
Spot Signage Design

This project is designed for the 3 AAAAA level scenic spots within the tourism area of Shanhai Pass — the Top Pass, Old Dragon Head, and Lady Meng Jiang Temple.

The design uses the Great Wall as the main clue. Based on the different characters of the 3 spots, the designer desires a variation in unification and a unification in variation so as to achieve a good balance in its wholesome. The application of crystal materials fully expresses that the part of the Great Wall in Shanhai Pass is the only Great Wall connecting to the sea in China and thus has a very strong local style. The stone used is fused with the Great Wall and the archaized carving map depicts the history of Shanhai Pass. While the white stone is a symbol for the pure and steadfast love of Lady Meng Jiang.

影视厅

Buqiaoan
Movie Theater | ビデオロビー | 무비홀

孟姜女庙
Meng Jiangnv Temple

景区
入口

Entrance
观光区入口
Вход в экскурсионную зону

→

出口

Way out | 出口
출구 | Выход

与文明同行　为你我喝彩

Keep a civil manner during your visit

Сопровождаетесь с цивилизацией, выражаете одобрение　за вас и нас.

接待处

고소접대 | приём жалоб
Complaints Reception | クレームの受付

Shandong Canal Park Scenic Spot Wayfinding

Design Agency:
Sinyu Signage Design

China enjoys a long history of canal construction; it owns one of the longest, biggest and oldest canals in the world.

Shandong Zaozhuang Canal Park is a canal culture themed park. With the concept of modern humanization, the project highlights how huge the manmade canal project can be. The Chinese traditional wave pattern expresses a glory of the past canal transportation. The wood and the modern materials are applied together to show that the canal is a combination and connection of the manmade waterway and the natural waterway. Decorated with ship mast and hemp road, the signage in detail emphasizes the theme of canal. The natural wood fits well with the environment.

Wuzhong Tai Lake Scenic Spot Signage Design — The Garden

Design Agency:
Sinyu Signage Design

This project was designed to assist Wuzhong Tai Lake in achieving to be a biggest AAAAA level scenic spot in China. At the same year, it was awarded the 5A level by China National Tourism Administration.

Due to the various spots in this tourism area, the design is assorted in accordance to the main 13 spots, realizing a "many but not disorderly" result and enjoying a strong sense of unity.

The signage here is for one of the spot, the garden. With Suzhou classical garden as the theme, it highlights the feature of Jiangnan, that is the scenery is usually like a Chinese ink painting; the design is planed in traditional Chinese painting techniques which can fully express the local culture of Jiangsu. Inlay is also a common technique in Jiangnan decoration style. The application of Tai Lake stone deepens the local characteristics. The color choosing, black, white and grey are in a good harmony with the environment.

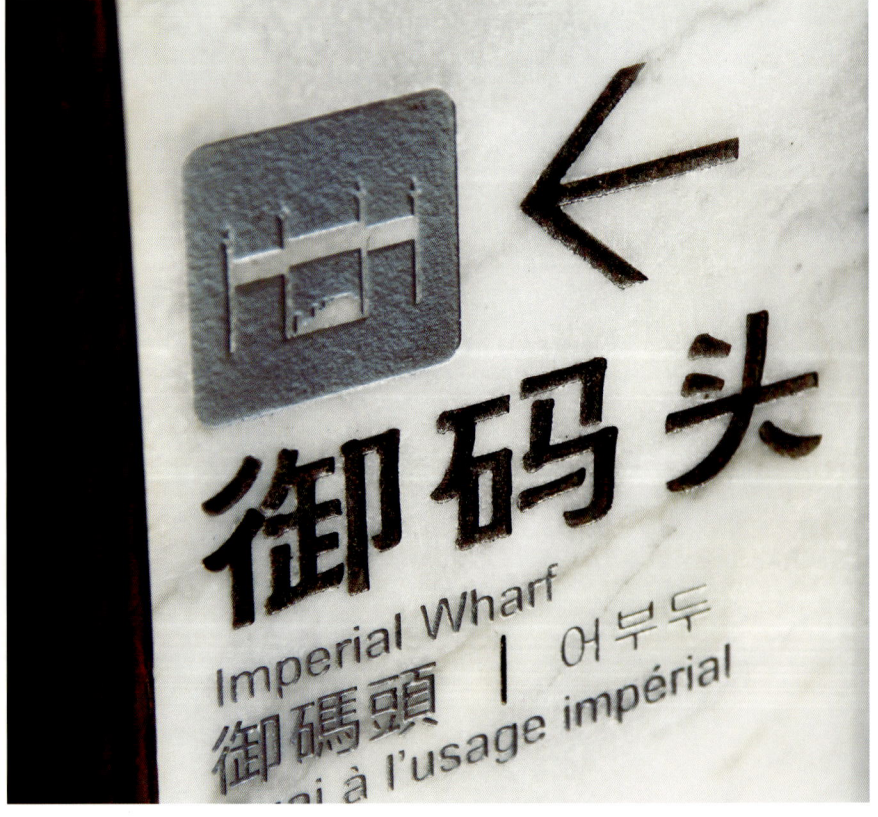

Wuzhong Tai Lake Scenic Spot Signage Design — The Temple

Design Agency:
Sinyu Signage Design

This is the signage design for another spot within this tourism area — the temple.

Corvin Wayfinding System

Design Agency:
Air Design

Designer:
Keith Evans

Brief
Air was appointed to develop the brand expression, interior design, wayfinding, signing and touchscreens for this exciting new scheme in central Budapest.

Solution
The centre logo inspired our solution – the circles forming a fundamental part of sign pattern designs and our bespoke Corvin furniture. A slick font and colour palette combination was also developed for use across the centre to ensure total brand consistency.

Result
Recent market research has found that customers feel Corvin is a unique shopping centre with plenty of space, which due to the wayfinding system, people feel they can easily navigate. The quality of the interior design (especially in the toilets) also contributed to perceived levels of customer service.

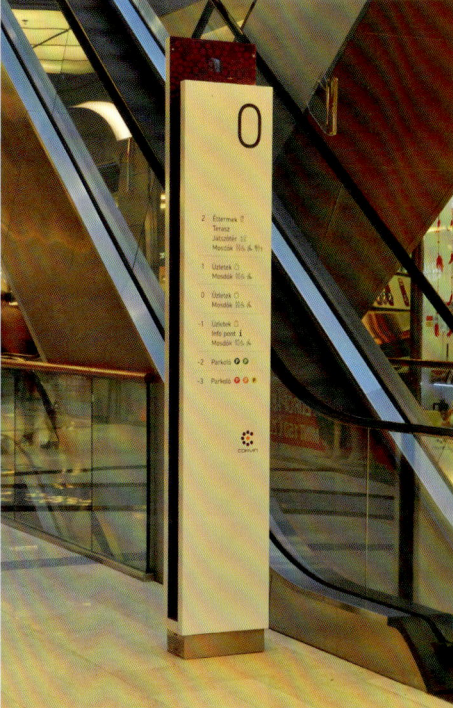

Novy Shmícov
Wayfinding System

Design Agency:
Air Design

Designer:
Jonny Ellison

Brief
With the third highest footfall in the Ségécé portfolio our brief for the famous Novy Shmícov in Prague was to not alienate the loyal customer base, but create a place that was even more welcoming, comfortable, modern and easy to use. The centre was built over ten years ago and so was in need of an uplift to maintain its prestigious reputation and compete with nearby centres.

Solution
Across the signage, interiors and digital touchscreens we have created a bright and fresh environment, using slick white corian with vivid details. As well as being an attractive solution, this aids legibility and visitor recognition. Corridors are no longer bland and unwelcoming, but visually stimulating and encourage customers to use the facilities. Unused spaces have been transformed into comfortable seating areas where visitors are able to relax before hitting the shops again.

Result
Our designs have been met with positive feedback from both centre management and visitors themselves. LED lighting has contributed to a 20% reduction in electricity costs, whilst simultaneously brightening up the mall. The seating areas in rest spaces are always in use, so rather than being a place to simply shop, Novy Smíchov is now a place in which people wish to spend their time.

Exit Štefánikova

Tesco
Exit Pl...

Fenway Park

Design Agency:
Ashton Design

Designer:
Ronald Younts, Jonathan Han,
Angelo Alcasabas, Alison Grissinger

Client:
Boston Red Sox

Ashton Design joined the Fenway Park restoration project in 2002 and over 10 years, the firm had an impact on every aspect of the visitor experience at the stadium billed "America's Most Beloved Ballpark." The project teamed Ashton Design with the same architects and management team with whom they had collaborated on several other projects, and the designers moved into a makeshift office at Fenway for months at a time during the off seasons so that they could apply the ethos of good design to every aspect of the renovation- directional signage, the branding of restaurants, the look of the new Green Monster Seats, the typeface on the scoreboard, sponsorship ads (ranging from a skyline-dwarfing, environmentally friendly Coca-Cola sign to the reintroduction of painted ads on the Green monster). The close collaboration of the designers, architects, and management team resulted in a ballpark that maintained the soul and century-old Fenway spirit while accommodating the needs of 21st-century baseball fans.

GREEN
MONSTER
3

GREEN
MONSTER
4

MONSTER
5

6

STATE STREET PAVILION
EMC LEVEL
GREEN MONSTER
COCA-COLA CORNER
GRANDSTAND

STEINER SPORTS
3RD BASE DECK
WWW.STEINERSPORTS.COM

CONCESSIONS
ABSOLUT CLUBHOUSE
YAWKEY WAY

Peoples' park - Peoples' signs

Design Agency:
2+1 Ideas Agency

Partner:
Rasmus Rune Nielsen

Project manager:
Anette Grønbeck

Creatives:
Helene Dalgaard, Rasmus Engelhardt & Britt Gundersen

Photography:
Ty Strange

Fælledparken is the largest park in Copenhagen, and one of the most popular spots in the city, boasting playgrounds, a dance pavilion, the National Stadium, lakes, green lawns and the biggest skatepark in Northern Europe.

The park is truly a place for the people. All people. Every year, hundreds of events and gatherings are held in the park, which is one of the oldest in Copenhagen. Until now, the signs in the park have been limited, and restricted to bans and regulations: No biking, No barbecuing, Dogs on a leash.

With the People's park - People's signs project, we invited everybody in to the park, focusing on easy navigation and clear access to the many destinations and activities in the park. The aim was to highlight the hidden treasures of the old park and make it easy and fun to explore it. We emphasized a timeless and clean design with clear references to the nature colors of the park. Further, the bright and sparkling colours of the park attractions give the user an impression of lively and diverse park for everyone.

Løberuter

På kortet kan du se forslag til løberuter og placeringen af de tre motionspladser i Fælledparken.

Stierne med løberuterne er markeret med pullertlamper.

Løberuten på Klosterfælleden er 1.25 km. Hvis du løber den 4 gange giver det en løbetur på 5 km.

Løberuten på Blegdamsfælleden er 1.66 km. Hvis du løber den 3 gange giver det en løbetur på 5 km.

På Øster Allé er der afmærket en løberute på 1 km.

KLOSTERFÆLLEDEN

ØSTER ALLÉ

BLEGDAMSFÆLLEDEN

Velkommen i det fri!

Stierne sneryddes og gruses kun lejlighedsvis

VEGA Building

Design Agency:
Yelo Wolf

Designer:
Andy Parsons, Richard Wolfströme

Client:
Southern Housing

Photography:
Jim Stephenson

The new social housing apartment block at 331 Kingsway, Hove was given the name The Vega Building to fit with the art deco styling of the proposal.

The brief for the building identity and brand was to hint at the clean line of the art deco style, in a contemporary way. We researched the lettering style from the period and developed the design strategy.

Building on the narrative, we developed a system that utilised the elegant form of the plane and chose a font that is modern, legible and contemporary, and which complemented the building and the developing story.

We wanted a 'light touch' to the design, avoiding 'blocky' signage panels, proposing a sensitive approach that used an accent colour for each floor and signage lettering that was mounted directly to building surfaces, respecting the architectural lines.

VEGA plane silhouette shapes have been used as navigational devices and the information and signage lettering laser cut from stainless steel and installed as individual letters raised from the wall surfaces giving a modern take on the industrial clean nature of the style and time.

The car park continues the theme where dotted lines indicate parking spaces with the VEGA plane motif labelling the space numbering system. Planes on the floor surface also direct users to bay areas and four disabled bay areas are clearly marked in blue.

Secondary signage throughout the building is signed using a matt black vinyl and statutory signage silk-screened onto stainless steel panels to maintain the aesthetic.

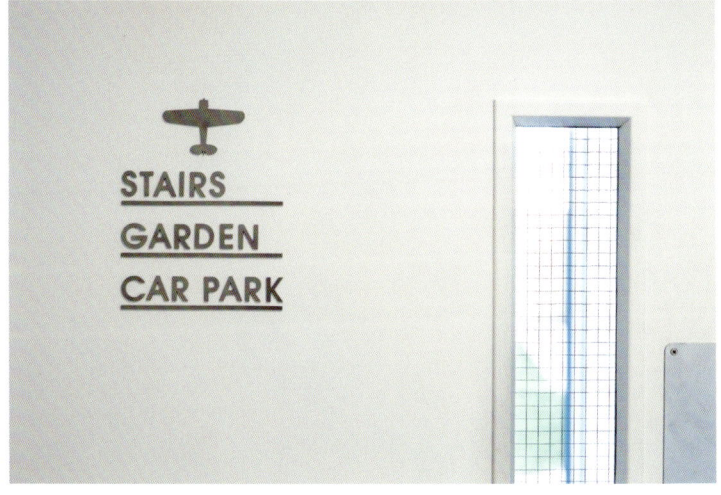

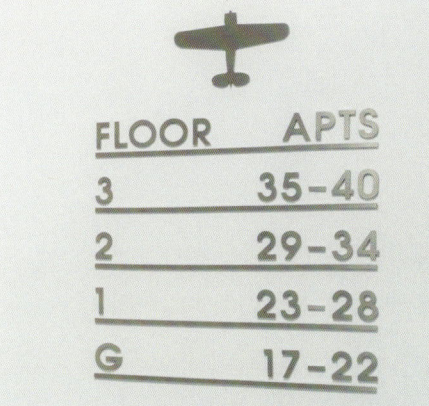

FLOOR	APTS
3	35–40
2	29–34
1	23–28
G	17–22

CONTRIBUTOR »

api(+)

Founded in 1990, api(+) is an award-winning multidisciplinary design firm offering strategy, architectural, interior, graphic, and signage design, and focusing on the development of consumer-centric concepts for retail driven environments. api(+) has developed some of the industry's top performing retail environments in the fields of shopping centers, consumable goods, specialty shops, and restaurants nationally and internationally.

api(+) is recognized as a leader in food retail design. The firm has created new concepts for the leaders in food retail and is creating the most captivating and engaging designs in the industry. Its strategic designs focus on achieving the clients' goals: customer volume, shopping frequency, and basket size. api(+) digs deep to position you distinctively within competitive markets. Cross channel formats are blurring the categories.

Air

Based in London, we created Air in 1998 with the single-minded objective of offering our clients a design service that could genuinely change their business through creativity and originality; and to do that within a happy studio environment where collaboration and cross-pollination (intellectual that is) between design disciplines is positively encouraged. We now have a presence in Moscow and Shanghai and operate across the globe, bringing innovative solutions to clients in the retail, real estate, law, professional services and public sectors.

Ashton Design

Ashton Design was founded in 1985. While the firm remains small, recognition has grown steadily. Today, organizations large and small throughout the mid-Atlantic region and across the country seek out our graphic design expertise.

In recent years, the trend among design studios has been toward specialization. Continuously broadening our horizons, we have chosen another path. Whether we are commissioned to create a new graphic identity or logo, a corporate annual report or brochure, college admissions and development publications, a website, environmental graphics for major league sports facilities, even prototypes for public sculpture, we apply the same basic principles: bring together a close-knit team of highly creative minds in a collaborative environment, strive for good taste always, and solve the communications challenge with élan, grace, and purpose.

Bloom Identity

Bloom Identity starts at the core of a brand and helps companies to recognise and evolve the emotional power of their own brands — from the budding flower to the magnificent blossom. Owners: Maneka Fahrer Bruno, Rahel Grünig.

Calori & Vanden-Eynden/Design Consultants

Calori & Vanden-Eynden (C&VE) is an internationally recognized, award-winning design firm specializing in the planning and design of signage, wayfinding, branded environments, identity, and user navigation systems.

C&VE's clients include many of the world's foremost architects, institutions, and developers. C&VE is widely recognized as one of the premier signage and environmental graphic design firms practicing today.

C&VE's principals, Ms. Chris Calori and Mr. David Vanden-Eynden, are Fellows of the Society for Environmental Graphic Design. Each has over 25 years' experience in solving signage and environmental graphic design problems. The firm purposely maintains a broad project mix, applying its talents to a wide range of facility and building types, including cultural, civic, commercial, educational, hospitality, retail, and transportation facilities.

Culminating years of its expertise, C&VE literally wrote the book on Environmental Graphic Design (EGD). Chris Calori's highly acclaimed *Signage and Wayfinding Design: A Complete Guide to Creating Environmental Graphic Design Systems* has become the essential reference book for EGD professionals and educators.

Christian Salic, Werbe- und Designagentur

Christian Salic, Werbe- und Designagentur is an award winning design and ad agency with a clear focus on ideas. The agency combines creative services and brand consultancy in order to create vibrant brand experience.
The agency is working for clients as: Audi, Porsche Austria, City of Salzburg, Schloss Hellbrunn, Salzburg Chamber of Commerce and Rewe International AG, to name but a few.

Christian Salic, Werbe- und Designagentur is founded in 2003 and located in Salzburg, Austria.

Collider

Collider is a firm and design collective based in Sydney, Australia. The ability to function as a hybrid between design and digital studio and production company puts the team in a unique position to facilitate and foster honest and original creative process. The result is powerful cross-pollination between creative spheres that would traditionally not always mix. Like our clients, our projects vary from TVC direction for global brands to creative direction for arts and culture organisations to digital information design projects for top tier developers and encompass all aspects in between.

Collider is guided by the belief that a company is only as good as its operational philosophy and practice. The ability to attract and inspire a talented core of creatives, while exciting clients and evolving its collective creative voice has pinned Collider as an internationally significant collective. Collider's creative participation is global, evident through its award-winning portfolio of projects and a widely dispersed client list.

Deuce Design

Founded in 1999 by Bruce Slorach and Sophie Tatlow, Deuce Design is a graphic design studio specialising in creative concepts, strategy, research and copywriting. The studio has a reputation for producing projects that are both contemporary and culturally significant, from graphics for public domain and environmental design to branding, print, Web, fashion, fabric and lighting. Collaboration with designers and architects across numerous disciplines plays a large part in Deuce's creative process. The studio endeavours to maintain a small team to nurture creativity and preserve creative integrity, securing the best client and team outcomes.

As primary creative director of Deuce Design, Bruce Slorach is an accomplished designer and visual artist whose works have been exhibited at the V&A Museum (London), The Victorian Gallery, The Australian National Gallery and the Powerhouse Museum. Bruce studied Fine Art at the Victorian College of the Arts and has enjoyed an extensive and rewarding career both in graphic design and in the arts. Apart from a five-year period as Creative Director at Mambo Graphics, Bruce has been a self-employed graphic designer and artist, beginning his career in the early 1980s with the design and fabric studio, Abyss Studios.

Dodoplan

Dodoplan is the place making design studio. They design signage and wayfinding systems for public spaces, such as malls or stadiums. You can also see some interesting retails and event scenography in their portfolio. The main goal in their projects is to integrate the visual identity of a company with space and to enrich user's experience. Their design is often inspired by material, anthropological, ethnographical or technological researches. Dodoplan considers beauty as a must, trend awareness as a good manner and technology as obviousness. Some of their projects involve handmade elements which is quite unusual in public spaces.

Drive Design

Established on an approach based on the common sense to define needs, aestheticism to conceive an effective line and in connection with its environment, the pragmatism to end in the realization, our methodology allows to end in projects in which every element complements itself perfectly, associating originality, relevance and coherence.

Our job between the skills and halfway between the produced design and the pure road marking, consists in imagining tools necessary for the guide and for the information according to a given, internal or outside environment.

My objective: make visible what the others do not see.

To observe, to give meaning, to offer a questioning in order to create a break and at the end, the value!

Filippo Partesotti

Filippo Partesotti was born in 1954. "Son of Arlequin!" (the ancient Italian mask whose dresses was made by multicolored fabrics), he loves colors and joyful, non-minimalist graphic design.

He is an architect, who works as visual designer especially for cultural events or institutions. His clients are mostly Museums, Libraries, Theatres and Cultural Centers, for whom he designs institutional identity, infographics, books, exhibitions and communication campaigns. He has been invited to show his works in several exhibitions all over the world and his works have been published on books and magazines.

FROST*

Frost* is an independent creative agency collaborating with clients around the globe in disciplines as diverse as design, branding, advertising, environmental graphics and digital. Founded in London in 1994 by Vince Frost and now based in Sydney, our philosophy is "Inspiring ideas to life". The Frost* team designs everything from postage stamps to the built environment.

Gourdin & Müller

Collaboration of Katy Müller and Nathanaël Gourdin in 2003 leads to the fondation of Gourdin & Müller office in 2006.

Gourdin & Müller is at the interface of urban space, architecture, product and graphic design; information, guidance and orientation systems can impart more than information.

The office's conceptual approach enables the creation of unusual responses, reflecting place, theme or client, i.e. a specific context, which is also represented appropriately. The adequate interaction between materiality, form, graphics and typography facilitates the realisation of identity-promoting solutions.

In addition, user friendliness, the representation of complex content and the taking into account of heritage conservation aspects form the focus of its considerations.

Sophisticated design and a high degree of functionality make signage systems a key communication instrument for companies and institutions.

Gourdin & Müller plans signage systems from conception to realisation, accompanying all project phases with the greatest of care and attention.

Intégral Ruedi Baur

Intégral Ruedi Baur at Paris, Zurich and Berlin are multidisciplinary studios created in 1989, 2002 and 2007 respectively. While graphic design represents a major part of the business, the field of application includes also 3D design, stage design, exhibition conception, signage systems and urbanism. If the business had to be defined, one would say that Intégral tries to solve identification problems, orientation difficulties and information communication challenges, by using all appropriate techniques and disciplines. Interdisciplinary cooperation is the principle characteristic of the Intégral design studios.

John Peachey & Associates

Capably led by Design Manager Amanda Wilbur, a team of talented designers use their diverse knowledge, experience, passion and creativity to produce signs that turn a vision a reality.

They collaborate with the clients to create unique designs with practical solutions to fit their budget. Their consulting service is tailored to suit the client's needs and they have extensive experience providing:
· Unique designs for individual signs
· Comprehensive sign plans for large scale projects
· Detailed sign guidelines for commercial developments and municipalities

From concept to completion they keep the clients informed throughout the process. The clients' opinions and input are always welcomed. They take the mystery out of creating great signs, drawing on our wealth of experience and specialized knowledge.

Kishino Shogo

Kishino Shogo was born in Tokyo in 1975. He joined the Hiromura Design Office, and he launched his own design office 6D in 2007.

Kishino has received JAGDA New Designer Award and ADC Award in 2010, KIDS DESIGN AWARD / Reconstruction Support Design Award in 2012, DFA Silver Award in 2012, One Show Merit Award in 2013, D&AD Yellow Pencil in 2013.

Along with teaching Corporate Identity (CI) and Visual Identity (VI) sign planning as a part-time lecturer at Tokyo Zokei (Art and Design) University, he has been involved in corporate branding for enhancing corporate image, such as VI Planning of "JA Minds". Other projects are art direction for the "Tokyo International Film Festival" etc.

Mayúscula

Mayúscula is a branding and design studio in Barcelona specialized in the creation of brands and the development of visual identity systems for local and international clients. They work in projects of diverse complexity, format and sector, such as new media, television, wayfinding, packaging or retail. Their goal is to shape creativity into a strategic tool for businesses to be unique, innovate and communicate.

Notice Kommunikation & Design

Notice, the communication and design agency, is led by Gilles Bachmann and Helen Hüsser who have been developing design and communication strategies for clients in various industries for more than 20 years. In 2011, they founded Notice.

The Notice designers agree that good design should make perfect sense and at the same time stimulate our senses. Design is not an end in itself; rather, it is an expression of appreciation toward people and objects. And good design is the key to standing out in local and global competition and a vital selling point.

Notice's portfolio focuses on signage design and systems for public and private buildings. The team always develops original solutions, taking into account aesthetics, functionality and cost efficiency.

Plus X

Plus X is an experience design and marketing company in South Korea, founded in 2010. Plus X has a connotation of the message that "We Add Experience for Your Brand." Brand experience design means providing consumers with valuable brand experience through consolidated online and offline designs based on the consistent brand strategy. The company mainly directed design projects of large company in South Korea such as SK telecom, Hyundai card, and Samsung. Plus X focused on integrated experience design, not just a design of one field.

Rama Studio

Rama Studio is a graphic design studio working in a broad range of media, often with collaborators from other creative disciplines. With a background in art and music Rama Studio maintains a creative and critical approach with ambitious and personal results.

Architecture has been a continued field of interest and collaboration, working with visual identity and spatial design for cultural institutions and architectural offices. Rama Studio's work combines the precision of digital tools with the spontaneous and analogue, creating living and diverse visual solutions — ranging from clear, simple communication to curious and challenging design.

Rama Studio was founded in 2007 by designers Stefan Mylleager and Thomas Frederiksen, both MA in design from the Danish Design School.

Roseta y Oihana

Roseta y Oihana is a graphic design studio created in 2010 by Roseta Mus Pons and Oihana Herrera Erneta, with offices in Barcelona and Pamplona.

The studio fits well the clients' needs, working closely with them and building a team with all the people that participate in the project. Roseta y Oihana works with enthusiasm and dedication, doing all the design process, taking care of each detail and supervising the production and implementation. They are not only specialized in sign design, they also design graphic identities, publications, webs, exhibitions and posters, and they focus their projects not only solving the needs of the project, but also with a mix of rationality and the will of creating graphic works that are simply nice and special to the people.

Roseta y Oihana's clients are some of the more renowned Spanish design, cultural and academical institutions and organizations, such FAD (Fostering Arts and Design), CCCB (Centre de Cultura Contemporània de Barcelona), Elisava (Barcelona School of Design and Engineering), Gran Teatre del Liceu and UPNA (Public University of Navarre).

Roseta y Oihana's works have been published in international blogs and magazines (Aisle One, It,It's nice that, Design inspiration, Ffffound, Chois Gallery, etc.) and exhibited in various exhibitions, among them highlight "Helvetica. A new typeface?" at Design Hub Barcelona.

Screenlounge

For over ten years Screenlounge has developed visual concepts for projects and companies of any kind and size. Focusing on design and typography they create visual identities, print and screen designs, interactive projects, book design, exhibition design and wayfinding systems.

SIDO DESIGN

SIDO DESIGN is focused on the environmental signage system design and solution. Signage is an indispensable part of the corporate environment and the impartment conveyor for the company profile. Reasonable and optimized signage system carries the info for orientation, communication and forges the corporate culture and improves the corporate profile.

Relying on the effective analyzing and positioning, and the sophisticate visual creating ability, SIDO, together with its clients, creates the excellent signage designs.

[sic]

[sic] was founded in 2005 and has been working in three areas since: architecture, design and signage.

In architecture, [sic] has developed and coordinated large scale projects in association with important architectural offices and construction companies in Brazil, such as Aflalo e Gasperini, Camargo Correa and Yuny.

In the design area, [sic] creates editorial projects for national and international publishing houses. This work has included the production of visual identity and institutional design for these corporations.

In signage, [sic]'s differential is the multidisciplinary team of designers and architects which rapidly attracted costumers like PDG, Viver, Camargo Correa, Hines, Lindencorp, Odebrecht, Supricel, TPA e Firmenich.

 ## Sinyu Signage Design

Sinyu Signage Design is professionalized in signage design and execution for the high-end scenic spots and the design for their brand profile. Sinyu combines its creation concept with the local characteristics and becomes the top design and execution company in China. They have offered the high quality service for about one hundred international famous scenic spots already.

Sinyu has a team of top talents, which enables their design original, special and novelty. From the brand forge, personalized design to scientific planning, they show their professionals for their clients.

 ## STUDIO 360

Studio 360 is an independent creative agency providing dynamic, integrated solutions in the fields of visual communications and architecture. We do corporate identities, packaging, signage, illustration, web, interaction and graphic design. Our fields of expertise are: branding, advertising, architecture, interior and event design. We love creativity.

Studio 360 is dedicated to efficient solutions. We do ideas with a meaning and give meaning to ideas. Our philosophy is communication in a fresh and sophisticated style, focusing on user satisfaction, attention to detail and higher quality of living. We aim to achieve more with less, and creatively transform constraint into opportunity.

15 years of experience ensure our excellence: Studio 360 projects have been featured in distinguished publications worldwide and have won many international awards.

 ## TGG Hafen Senn Stieger

The designers Dominik Hafen, Bernhard Senn and Roland

Stieger founded the TGG Hafen Senn Stieger agency for visual communication in the Swiss town of St.Gallen in 1993.

They had met while training together to become typographical designers – students of the book designer Jost Hochuli – at the School of Design in St.Gallen. Alongside the work in their own design agency, which now employs around a dozen designers, they are also involved in teaching. In the area of visual communication, the agency focuses on book and editorial design, signage, exhibition organisation, corporate, web and type design.

 ## ujidesign tokyo

ujidesign was founded in 2005 by Yutaka MAEDA in Tokyo, JAPAN. We are involved in various fields of design work. Graphic, Sign, Exhibition graphic, Package, Book, Web-site and so on.

 ## White Studio

White Studio is a multidisciplinary design studio, based in Porto and more recently in London.

White Studio runs with a small team, which works in a wide range of areas, such as packaging, editorial, signage, corporate identity and web design.

The studio believes that design should be white, always based on concept and ideas, always adapting to each client's needs.

The relationship with each project is unique as a result of a close partnership and dialogue with the client.

White Studio has been around for more than decades.

Woodhouse

. . . .

Woodhouse, based in the UK, design, manufacture and install contemporary street furniture, lighting and signage that provide architects, designers, specifiers, planners and engineers with innovative and exceptional design solutions for today's public spaces. A reputation of excellence has been built over 25 years for delivering bespoke designs, in-house and partner products that truly enhance landscapes.

Projects include urban landscapes such as the London Canary Wharf financial district, innovative lighting columns for Exhibition Road, Kensington in London, bespoke internal and external signage for Cabot Circus Shopping Mall, Bristol, an iconic nine-metre high LED illuminated monolith sign in Newport, Wales and hosts of other waterside, city street, campus, shopping mall, prestigious commercial and public developments.

2+1 Ideas Agency

. . . .

2+1 is a Danish agency, specializing in design and communication for cities, citizens and companies. Through strategic work on communication, identity and experience design, 2+1 helps private and public clients change attitudes and actions among citizens, users and consumers.

2+1 call themselves an ideas agency because they nurture and refine ideas that give the simplest solutions to the biggest challenges. Ideas that make people come together, sets the agenda and creates results. Ideas take on a life of their own.

Yelo Wolf

. . . .

Yelo Wolf is specialised in branding buildings and place by creating sympathetic modern contemporary design for building identity, signage and wayfinding. As well as delivering into the 'real' environment, they also include supporting augmented reality and wayfinding digital solutions. Yelo Wolf ensures that buildings have a coherent, appropriate and desirable approach to environmental and spatial information design.

About ARTPOWER

BOOK PUBLISHING

Independent plan, solicit contribution, printing, sales of books covering architecture, interior, graphic, landscape and property development.

BOOK DISTRIBUTION

Publishing and acting agency for various art design books. We support in-city call order, door to door service, mail and online order etc.

COPYRIGHT COOPERATION

To further expand international cooperation, enrich publication varieties and meet readers' multi-level needs, we stick to seeking and pioneering spirit all the way and positively seek copyright trade cooperation with excellent publishing organizations both at home and abroad.

PORTFOLIO

We can edit and publish magazine/portfolio for enterprises or design studios according to their needs.

BOOKS OF PROPERTY DEVELOPMENT AND OPERATION

We organize the publication of books about property development, providing models of property project planning and operation management for real estate developer, real estate consulting company, etc.

INTRODUCTION OF ACS MAGAZINE

ACS is a professional magazine specializing on high-end space design. It is a color printing bi-monthly with 168 pages and 245*325mm format. There are six issues every year which are released in the even months. Featured in both Chinese and English ACS is distributed nation-wide and overseas. As the most cutting-edge counseling magazine ACS provides readers with the novelist works of the very best architects and interior designers and leads the new fashion in space design. "Present the best whole-heartedly with books as a media" is always our slogan. ACS will be dedicated to build the bridge between art and design and create the platform for within-industry communication.

Artpower International Publishing Co., Ltd.

Add: G009, Floor 7th, Yimao Centre, Meiyuan Road, Luohu District, Shenzhen, China
Contact: Ms. Wang
Tel: +86 755 8291 3355
Web: www.artpower.com.cn
E-mail: rainly@artpower.com.cn

QR (Quick Response) Code of ACS Official Wechat Account

Acknowledgements

We would like to thank all the designers and companies who made significant contributions to the compilation of this book. Without them, this project would not have been possible. We would also like to thank many others whose names did not appear on the credits, but made specific input and support for the project from beginning to end.

Future Editions

If you would like to contribute to the next edition of Artpower, please email us your details to: artpower@artpower.com.cn